THE
HISTORY OF
ICELAND

ADVISORY BOARD

THE
HISTORY OF
ICELAND

Guðni Thorlacius Jóhannesson

The Greenwood Histories of the Modern Nations
Frank W. Thackeray and John E. Findling, Series Editors

BLOOMSBURY ACADEMIC
NEW YORK • LONDON • OXFORD • NEW DELHI • SYDNEY

BLOOMSBURY ACADEMIC
Bloomsbury Publishing Inc
1385 Broadway, New York, NY 10018, USA
50 Bedford Square, London, WC1B 3DP, UK
29 Earlsfort Terrace, Dublin 2, Ireland

BLOOMSBURY, BLOOMSBURY ACADEMIC and the Diana logo
are trademarks of Bloomsbury Publishing Plc

First published in the United States of America by ABC-CLIO 2013
Paperback edition published by Bloomsbury Academic 2024

Cover photo: An aerial view of Reykjavik, Iceland, with the sea and Esja volcanic
mountain range in the background. (Jeremyreds/Dreamstime.com)

Bloomsbury Publishing Inc does not have any control over, or responsibility for,
any third-party websites referred to or in this book. All internet addresses given
in this book were correct at the time of going to press. The author and publisher
regret any inconvenience caused if addresses have changed or sites have
ceased to exist, but can accept no responsibility for any such changes.

Library of Congress Cataloging-in-Publication Data
Guðni Th. Jóhannesson, 1968–
The history of Iceland / Guðni Thorlacius Jóhannesson.
pages cm. — (The Greenwood histories of the modern nations)
Includes bibliographical references and index.
ISBN 978-0-3133-7620-7 (hardcopy: acid-free paper) — ISBN 978-0-3133-7621-4 (ebook)
1. Iceland—History. I. Title.
DL338.G864 2013
949.12—dc23 2012031759

ISBN: HB: 978-0-3133-7620-7
PB: 979-8-7651-1486-5
ePDF: 978-0-3133-7621-4
eBook: 979-8-2160-9754-9

Series: The Greenwood Histories of the Modern Nations

To find out more about our authors and books visit www.bloomsbury.com
and sign up for our newsletters.

Contents

Series Foreword

The Greenwood Histories of the Modern Nations series is intended to provide students and interested laypeople with up-to-date, concise, and analytical histories of many of the nations of the contemporary world. Not since the 1960s has there been a systematic attempt to publish a series of national histories, and as series editors, we believe that this series will prove to be a valuable contribution to our understanding of other countries in our increasingly interdependent world.

Some 40 years ago, at the end of the 1960s, the Cold War was an accepted reality of global politics. The process of decolonization was still in progress, the idea of a unified Europe with a single currency was unheard of, the United States was mired in a war in Vietnam, and the economic boom in Asia was still years in the future. Richard Nixon was the president of the United States, Mao Tse-tung (not yet Mao Zedong) ruled China, Leonid Brezhnev guided the Soviet Union, and Harold Wilson was the prime minister of the United Kingdom. Authoritarian dictators still controlled most of Latin America, the Middle East was reeling in the wake of the Six-Day War, and Shah Mohammad Reza Pahlavi was at the height of his power in Iran.

Since then, the Cold War has ended; the Soviet Union has vanished, leaving 15 independent republics in its wake; the advent of the computer age has radically transformed global communications; the rising demand for oil makes the Middle East still a dangerous flash point; and the rise of new economic powers like the People's Republic of China and India threatens to bring about a new world order. All of these developments have had a dramatic impact on the recent history of every nation of the world.

For this series, which was launched in 1998, we first selected nations whose political, economic, and sociocultural affairs marked them as among the most important of our time. For each nation, we found an author who was recognized as a specialist in the history of that nation. These authors worked cooperatively with us and with Greenwood Press to produce volumes that reflected current research on their nations and that are interesting and informative to their readers. In the first decade of the series, more than 40 volumes were published, and as of 2008, some are moving into second editions.

The success of the series has encouraged us to broaden our scope to include additional nations, whose histories have had significant effects on their regions, if not on the entire world. In addition, geopolitical changes have elevated other nations into positions of greater importance in world affairs, and so, we have chosen to include them in this series as well. The importance of a series such as this cannot be underestimated. As a superpower whose influence is felt all over the world, the United States can claim a special relationship with almost every other nation. Yet many Americans know very little about the histories of nations with which the United States relates. How did they get to be the way they are? What kind of political systems have evolved there? What kind of influence do they have on their own regions? What are the dominant political, religious, and cultural forces that move their leaders? These and many other questions are answered in the volumes of this series.

The authors who contribute to this series write comprehensive histories of their nations, dating back, in some instances, to prehistoric times. Each of them, however, has devoted a significant portion of their book to events of the past 40 years because the modern era has contributed the most to contemporary issues that have an impact on the U.S. policy. Authors make every effort to be as up to date as possible so that readers can benefit from discussion and analysis of recent events.

In addition to the historical narrative, each volume contains an introductory chapter giving an overview of that country's geography, political institutions, economic structure, and cultural attributes. This is meant to give readers a snapshot of the nation as it exists in the contemporary world. Each history also includes supplementary information following the narrative, which may include a timeline that represents a succinct chronology of the nation's historical evolution, biographical sketches of the nation's most important historical figures, and a glossary of important terms or concepts that are usually expressed in a foreign language. Finally, each author prepares a comprehensive bibliography for readers who wish to pursue the subject further.

Readers of these volumes will find them fascinating and well written. More importantly, they will come away with a better understanding of the contemporary world and the nations that comprise it. As series editors, we hope that this series will contribute to a heightened sense of global understanding as we move through the early years of the twenty-first century.

Frank W. Thackeray and John E. Findling
Indiana University Southeast

Preface

It was in early 2008 that I agreed to write a volume on Iceland in the *Histories of the Modern Nations* series. At that time, most observers felt that the rich, modern welfare state on this rugged, isolated island was a nice example of a rags-to-riches tale. Despite literary achievements and alleged affluence in the first centuries of settlement, human settlement in Iceland had mostly been marked by abject poverty, foreign rule, deadly epidemics, and natural disasters. At the start of the twentieth century, the Icelanders still counted among Europe's poorest countries, backward subjects of a foreign power. But then, everything changed. Independence was achieved, relative prosperity as well. By the end of the century, tiny Iceland, with a few other states, topped the UN Human Development Index. The Icelanders seemed to be better off and more content than most other people on the planet. Their history seemed to be one of rise, fall, and rise, with success directly attached to independence but destitute to foreign rule.

The initial outline of the work bore witness to this traditional frame. In late 2008, however, the Icelandic banking system collapsed in spectacular fashion. State bankruptcy was avoided only by drastic last-minute measures. Although progress has been made since, the impact of this shock can still be felt, not only in financial, economic, and political terms. In the immediate years before the collapse, as the devastating events came to be known, many Icelanders had been blinded by the apparent success of their bankers and entrepreneurs abroad. Was it not a fact that this nation was capable of more success on the international scene than its small size—around 280,000 people at the turn of the millennium—would indicate? Had the Icelanders not been hardened in their centuries-long struggle with a harsh nature? Were they not embedded with the adventurism and courage of their forefathers, the Vikings, who sailed far and wide? Were they not just better than the rest?

The collapse was a psychological shock, a slap in the collective face of Icelanders, so to speak. Had this book been finished before 2008, it would have been different in many respects. At least it would not have been structured on the new lines, which now seem to be necessary, of rise, fall, and rise but followed with another fall. Working on this book has been a case study in the importance of the present in historical writing.

While the roller coaster ride of the Icelanders in the last years should make interesting reading, I also hope that the readers of this book will appreciate the marvels and contradictions of Icelandic history—the constant struggle against adverse nature versus the use of its resources; foreign rule and oppression versus the vital reliance on strong links with the outside world; the pride of a nation that strives to survive in a globalized world versus the minority complex that comes with being among the smallest on the international stage.

A number of colleagues have assisted me, and I am grateful to them all. I will mention only Helgi Skúli Kjartansson and Sverrir Jakobsson, with the important addition that they are in no way responsible for any mistakes or injudicious interpretations that may be found in the book. I also thank Kaitlin Ciarmiello and other staff at ABC-CLIO for their assistance and patience. Lastly, I express my heartfelt gratitude to my wife Eliza. She has been my rock, as always.

A NOTE ON SPELLING AND NAMES

In the text, the Icelandic letter ð is replaced with d, and the letter þ with th. In foreign works on contemporary Iceland, Icelanders are usually referred to by their surname, although the locals refer to each other by given names. In this work, surnames are used in the chapters on the modern period but first names for previous times.

Timeline of Historical Events

Around 400 BC	Greek explorer Pytheas travels to Thule near the frozen sea
Around 825	Irish monk Dicuil tells of hermits' voyages to islands in the north
Around 871	Settlement in Reykjavík
Around 930	Foundation of the *Althing*, a countrywide court and legislature
Around 980	Discovery of an island west of Iceland, named Greenland
999	Christianity accepted at the *Althing*
Around 1000	Discovery of lands west of Greenland
1056	First bishop of Iceland consecrated, resides at Skálholt, which also becomes a seat for education
1230s–1262	Civil strife
1262–1264	The Old Covenant, a pledge by Icelandic chieftains to become subjects of the Norwegian king

1271 and 1281	New legal codes adopted
1402–1404	Outbreak of the plague, again in 1494–1495
1400s	English fishing off Iceland begins
1550	Execution of Jón Arason, the last Catholic bishop in Iceland until the twentieth century
1602	Beginnings of trade monopoly
1631	First Anglo-Danish agreement on fishing limits off Iceland
1662	King Frederick III has absolutism imposed in Iceland
1707–1709	Smallpox epidemic kills around a quarter of the population
1783–1784	A massive volcanic eruption results in the death of around 20 percent of the population
1800	The *Althing* terminated by royal decree
1845	Restoration of the *Althing* as an advisory body, residing in Reykjavík
1851	National assembly, led by Jón Sigurdsson, calls for increased rights from Danish rulers
1870–1914	Emigration to North America
1874	Iceland granted a constitution, with limited legislative authority and powers of appropriation
1890s	Beginnings of British and German trawling near Iceland's shores
1901	Parliamentary democracy established in Denmark
1904	Home rule, with the minister for Iceland residing in Reykjavík; Iceland Bank founded, primarily with foreign capital
1915	Women receive the right to vote in parliamentary elections; flag for Iceland legalized
1918	Union Treaty with Denmark grants Iceland sovereignty in a personal union, but Denmark still handles Iceland's foreign affairs; an influenza epidemic kills 0.5 percent of the population

1940	Nazi takeover of Denmark, parliament assumes royal powers and takes over handling of foreign affairs; British occupation of Iceland begins
1941	United States–Icelandic defense agreement; arrival of U.S. forces
1944	Republic of Iceland founded at Thingvellir; Sveinn Björnsson becomes the country's first president
1949	Membership of NATO
1951	Return of U.S. troops
1955	Halldór Laxness awarded the Nobel Prize for literature
1958–1961	First "Cod War" with Britain
1970–1976	Two "Cod Wars" with Britain
1973	Eruption on Westman Islands destroys a third of the town
1980	Vigdís Finnbogadóttir becomes the world's first democratically elected female head of state
1994	Iceland enters the European Economic Area
2003–2006	Rapid expansion of Icelandic banks, mostly based on easy access to loans on the international market
2006	U.S. forces leave Iceland
2008	Collapse of the *króna* and the three Icelandic banks, emergency law to stave off state bankruptcy; application for a seat on the UN Security Council fails; first year in (recorded) history without fatalities at sea
2009	Pots and pans revolution; new left-wing coalition applies for EU membership

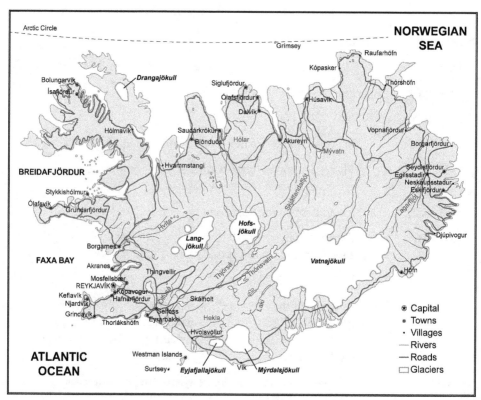

Iceland. (Cartography by Jeff Dixon.)

1

Norse Iceland: Discovery, Settlement, and Vengeance (874–999)

THE DISCOVERY OF A DISTANT LAND

The history of Iceland is a story about a young nation and a young state. It is also about one of the most recent lands on earth. Today, Iceland's oldest rock formations date from around 16 million years ago, just a flash from the present when compared with the world's most ancient rocks, which are more than 4 billion years old.

Iceland is a remote island, touching the polar circle in the North Atlantic. It lies nearly 200 miles from Greenland's eastern shores, 400 miles from the Faroe Islands, and 500 miles from the northern coast of Scotland. It is around 40,000 square miles in size (similar to Cuba or the state of Kentucky). The island's oldest parts—mountain plateaus in the northwest and along the east coast—consist of basalt lava, which streamed from a hot spot on the North Atlantic ridge between the drifting Eurasian and American tectonic plates during the tertiary period in the world's geological history. The basalt continued to stream until the ice age began, some three million years ago. Then the volcanic activity persisted, but glaciers covered the emerging landmass and tuff stone, and dolerite lava was created instead of basalt. Volcanoes also emerged.

At times, an ice shield covered almost the whole of the island, and advancing glaciers shaped the land by their enormous weight and force, forging deep valleys and fjords. During the ice age's warmer periods, the shield shrunk and the land formation took a different turn. Long canyons were created where glacial water suddenly burst forward, and glacial rivers carried forth soil and sand, creating lowlands, primarily along the south coast.

The ice age ended 10,000 years ago. As temperatures rose permanently and most of the ice cap melted away, the land began to ascend so that, today, signs of old sea levels can be found in places at an altitude of more than 300 feet. The southwestern part of Iceland has even begun to descend again.

After the end of the ice age, lava continued to flow from the two volcanic belts that lie roughly from the island's southwestern tip to the western part of the interior, and from the islands to the south of the mainland through Vatnajökull glacier and beyond the northeastern coastline. Thus, the volcanic formation of Iceland has gone on unabated for millions of years. The process has in fact been compared with a conveyor belt: Since the Eurasian and North American plates continue to drift apart, at the present rate of one-third of an inch in each direction per year, new lava continues to flow from the hot spot astride the North Atlantic ridge. Older rock formations are pushed outward, where, ultimately, they sink into the sea, millions of years after their creation.[1]

The history of the island's flora is also short in comparison with most other parts of the globe. The oldest tree fossils date from 10 million years ago, near the end of the tertiary period. Remains of up to 50 types have been discovered, including broad-leaved and pine trees, indicating that the flora was then similar to the present vegetation on the east coast of the United States and central Europe. During the ice age, the trees all but vanished, and afterward, birch wood was the prime type of tree on the island. Some plants may also have survived the ice age, and the seeds of others arrived later with wind, birds, ocean currents, or drift ice. Drastic changes in climate still occurred, and sudden drops in temperature could gravely affect vegetation. Natural forces have therefore made their mark on the land in more ways than humans have ever been able to—but of course over a much longer period.

The remoteness of the island also affected its animal life. After the ice age, foxes and field mice were the first land mammals to appear, presumably making their way with drift ice from Greenland. Seals and whales swam in the adjacent waters, which must also have abounded with fish. Migratory birds discovered the island and also those insects that could survive in the relatively cool climate.

But what about humans? By the start of the first millennium AD, humankind had settled in all corners of the world. Archaeological evidence suggests that only the most isolated islands remained uninhabited, like the many small islands of the Pacific and the larger islands that are now known as Madagascar, New Zealand, and Iceland. Of these, the first two may have been discovered in the first centuries AD. Madagascar was settled only around AD 700, however, and New Zealand even later, possibly about AD 1,300. As for Iceland, it cannot be ruled out that well before these dates, an adventurous voyager or a merchant who drifted off course may have sighted the island, gone ashore, and even stayed there. Around 400 BC, the Greek explorer Pytheas claimed to have sailed north from the British Isles to a country he called Thule, near the frozen sea where the sun never set. Still, if this is true, it seems more likely that Pytheas sailed to Norway rather than Iceland.

In the southeastern part of Iceland, a few Roman coins from around 300 BC have been unearthed. While it is possible that a vessel on its way to or from Britain, a Roman province at the time, strayed north, the coins most likely belonged to settlers who arrived much later. In the early sixth century AD, the renowned Irish monk Brendan allegedly sailed to new lands to the north of Ireland, where he witnessed volcanic eruptions on land and at sea. It has been suggested that he may have witnessed these events off Iceland. This seems most unlikely, however. Overall, the tales of Brendan's voyages have a legendary air to them, in some ways reminiscent of the travels of Sindbad and Ulysses. Furthermore, the descriptions of volcanic activity seem rather to originate from Italy, where the island of Stromboli was constantly erupting and other volcanoes were active as well.[2]

Around 730, the English monk Bede, known as the first writer of British history, recounted stories of the island of Thule in the north. Again, the land in question was probably Norway. Even so, there can be little doubt that by the eighth century AD, Irish hermits had settled in Iceland. Seeking solitude in their religious fervor, they dared to sail out into the ocean on small boats, wood framed and covered with animal skins (the Gaelic word is *curach*). In 825 or so, the Irish monk Dicuil stated that for more than 100 years, hermits had stayed on islands in the north but that they were then being driven away by Norse intruders. Here he must have been referring to the Faroe Islands, which probably began to be settled by Norsemen in the early ninth century but may have been populated by others up to 500 years before. Dicuil then went on to recount descriptions he had heard from other monks 30 years before, of another island where the sun was so bright at midnight in the summertime that people could easily pick lice from their shirts. This must have been Iceland.

The presence of Irish monks on the island has not been confirmed by archaeological finds. Still, there is inconclusive evidence of a man-made cave on the south coast before the recorded Norse settlement. Also written accounts from the twelfth century contain stories of Christian hermits who left the island because they did not want to interact with heathens. Presumably, they may just as well have been driven away by the newcomers, but these chronicles, along with a number of place-names (like *Papey*, Papal Island, off Iceland's south-eastern shore) must support the contention that the first humans on the island were Irish monks in search of solitude and intimacy with their god.

These pioneers probably survived on fishing and hunting. They sailed in small groups, no more than a dozen or so on a boat, and it is almost certain that no women were among them. No permanent settlement therefore occurred. That was left to Norse chieftains and farmers and their entourage, both captive and free.

When did those settlers of Iceland arrive? That has been among the most hotly debated issues in Icelandic history. Was it in the late ninth century AD, as has long been believed, or even up to two centuries before? The various answers have depended on the types of sources used, including written records from the first centuries of settlement, excavations, and scientific means to date archaeological and geological samples.

Who settled the island? Were they mostly Norse or did a significant number of Celts also move to Iceland? Again, the answers rely on the type of information at hand, much enhanced since the late twentieth century through advances in genetic research. And, finally, why did people decide to move to this faraway island? While some went against their will, the voyagers who took the lead must have had solid reasons to risk their lives on a treacherous journey across the North Atlantic.

First, reasons and incentives. By the seventh century AD, new trade routes had developed in Scandinavia, the modern territory of Norway, Sweden, and Denmark, which was primarily populated by people called Norse or Norsemen. After the fall of the Roman Empire, southern routes were abandoned, and trade increased with peoples around the North Sea, the Baltic, and even farther, to Russia and beyond. Simultaneously, sailing techniques improved. The Norse learned to build two types of ships: the long ships that were light, shallow, and fast warships, and used oarsmen as the main source of power; and the shorter and bulkier merchant vessels, the *knörr*, with only a few oar ports. Both had a large single sail.

In AD 793, Norse raiders ransacked a monastery on the island of Lindisfarne, off England's eastern coast. While such attacks had undoubtedly taken place before, this one has lived in history because extensive accounts of the brutality have survived. Monks were killed and valuables destroyed or stolen. In modern historiography, the Viking Age had begun. For almost three centuries, the Vikings (probably the name was originally used in the Norse language over someone who sailed to unknown destinations in search of fame and glory) pillaged and brought fear to peoples in the British Isles and elsewhere in Western Europe.

While it is sometimes said that history is written by the victors, this was a case of history being written by those who could write. Apart from primitive

runic inscriptions, the marauding Vikings did not have a written language like the victims did, leaving us with a rather one-sided version of events, admittedly. In the late eighth century, to compare, heathens in Saxony were massacred in the name of Christianity.

Besides, trading voyages continued as well. Some Norsemen focused on raids, others were merchants, and some may have switched professions as opportunity and desire demanded. Norse trading posts and power centers were established, for instance, in Dublin and York. Furthermore, the Norsemen began to colonize regions on the British Isles: the Shetland Islands, Orkney Islands, and the Hebrides, along the Scottish coast and in various other settlements. Shortage of land, especially in Norway, may have led to this development.

Finally, consolidation of power in Norway probably contributed to the settlement of distant lands. There were a number of small kingdoms, local earls also had considerable authority, and farmers could have a say in important decisions at the *things,* the regional assembly of free men. In the seventh and eighth centuries, leading chieftains began to amass wealth and power in Norway and elsewhere in Scandinavia. As this process continued, an increasing number of men must have lost power or found themselves threatened by the victorious leaders.

In short, there were many reasons why the various Norsemen decided to move to Iceland. A sense of adventure or the wish to build a new life may even be added, but a definite answer cannot be given. That conclusion leads to both a consideration of the sources at hand and the timing of the settlers' arrival. Archeological remains confirm theories of social upheavals, changing trade routes, and the consolidation of power in Scandinavia. Written accounts from the British Isles, often by eyewitnesses, tell the story of Viking brutality. And then there are the sources from Iceland itself.

Around 1130, Ari the Learned Thorgilsson, a chieftain, scholar, and priest, wrote the *Book of Icelanders,* a brief chronicle of the island's history. A longer work, the *Book of Settlements,* is a catalog of the original colonizers and a joint work of numerous authors. The oldest existing versions of the compilation date from 1275 to 1280. In this work and some other written sources, emigration from Norway to Iceland was explained by the aggressive unification of Norway by Harald Fairhair, a local king who ultimately conquered the whole country and created the Norwegian Kingdom. While some present scholars doubt whether Harald actually existed since the oldest sources that mention him date from the twelfth century, the fact remains that by the tenth and eleventh centuries, the separate kingdoms of Norway, Denmark, and Sweden had been established.[3]

The *Book of Icelanders* and the *Book of Settlements,* along with other sources from the twelfth century and beyond, also time the Norse discovery and settlement of Iceland. First, some Norwegians were said to have become lost on their way to the Faroe Islands, probably around the middle of the ninth century. Ultimately, they reached an unknown land. They scaled mountains and searched for human settlements; they found none but praised the country when they returned to Norway. Among the men was a Norwegian by the name of Naddoddur, who gave the new country its first name, *Snæland* (Snowland). A Swedish man, Gardar Svavarsson, heard the tale and decided to search for this land. That he did, sailing around the island, building a house on the northern shore, and wintering there. In the spring, as Gardar was to depart again, one free man, Náttfari, and two slaves, a man and a woman, stayed behind and established a farm.

Next, a Viking by the name of Flóki decided to seek the new island. He was said to have released ravens on the journey and, following their lead, was brought safely ashore. Hence he became known as Raven-Flóki. According to the written tales, his livestock died during a harsh winter. Before he left the country for good the following spring, a frustrated Raven-Flóki therefore gave it a cold and unsympathetic name, *Ísland* (Iceland).

The next voyager stayed, however, and was given preeminence in the *Book of Settlements*. In the two main versions, Ingólfur, the son of Örn, sailed with his blood brother Leifur to the island, which Raven-Flóki had discovered. They were warriors and had become involved in slayings; a move to a new island seemed sensible in the circumstances. Still, they returned to Norway, and Leifur went on a raid to Ireland, where he found a sword in a burial mound and also brought 10 Celtic men back as slaves. After this venture, Leifur became known as Hjörleifur (*Hjör* meaning sword). He and Ingólfur then decided to move permanently to the new island in the north.

Stories of their journey describe how they safely reached their destination, although Hjörleifur had neglected to make a sacrifice to the Norse gods. After the first winter, however, his slaves killed him and other free men in his company. Ingólfur, on the other hand, had honored the gods and fared well. As he saw the island rise from the sea, he cast his high-seat pillars (wooden columns on either side of a chieftain's seat) overboard and promised to build his farm where they would be washed ashore. This happened to be by a small bay on the southwestern coast, which Ingólfur named *Vík* (bay) or *Reykjavík* (smoke bay), the latter version possibly because of steam from hot springs nearby. Ingólfur was also said to have avenged Hjörleifur, killing the slaves on a cluster of islands to the south of the mainland where they had sought refuge. Subsequently, these islands were called Westman Islands (Westman being the Norse name for a Celt).

When did all this happen? Ari the Learned wrote that Ingólfur's settlement began around 870. The *Book of Settlements* puts his first arrival in Iceland at 874 and permanent residence from 877. Nonetheless, the year 874 has since been established—semiofficially and in the collective memory of contemporary Icelanders—as the first year of the settlement of Iceland. Even so, on closer look, the stories described earlier about the Norse discoverers of Iceland, culminating in the tales of Ingólfur and Hjörleifur, provide a weak basis for this history of the island's founding fathers as it were. First, if the written accounts are indeed to be believed, then Náttfari must be granted the honor of being the first settler of Iceland, along with the unnamed slaves who parted with Gardar Svavarsson. Second, the story of Raven-Flóki is obviously apocryphal and similar to the biblical description of the doves who led Noah to a solid ground after the deluge. And Hjörleifur is most likely a fictional character. Ingólfur, on the other hand, probably existed, although he was probably not the son of Örn but of Björnólfur, another Norse chieftain. Moreover, the stories of the high pillars can hardly be believed. In 1974, when 1,000 years of settlement in Iceland were celebrated, more than 100 marked pillars were put at sea along the island's southeastern and southern coast. None of them drifted to Reykjavík or anywhere nearby.

Furthermore, the timing of the settlement of Iceland, as given in the *Book of Icelanders* and the *Book of Settlements*, may be compared with archeological findings. This is also where science meets history. To begin with, since volcanic eruptions have occurred countless times on the island (every five years on average in the last several centuries), the soil is marked by layers of tephra (volcanic ash). These layers, and remnants of habitation between them, can be timed by measuring the remaining amount of the radioactive isotope carbon 14, which decreases gradually over time. Pollen analysis can also denote sudden changes in vegetation due to farming by humans.

Most recently, layers of ash have been dated by comparison with ancient ice cores drilled from the Greenland glacier, which also contains the tephra. This method provides dates within the span of four years, and it has been confirmed that a layer of tephra, which lies just beneath remains of human habitation in Reykjavík and elsewhere, dates from 871, give or take two years. This layer and the ice from the Greenland ice cap—snow that fell around 871—seem to validate, if not to a year, the timings given in the *Book of Icelanders* and the *Book of Settlements*. It does not prove, however, that Ingólfur was the first settler. Moreover, remnants of a wall in Reykjavík seem to be older than the tephra layer. Maybe it was built a few years before, say, in 867, or maybe much earlier.

Indeed, some archeologists have been convinced that their excavations, for instance, in the Westman Islands, confirm an earlier settlement. Pollen analyses and carbon 14 calculations may therefore suggest that the island was inhabited decades, or even centuries, before the late ninth century. Then again, these findings are never as precise as the drilled ice method. In addition, remains that date from before the settlement layer may be signs of brief encounters rather than permanent inhabitance. Also the oldest swords and artifacts in pagan graves in Iceland date from the latter half of the ninth century, and the enumeration of ancestors in the *Book of Settlements* and other accounts indicates that an extensive movement of people to Iceland began only in the last decades of the ninth century. Lastly, it must seem logical that the island was settled some time after the Norse settlements on the British Isles and the Faroe Islands.

It is therefore impossible to state definitely the timing of the first settlement of Iceland, just like the first human to set his eyes on the island (it seems most likely, still, that it was a man rather than a woman) will never be identified. Nonetheless, the general period of settlement probably began around the period identified in the written sources at hand.

In this connection, the composition of the original population may also provide some clues. In itself, the origin of the settlers of Iceland is a fascinating issue and, again, the written accounts provide a certain version. The *Book of Settlements* contains information about 435 original settlers, their lineage, where they came from, and where they established themselves in Iceland. Most of the settlers are said to have come from the regions of western Norway, while some arrived from the Norse settlements in the British Isles. Most were men, leading personalities like the famed Ingólfur or Skallagrímur, a forceful chieftain who settled in Borgarfjördur, north of Ingólfur's wide-reaching settlement, and Helgi the lean, who had an Irish mother, Rafarta, said to be the daughter of Kjarval (Cerbhall), a king in Ireland. Helgi claimed the whole of Eyjafjördur in the north for him and his people. The work also mentions a few women, most notably Audur the Wise, who allegedly fled from Scotland after her son had been killed there and made her farm in the western part of Iceland.

In all, the *Book of Settlements* contains more than 3,000 names and some 4,000 place-names, most of which are still in existence. This has given credence to the collection although it can clearly not be believed in its entirety, written as it was at least more than 200 years after the events it describes. Recently, some scholars have even gone so far as to call the *Book of Settlements* a work of fiction.[4]

Besides, the *Book of Settlements* focuses on leading farmers and chieftains, not ordinary people, and certainly not the Celtic slaves or women who were married to Iceland-bound Norsemen, more often than not against their will. The book and other written accounts only confirm that these people existed; apart from that, they have almost no history. Their subjugation, fear, or fortitude was surely real but must be imagined rather than confirmed by historical sources. Scientific advances have also confirmed the strong Celtic composition in the original body of people in Iceland. If the *Book of Settlements* is to be believed, around 86 percent of the first settlers were Norse and the remaining 14 percent were Celts. Although the findings have not been undisputed, genetic research has since suggested that in fact only around two-thirds of the male population were of Norse ancestry, whereas 60 percent of the women were of Celtic origin.

The journey across the ocean was undoubtedly a risky affair. The voyagers had few means to know whether they were heading in the right direction, especially if the skies were overcast as they often are in the North Atlantic (presumably that was also the case in settlement times). They did learn to read into cloud banks, and it is has been argued that they made use of sunstone, a rock crystal that could have indicated their location. On closer look, this seems very unlikely.[5] Luck had to be with seafarers—or as they must have wished for, the goodwill of their god or gods.

The vessel used, the *knörr*, was 50 to 80 feet long and could carry dozens of people. On each journey to Iceland, which usually took some four-to-seven days' sailing from Norway, there were probably 20 to 30 persons on board, with water and food that needed to last them for weeks. The company carried livestock with them—cows, sheep, goats, and pigs—and probably a few horses. The prospective farmers must also have brought with them farming tools and weapons like axes and swords. Embers were kept alive in a tub.

The number of the first Icelandic settlers cannot be ascertained. Maybe there were about a hundred new arrivals each year, and there is general agreement that by the end of the tenth century, the influx had more or less ceased. Although it has been argued that by the middle of that century, some 50,000 people lived in the country, a lower number of even 10,000 to 15,000 seems plausible as well. Apparently, that left space aplenty for all, but as the newcomers were to realize, many parts of the island were uninhabitable and some regions were richer than others. The land and its resources were not unlimited, especially as time passed. Soon, the inhabitants of the island would also be astonished or marred by volcanic eruptions, cold winters, avalanches, and other natural assaults.

Moreover, some settlers had grown used to making their living as pillaging Vikings and others were on the run after feuds and killings in Norway. Brutality and ruthlessness were their way of life. Others wanted nothing but a peaceful existence on their new farm but may have found it necessary to defend themselves. This they had to do, however, in a country without law, order, and established leaders. A new society rarely establishes itself in an orderly and peaceful manner. After a hazardous voyage, an equally unsafe life may have awaited the settlers of Iceland.

AN EMERGENT SOCIETY

It was a pristine place, all but untouched by humans. Whales, walruses, and seals swam in the seas as they had done for hundreds of thousands of years. Driftwood covered many coasts. Ocean birds like the seagull, gannet, puffin, and great auk abounded. Seasonal birds arrived in spring. Foxes ran wild. Freshwater rivers were full of salmon and trout. The settlers quickly realized that they did not have to fear bears or wolves, although in the extreme north and the west, they may have encountered the occasional polar bear.

The average temperature was apparently similar to conditions in the twentieth century. It was and is higher than the island's latitude would suggest because of the Gulf Stream, which runs up to its shores. Vegetation covered about two-thirds of the country. Woodland and shrubbery reached up to an altitude of 2,500 to 3,000 feet, with birch predominant. In the wet and windy maritime climate, trees rarely exceeded 6 to 10 feet. Centuries later, stories survived in Iceland of settlers who had to bring wood for house construction to the country. In the interior and other mountainous regions, heather and moss grew. Marshes were also common as well as black sands, lava fields, lakes, waterfalls, glaciers, hot springs, and seemingly impenetrable rivers and mountain ridges.

The land was in many ways unlike anything the newcomers had seen before, whether they came from Norway or the British Isles. Still, they had to base their existence to a large degree on what they knew and had learned at home. It may safely be assumed that the first settlers established their farms near the sea or on islands and headlands where it was not necessary to clear the woods or cultivate hayfields for the livestock. The farmstead Reykjavík fits that scenario well; it was on open lowland with a good anchorage. There must have been plenty of driftwood and birds to exploit and probably seals and walrus as well. Nearby, there was a fine salmon river and the weather was usually mild. The gods' guidance of Ingólfur's pillars is not needed to explain why a farm was established in this excellent region.

Western Norway is a mountainous region, with little lowland. Many settlers were therefore used to farming in hilly environs, and some of them must have contended themselves with land on higher ground in Iceland. Most parts of the country were probably settled in groups, led by chieftains who founded an estate with smaller farms and cottages attached. Alternatively, settlements where a few farmsteads were similar in size may also have developed. Soon, the inhabitants began to clear the woods, aided by their livestock, which gnawed at the birch as best they could. In the first two centuries after the arrivals of humans, cows, pigs, horses, and sheep, fields and pasture apparently replaced birch as the main feature of Icelandic flora. Gradually, sheep farming became dominant, since they adapted best to the relatively harsh climate, although cattle continued to be raised, especially in the southern, and slightly warmer, part of the island. Acres were also cultivated, as confirmed by the remains of a scratch plow, which was excavated in Reykjavík and place-names like Akranes and Akureyri (*Akra-* and *Akur-* meaning field). Barley was grown for the production of ale.

The *Book of Settlements* described clear rules for the original demarcation of land in Iceland: a man was allowed to lay claim to areas inside all bonfires he could light within sight of each other in a day. Women could claim land by leading a heifer around it from sunrise to sunset. Overall, the image is given of an orderly and peaceful process. That may certainly have been so in many cases, in particular where a powerful leader and his entourage could not be attacked or intimated. Furthermore, no remains of fortifications have been discovered from the settlement period. Still, the processes that are described in the *Book of Settlements* are obviously fictional, and the notion of violent fights over precious land cannot be discounted, even if no direct evidence for such episodes exists. Indeed, the location of the earliest burial mounds suggests that in some places people buried their kin not on the outskirts of a property, so as to assert their ownership, but instead near the farmhouse, a conceivable sign of fear and encirclement.

Most of the Norse settlers adhered to the pagan faith, a polytheistic religion where Odin ruled supreme, but Thor, the god of thunder, was probably most popular. Ingólfur and Hjörleifur were heathen, as has been mentioned, and the latter was deemed to have suffered for his disrespect toward the gods. The devout Ingólfur fared better. Conversely, Audur the Wise had adopted the Christian faith, as had the Ireland-born Helgi the Lean, one of the most prominent settlers in the northern part of the country. He vacillated, still, between the new and the old faith, allegedly pledging sacrifice to Thor before he set sail from Ireland but naming his estate *Kristnes* (Christ's cape). By the ninth century, the division between heathendom and Christianity was therefore not always clear-cut.

The pagan faith was not uniform, as indicated by differences in burial mounds. In addition, most knowledge about it can be gleaned only from later sources, especially the two *Eddas*, one a textbook on poetry, written in the thirteenth century by Snorri Sturluson, a chieftain and writer in Iceland, and the other a collection of poems from the same age (although the poetry was probably composed centuries before). While both works were almost certainly contaminated by the influence of Christendom, they describe a complex collection of deities, 12 male gods and the same number of goddesses. The faith clearly involved sacrificial customs, not of humans, though. It was fatalistic and animistic, with people believing in predestination and the supernatural powers of trees, mountains, or waterfalls.

So life in a new land had begun. How was it lived? How did people survive? How did they interact? How could they express emotions like fear, anger, and love? How did they die? Or, to begin with, how were they born? Birth was probably the only event in life that came about in a way irrespective of social status. When women gave birth, they presumably positioned themselves as nature taught—standing on two feet and more often than not, often, leaning on someone, or squatting or kneeling. Sometimes delivery occurred during travel or out in the open.[6]

For mothers, labor was often life-threatening. For the newborn, life could also end almost as soon as it began. Infant mortality was high; out of 25 skeletons in an eleventh-century graveyard, about half were of children under the age of two. Infanticide was also a known feature in the world of Norsemen. This could be the fate of a child born out of wedlock, or simply with a cleft lip or other irregularities. Moreover, the stark knowledge that the parents would not be able to feed the child may have forced them to let the newborn die. It may be asked, therefore, whether parental love even existed. Those scholars who have more or less denied its existence in medieval Europe have quoted countless records of brutality and abuse, concluding that compassion of this kind is a trait established by modern society. Furthermore, the high degree of natural infant deaths may have discouraged mothers and fathers from establishing immediate and close relations with their offspring. Still, the prevailing opinion holds that parental and especially motherly love is a natural instinct. Despite clear signs of a rough life and harshness, we must assume that children in early Iceland were more loved than disliked.

For those who survived infancy, the hierarchical division of people immediately began to influence or dictate their fate and well-being. The farm was everyone's universe, as it were, a self-sufficient unit. Practically, all the first inhabitants lived off the land and had no reason to wander far from home. Housing was simple, in line with the Norse tradition. Inside an oblong chamber, an open fire lay in the middle of a mud floor. The walls were made of stone and turf, with a single roof sustained by beams. The houses were probably 130 to 330 square feet. Bedsteads were along the walls, and the whole space was divided into a few sections by wooden panel. The chamber was a place for work, sleep, and nourishment. With the exception of the slaves, they were one "family" for at this time that term was mostly used to denote a single unit of production and consumption rather than a body of people related to each other.

The average number of persons on an affluent farm in the first centuries of settlement was probably around 15. A typical farmer may have owned some 6 cows and 25 ewes. Dairy products were consumed and the meat of cattle, sheep, and pigs. Fish and fowl were eaten as well. For storage in wintertime, foodstuffs were salted or soured. Meat was sometimes smoked and fish was dried. Ale was enjoyed, sometimes in excess, as recounted in numerous tales. In good years, there was probably ample food for all. In hard times, famine set in. According to the *Book of Settlements,* in one austere year, many people starved to death and stories were told of the sick and the elderly being thrown off cliffs in order to leave more food to abler persons.

Little is known for certain about clothing except that people dressed in wool and wore shoes made of animal skins. Presumably, they wore underwear and protective clothes in bad weather, like mittens, hats, and oilskins. Still, wet feet and numb fingers must have annoyed or hurt the inhabitants of Iceland, as was going to be the case for the next thousand years or so.

Hunger and cold had to affect slaves the most. They were an essential factor in the running of a farm but could be treated like livestock. When food was scarce, they received little or none, and their diet must have been poorer than that of free persons. As it turned out, slavery proved not to be economical on the island since farming was primarily seasonal. Some historians maintain that many slaves may fairly soon have become tenants with the limited freedom that that entailed, including the right to enter into marriage. Others find that hard to believe.

Free laborers fared little better than slaves and tenants. They were obliged to be engaged to a landowner on an annual basis. Women worked for food, clothing, and shelter, while men could earn up to half the price of a cow in a year. Some laborers were employed in fishing for their farmer when other duties allowed. Although there may have been respite in wintertime, it was hard work. The laborers would have to run after sheep; milk the cows; clear the woods; bring home firewood, peat, and charcoal; gather hay for the winter; plow the soil; and finish various other chores.

Worn and marred bones from the settlement period can give an indication of endless drudgery. Adding disease, epidemics, and violence to malnutrition and hard labor, it is no surprise that the life expectancy of people in Iceland in the first centuries of settlement was probably around 30 years, including infant deaths, but 40 to 50 years with that excluded. Then again, this was similar to the rest of Europe, and averages cannot tell the whole story.

Presumably, farmers and chieftains had a slightly better chance of a long life. They could also purchase fancy clothes and other luxuries from abroad. The landowner was the head of the household, the one whom others had to obey. He could kill his slaves without impunity and punish free laborers or expel them, a cruel penalty in a land where there seemed little chance of survival outside the farm universe. The landowner also ruled the lives of his children and wife. He determined whether newborns should live or die, and he chose their name. There are indications that free children played with toys like animal bones and enjoyed games where one was a soldier and the other a bishop, for instance. Still, childhood in settlement Iceland was brief and more filled with work than play. By the age of 12 or so, children were considered adults and were expected to provide their share rather than be a burden in the household. In a similar vein, old age did not bring ease of mind and the respect of others. There were of course exceptions to this generalization, but, like the young, the elderly were usually considered an inconvenience, helpless, even senile, and unable to support the family.

Women were not a single unit, any more than men. Nonetheless, their gender determined that they enjoyed less freedom and rights than the dominant sex. Admittedly, wives of farmers ran the indoor household, organizing the making and preservation of food and other domestic work, as well as the production of homespun cloth, the island's sole export. Housewives were also responsible for treating dignified guests in an honorable manner, and they could exert great influence, it is argued, by encouraging or dissuading their husbands in feuds with other men.

Even so, women were rarely masters of their own destiny. As with parental love, scholars have debated the notion of romantic love in medieval Europe. The innate existence of lust is never doubted, but did people fall in love? Harshness of life and scarcity of resources make it likelier that other considerations counted more. Marriage, especially in the upper echelons of the emergent society, was a political and economic contract between families. Fathers and prospective husbands decided wedlock although women must sometimes have had a say in the matter. Moreover, daughters could claim inheritance only if they had no brothers, and husbands or other close male relatives were to control their possessions. There were exceptions to this, and well-off widows could lead an independent life, but the general rule is clear: it was a world dominated by men.

All men were not equal, however. It was also a world where a small number of men—landowners and chieftains—dominated the rest of the population, male and female. At first, that domination was exerted solely or primarily within each farmstead or small units of farms. But as time went on, some kind of structure had to be imposed. A *society* was constructed.

LAW AND ORDER, HONOR AND HATE

Being accustomed to the practice of *things*, the Norse settlers could be expected to establish a similar structure in the new country. The *thing* was an assembly to settle disputes and mete out punishments, agree on boundaries and price levels, and discuss improvements in communications and other matters of common concern. It was also a place where men could drink and gossip, renew friendships, trade goods, and create alliances in feuds if need be. It was not a democratic gathering in the modern sense; it was only a convention of free landowners, possibly around 5,000 in the first centuries of settlement, led by the most noble chieftains. Those overlords knew the laws and were named *godi* (*godar* in the plural). They may also have played a role in the pagan faith, for example, by overseeing animal sacrifice to honor the gods. No direct evidence of this exists, still, and some scholars conclude that, despite the term, the *godar* had nothing to do with religion.

In the arena of politics and power, the *godar* clearly ruled the land. Farmers were not obliged to follow a certain *godi*, but they usually pledged allegiance to the nearest one, assuming that they would then receive his protection and goodwill. In the *Book of Icelanders,* Ari the Learned recounted that around 900, Thorsteinn Ingólfsson, the son of Ingólfur, the famed settler of Reykjavík, was prominent in establishing a *thing* in the vicinity, at the cape of Kjalarnes. Around the same time, another assembly was established at Thórsnes (Thór's cape) in Breidafjördur in the west and maybe more assemblies were founded elsewhere in the country. Gradually, farmers and chieftains from a sizable part of southwestern Iceland gathered at Kjalarnes, and by 930 or so, Thorsteinn Ingólfsson and other chieftains in the southwest took the lead in establishing a new assembly for the whole of the country, the aptly named *Althing* (general assembly). Allegedly, a man named Úlfljótur went to Norway and brought back the latest law code of western Norway. His blood brother Grímur surveyed the island for a suitable location and decided on fields near a lake in the south, which were subsequently called Thingvellir (assembly fields). Thorsteinn Ingólfsson was selected the first law-speaker, or assembly president, a sure sign of his authoritative role in the process.

This information derives from the *Book of Icelanders* and other sources, written centuries later than the events that they refer to. As with the accounts in the *Book of Settlements,* they describe an orderly process where, in fact, the story was more complex. Quite possibly, the chieftains of Kjalarnes formed their assembly, and then the *Althing,* in response to the rise of other settlers and their descendants. Likewise, while Úlfljótur may well have existed, his journey across the sea to collect the laws of the land seems more mythical than true, and the year 930 cannot be taken for granted. The foundation of the *Althing* may well have taken place years or even a decade or so before.

Nonetheless, the formation of one legislative and judiciary body for the whole country must be considered a logical development. By the first decades of the tenth century, the inhabitants of Iceland had gained a basic knowledge of the country, where mountain ridges could be passed, rivers forded, and marshes traversed. They had begun to clear the birch woods on a grand scale, and paths through the land had been created. Their horse stock was increasing. Communications, in other words, were becoming easier. Thus, the Kjalarnes assembly was moved from the original location by the sea to a new ground more inland, and Thingvellir were at a crossroads, easily reached by the farmers in the south and the west, although those in the north and the east had to travel further.

The *Althing* convened for two weeks in high summer. Little is known of its initial structure, but around 963, a revision of its workings led to the following composition: the country was divided into four quarters. In each quarter, there were three local *things,* except in the northern one where there were four. These local assemblies convened in spring. From each one of them, a *godi* came to the *Althing* to sit in a law council, with two men from his entourage as advisers. To maintain balance between the quarters, all of them except the northern quarter also nominated three additional *godar* each. Thus, there were 12 *godar* from each quarter in the law council. The law-speaker was its head. He recited the existing law, and the council changed or amended the law as it saw fit, presumably through a majority or unanimous vote. Apparently, a fair amount of negotiations and compromise were therefore needed.

The *Althing* was also a judiciary. At first, a single court was probably held there, but with the revisions of around 963, four courts were established, one for each quarter. A few decades later, a fifth court, a supreme court of sorts, was also formed. The *godar* nominated 36 judges for each regional court where unanimity was required before sentences were passed. The nominations for the fifth court were more complex, but there only a majority was needed to reach a conclusion. Women could not sit in the courts, and not even bear witness in disputes.

Most knowledge of this political and legal system is gleaned from the much-mentioned *Book of Icelanders* and a collection of the country's laws, first recorded at the start of the twelfth century but only surviving in manuscripts from the latter half of the thirteenth century. This lapse in time between events and sources must be kept in mind, but the law, as it is known, seems to have been extensive. It stipulated, for instance, how commodities that were considered common goods, like a beached whale, should be divided. It also contained provisions about the upkeep of paupers or assistance in case of fire or livestock losses. This help was arranged within local districts, which were probably formed in the tenth century. Aside from overseeing communal aid, the district leaders could prohibit marriages and the establishment of a new farm unless couples could demonstrate enough collateral, and, similarly, they could prohibit newcomers from settling in the district. The resistance to uncontrolled movements of people can perhaps most be inferred from the law that allowed the castration of vagabonds.

Obviously, the aim of the *Althing*, the local *things*, and the districts was to maintain order and stability, as determined by the island's chieftains and affluent landowners. For this, there was the law and the courts. But there was no executive. If the ruling class wanted to enforce their rules, they had to do it on an individual basis. They did not control a police force or an army. And although a wronged man could have his adversary convicted in the courts, it was up to him to enforce the ruling. In this context, the law stipulated punishment for various offences, primarily financial penalties or exile, either temporarily abroad or total banishment, in which the offender could be killed wherever he was. The right to kill without a previous ruling by the courts also existed. Thus, a man could slay another man if the latter had murdered a close relative or raped his wife, daughter, mother, or sister. Homosexuality was present as in all other societies, but its existence was proven in another way by damning references in the sagas, legal codes, and similar written sources.

Sexual relations with a person of the same gender were explicitly forbidden, and a man had the right to avenge by death claims of such affinity. Homosexual persons had no opportunity to express their genuine feelings.

Generally, revenge was a key component in the judicial framework. It might even be labeled the right to hate, as historian Gunnar Karlsson has put it.[7] In the same way, honor was a fundamental concept. A dispute over land demarcation might not involve much material assets but rather a quest for respect in the region. Rape, more revealingly, was not considered a crime against a woman but an assault on the honor of the husband and her closest male relatives as well, since women continued to belong to their parents' relations after marriage. Men also counted both their mother's and their father's ascendants as kin. The kinship system was therefore unlike the predominant structure in the southern parts of Europe, where a wife was simply ensconced into a man's family.

The societal emphasis on honor marked the mind-set and mood of chieftains and farmers. Men must have felt hurt, enraged, or feeble when they were faced with an affront of some kind. While women and laborers were subjugated in society, this mental pain of inadequacy and shame was primarily restricted to the ruling class of males. Then again, slighted men may well have vented their anger and frustration on weaker parties in their own household.

Despite the prominence of penalties, revenge, and honor, the underlying assumption was that society would disintegrate if men thought primarily about fighting each other, inside or outside the courts. Most disputes may therefore have been settled through informal arbitration and negotiation by a chieftain, or between two or more chieftains. A successful outcome included not only the avoidance of escalating conflict but also the preservation of honor on both sides. Subsequently, the chieftains—the *godar*—and the leading landowners in each district had to demonstrate their prestige and honor in other ways than by force. The more followers they had, the stronger they were perceived, and the more generous festivities they could throw the better. In the words of archeologist and historian Orri Vésteinsson, such gatherings were indeed among the most important functions in society, strengthening bonds in the community and respect for the local leader.[8] A seemingly straightforward action like the giving and receiving of presents also had underlying societal connotations. Such acts could be a sign of honor, strengthening friendships and stability. Conversely, they might also be construed as dishonorable insults, intentionally or not, with fateful consequences.

Put simply, fragility is another key word to describe the society, which had been created in Iceland by the late tenth century. It may even have carried with it its own seeds of destruction. But before the story is taken further, it is apt to look at how the creation of Iceland and Icelandic society has been remembered and used through the centuries until the present day.

THE VIKING SPIRIT

In contemporary Iceland, the geological origins and shaping of the island are evoked in the colors of the national flag, blue for the mountains, red for the volcanoes, and white for the glaciers. Moreover, the relatively harsh climate is habitually said to have shaped the Icelanders by exterminating weak individuals while those who endured became stronger through an endless fight with nature. By the same token, politicians and statesmen have used the Viking heritage to highlight alleged national characteristics like courage, innovation, and a yearning for freedom and triumph. Less is made of the legitimate question, whether marauding Vikings should perhaps be described as despicable terrorists of their time.[9]

The Norse discovery of Greenland and North America has also been cited as evidence of an inherent Icelandic bravery. The first settlers of Iceland gained a vague knowledge of a territory to the west of the island. A few of them undoubtedly strayed off their course and told stories of a mountainous land, covered with ice. Reputedly, two Norsemen nonetheless decided to move to this inhospitable place. The former one failed and the latter one was said to have set sail in 986. This was Eiríkur the Red, a fearsome man who had been forced to flee to Iceland after he was convicted of manslaughter in his native Norway. He fared little better in the new land, however, as he got into fatal feuds and was sentenced to a three-year exile. Since he could not return to Norway, the story went, he decided to journey further west with his retinue. He reached the desired destination and named the country Greenland so that others might be tempted to follow him. A number of people did, and the Norse population probably grew to a few thousand in the following centuries. The new inhabitants became Greenlanders, just like the Norsemen of Iceland became Icelanders. The story of their survival and eventual demise some time after the fifteenth century at the very latest is only indirectly a part of the history of the Iceland. The reasons for their disappearance are unknown but a combination of colder climate, diseases, and conflicts with the Inuit population is the most convincing explanation.

In the early days, the Norse settlers of Greenland seemed bound to reach even further westward. Stories of such travels are recounted in two of the Icelandic family sagas, epic tales that were written in the thirteenth and fourteenth centuries, and thus discussed in detail later. The *Saga of the Greenlanders* describes how a man went off course from Iceland to Greenland and caught sight of new lands, which must have been somewhere on the eastern coast of the present-day Canada. More famously, however, the *Saga of Eiríkur the Red* recounts that his son Leifur (known as the Lucky) went ashore on these lands around the year 1000. Furthest south, the terrain was fertile, with wheat and vine in abundance. Therefore, he named that country Vínland (Vine land). According to the two sagas mentioned here, another man, Thorfinnur Thórdarson, sailed to Vínland with a group of Norsemen and lived there for a few years. His wife, Gudrídur Thorbjarnardóttir, gave birth to a son, Snorri, but the settlement did not last. The new arrivals were too few in number, and they ran into conflict with the aboriginal population. In the next centuries, some voyagers most likely sailed to the new lands in the west, but there is no evidence that a lasting settlement was established. That is not to say that it did not happen and recent genetic research suggests that at least one native woman was taken to Iceland and had children there.

Although the sagas are not trustworthy when it comes to specific events and details, there is no reason to doubt the tales of the westward journeys that have indeed been confirmed by archeological findings, most notably at L'anse aux Meadows in Newfoundland. These travels were a true feat of navigation, individual resilience, and courage. Their overall importance is another matter. Throughout the twentieth century and up to the present day, Icelanders have prided themselves on the Icelandic discovery of North America long before Columbus, downplaying or ignoring the existence of the aboriginal population. The infant Snorri has thus been hailed as the first European born in North America or even the first white child there. Further-more, a semiofficial dispute arose about the origins of Leifur the Lucky since the Norwegians could point to the birthplace of his father. On Leif Erikson Day in the United States, the administration in Washington diplomatically calls him the son of Iceland and grandson of Norway. Arguably, however, the first Europeans on the Western continent would best be described as Greenlandic or just Norse.[10]

The Viking heritage of heroism and audacity is a good example of the role history can play in the shaping of national consciousness. As early as the sev-enteenth century, an author of Iceland's history, Arngrímur Jónsson (dubbed the Learned, like Ari), praised the virtues of the freedom-loving settlers. By then, the island had come under foreign rule, and from the beginnings of the struggle for Icelandic independence in the middle of the nineteenth century, the alleged inheritance of bravery and other merits was emphasized with even more gusto. For the next hundred years or so, the discovery and settle-ment of Iceland, as described in the *Book of Icelanders*, the *Book of Settlements*, the sagas, and other sources, were firmly believed by scholars and the general public alike. Ingólfur Arnarson (Arnar being the genitive form of Örn, de-scribed erroneously as Ingólfur's father) was celebrated as the first settler of Iceland, arriving in 874. The foundation of the *Althing* was deemed to have taken place in 930, and it was hailed as the oldest parliament in the world. Suggestions that it was undemocratic in the modern sense of the word were usually dismissed, and when the feeble communists in Iceland suggested in 1930—purportedly at the thousandth anniversary of the *Althing*—that the common man Náttfari was really the first man to make his farm on the island, they were met with derision or disgust. The first settler had to be a noble chieftain. In 1924, a statue of Ingólfur Arnarson was erected in Reykjavík, but there is no statue of his wife, Hallveig Fródadóttir.

Likewise, the ethnic origins of the initial settlers have been used, or abused, to support contentions about the nature of Icelanders. During the Nazi era, enthusiasts of Aryanism notoriously held that Iceland was a bastion of a pure, Germanic race. Some of them were greatly disappointed when they realized that the island was not full of blond-haired and blue-eyed idols. They also overlooked the Celtic influence, as indeed one author of the *Book of Settlements* had done when he wrote that the work's primary goal was to refute the claim that "we are descendants of slaves and thugs." In contemporary Iceland, conversely, the Celtic origins are recognized, and the arrogant notion can even be heard that they explain the poetic skills of men and the beauty of the women.

Fortunately, the ethnic origins of the Icelanders can be made beneficial in a more scientific manner. Notwithstanding debates about the moral aspects of genetic research, the fact that a small, fairly homogeneous group of people settled in Iceland and remained fairly isolated there for over a thousand years has provided fertile ground for such studies. Moreover, in recent decades, a more nuanced version of the settlement has emerged. Although politicians, tourist entrepreneurs, and, apparently, the general public still tend to favor a positive history of heroes and heroics, source criticism and an increased focus on the rugged life of the general population have led academics to discard or downplay celebratory dates as well as the achievements or even the existence of acclaimed notables. In fact, the more research there is done, the less seems to be known for certain. Single heroes fade as well and unnamed masses emerge.

Apart from questions about Viking brutality instead of heroics, the settlers' treatment of the land they discovered has even been criticized. In his widely read work *Collapse*, writer Jared Diamond pointed out that the first inhabitants of Iceland embarked on a merciless destruction of trees and vegetation, with the result that Iceland "became the European country with the most serious ecological damage."[11] While it is true that today, vegetation covers only a quarter of the country, and woods merely one-hundredth, the erosion cannot be explained only by human habitation. Worsening climate and volcanic eruptions were also at play, and recent research suggests that previous assumptions about widespread forests and their rapid destruction when the first settlers arrived seem exaggerated. Furthermore, they had to travel and get firewood, and they knew only sheep and cattle farming. Taking that into account, they simply had to clear the land.

The life of the past has to be seen in the context of its times, whether it involves Viking attacks during the sometimes brutal advancement of Christianity, the burning down of wood to survive in a rough country, or even the need of an emerging nation for stories about a proud heritage.

NOTES

1. Sigurdur Steinthórsson, "Hversu gamlir eru mismunandi hlutar Íslands?" [How old are the various parts of Iceland?], *Vísindavefurinn* June 11, 2000. http://visindavefur.is/?id=631.

2. Árni Hjartarson, "Hekla og heilagur Brendan," [Mount Hekla and St. Brendan], *Saga* 45/1 (2007), 161–171.

3. Sverrir Jakobsson, "'Erindringen om en mægtig Personlighed': Den norsk-islandske historiske tradisjon om Harald Hårfagre i et kildekritisk perspektiv," ["The memory of a mighty personality": A criticial perspective on traditional historical view on Harald Fairhaired in Norway and Iceland], *Historisk tidsskrift* 81 (2002), 213–230.

4. Sveinbjörn Rafnsson, "Hvad er Landnámabók?" [What is *The Book of Settlements?*], *Saga* 46/2 (2008), 179–193.

5. Árni Einarsson, "Sólarsteinninn. Tæki eda tákn?" [The sunstone. A tool or a symbol?], *Gripla* 21 (2010), 281–297.

6. Anna Sigurdardóttir, "Úr veröld kvenna—Barnsburdur," [From the world of women giving birth], Björg Einarsdóttir (ed.), *Ljósmædur á Íslandi* [Icelandic midwives] II (Reykjavík: Ljósmædrafélag Íslands, 1984), 139–145.

7. Gunnar Karlsson, "Tilfinningaréttur. Tilraun um nýtt sagnfrædilegt hugtak," [Emotional right. A trial concerning a new historical term], *Saga* 47/1 (2009), 75–101, (here 96–97).

8. Orri Vésteinsson, "'Hann reisti hof mikid hundrad fóta langt.' Um uppruna hof-örnefna og stjórnmál á Íslandi á 10. öld," ["He raised a large temple, 100 feet long." About the "hof" place names and Icelandic politics in the tenth century], *Saga* 45/1 (2007), 53–91 (here 89).

9. Helgi Thorláksson, "Sagnfraedin í heimi menningararfs og minninga," [History in the world of cultural heritage and memories], Benedikt Eythórsson and Hrafnkell Lárusson (eds.), *Thridja íslenska söguthingid 18–21. maí 2006* (Reykjavík: The Association of Icelandic Historians, 2007), 316–326 (here 323).

10. Gunnar Karlsson, "The Ethnicity of the Vinelanders," *Journal of the North Atlantic* 2 (2009–2010), 126–130.

11. Jared Diamond, *Collapse. How Societies Choose to Fail or Survive* (London: Allen Lane, 2005), 201.

2

Catholic Iceland: Consolidation, Conflict, and Flux (999–1550)

CHRISTIANIZATION AND CONSOLIDATION

Despite the foundation of the *Althing* sometime in the first decades of the tenth century, Iceland remained a country without a centralized authority. There was no king, no earls, and no chieftains with supreme power. Moreover, a majority of the free population adhered to the pagan religion, and the Catholic Church, with its growing powers in many parts of Europe, seems to have played a very limited role in society. Still, many or all of the Christian settlers kept their faith and passed it on to their descendants. Archeological excavations have unearthed remains of churches made of turf, as was the Celtic custom. Ruins of wooden churches, in line with Anglo-Saxon and Scandinavian culture, have also been discovered. This difference in construction suggests not only two strands of influence but also contrasting methods of Christianization. The former was, then, an accidental process of infiltration, from the bottom up and undocumented, and the latter was an organized mission that was specially aimed at the chieftains in the country. That determined effort is told in numerous narratives, but the most detailed descriptions are given in hagiographic tales, primarily from the thirteenth century. They provide the story of two missionaries, an Iceland-born man and a bishop from Saxony, who converted a number of chieftains in the 980s. Although impossible to verify, the account need not be untrue. Around the middle of the tenth century, the Catholic Church had begun an active campaign of Christianization in Scandinavia. Initially, the results were mixed, but the new faith was clearly on the rise. Significantly, in or around 995, Ólafur Tryggvason became the king of Norway. An eager Christian convert, he was determined to spread the faith both in his realm and the Norse settlements overseas. To Iceland he sent a new missionary, a native of the country, who was said to have demolished pagan relics before he was forced to flee. A Flemish priest followed. Although he managed to baptize a few chieftains, he too had to leave the island, having killed several men who protested his efforts.

In the summer of 999, however, a breakthrough occurred, according to the *Book of Icelanders*. King Ólafur, enraged at the resistance to Christianization, sent two converted chieftains to the *Althing* with the clear message that he would not tolerate any further defiance. Lest his will be doubted, the king kept captive four young men who had stayed at his court, sons of chieftains from Iceland. At Thingvellir, civil strife looked likely since neither the Christians nor the most assertive pagans were willing to give in. Ultimately the law-speaker, Thorgeir Thorkelsson, a *godi* from northern Iceland, was instructed to declare to which faith the population should adhere. After a daylong deliberation in solitude, Thorgeir announced that unless there was one law in the country, there could be no permanent peace. Therefore, the law-speaker decreed that all men in Iceland should be Christian, but those who wished could still worship the heathen gods in secret (and they could continue the blasphemous practice of taking the lives of newborns and consuming horse meat).

Conflict was averted. King Ólafur Tryggvason had his way, both in Iceland and in Norway, where the conversion to the Christian faith was completed sometime after 1015. As always, however, when the written narratives of long-passed events are recounted, caveats must follow. While pagan burial customs seem to have ceased in Iceland in the early eleventh century, the victory of Christianity was not necessarily as sudden and dramatic as the written sources suggest. Nonetheless, it seems safe to assume that as the eleventh century went on, a powerful entity, the Catholic Church, had taken hold in Iceland, with drastic impact on both the rulers and the ruled.

While some of the dates are unsure (for instance, the monumental decision at the *Althing* may possibly have been taken in 1000), a number of key events signaled the change. In 1056, Archbishop Adalbert consecrated Ísleifur Gissurarson, the son of Gissur Teitsson, as the first bishop of Iceland. Ísleifur resided in Skálholt, the family estate in the south of Iceland. His father had built a church there, and Ísleifur established a theological seminar. In 1082, he was succeeded by his son, Gissur Ísleifsson. During Gissur's reign, the

Church's powers increased noticeably. A cathedral was built, and although it was only 50 feet long, it must have been the biggest church in the country at the time.

In 1097, Gissur succeeded in having the *Althing* approve the introduction of the tithe, decades before it was established in Scandinavia. In the main, the tithe was a 1 percent property tax, equally divided among the bishopric, the priest, the local church, and the local district for use as poor relief. Around this time, the division of the country into parishes also began. Each parish church was not owned by the community, as was the case in Scandinavia. Instead, wealthy farmers built and ran churches on their own land. While the initial cost was high, they presumably aimed to please their god in this manner. Furthermore, they could ultimately benefit in material terms since they received two quarters of the tithe, those for the church and those for the priest. The farmer might well be a priest himself, and apart from the tithe, priests received imbursements for baptisms, burials, and other duties.

In 1106, the northern quarter of Iceland became a separate bishopric. This was due to pressure from chieftains in the north who probably did not want to have the local tithe taken southward. Jón Ögmundsson, a passionate priest who had studied at Skálholt and in convents abroad, became the first bishop of Hólar, a farmstead in the central region of the northern quarter. Jón founded a cathedral and a school and laid the ground for further advances. In 1133, the first monastery in Iceland was founded, a friary in the Hólar diocese. By the late thirteenth century, there were four monasteries in that bishopric and at least another four in the Skálholt bishopric. In 1152, both sees came under the new archiepiscopal seat at Nidarós (now known as Trondheim) in Norway.

The monasteries and the seminaries at Hólar and Skálholt were the only seats for formal education in the country. Apart from theological instruction, they presumably offered teaching in the Seven Liberal Arts as they had by then been codified: grammar, rhetoric, and logic; and arithmetic, geometry, music, and astronomy. And although poor relief had probably been organized to some degree in local districts before the Christianization of Iceland, the Catholic Church regulated and increased that effort. Furthermore, the poor and the sick often sought refuge at Skálholt, Hólar, and the monasteries.

Slowly but surely, the Church strengthened its hold on society. The general population felt this interference most clearly in the small but precious sphere of pastime and entertainment. After the initial settlement period, communications improved. Although self-sufficiency was paramount in the agricultural community on the island, internal trade in local goods was established, for instance, in salt, wheat, or iron, which could be produced by burning coal. Merchants from Norway provided other products, like linen, wax, incense, tar, kettles for cooking, and timber, which was soon needed from abroad, despite the steady flow of driftwood. Silver was the main currency in Iceland until the early twelfth century when it was replaced by homespun cloth.

Furthermore, once local districts and parishes had been established, people could regularly gather for festivities. There were ancient feasts around the winter and summer solstices. Horse fights were popular, as were various trials like wrestling, sprinting, and jumping, tug-of-war, fencing, and other weaponry skills. A primitive game on ice, where the aim was to put a puck behind the opponent's line, was also played. All these events could be bloody by modern standards. Horses suffered a gruesome death, and the physical games sometimes ended with serious injuries or slayings.

Naturally, singing, drinking, and dancing were a prominent feature of any proper feast. String instruments were sometimes at hand. The songs and dances had either Celtic or Norse origins, and some of them were imbued with erotic overtures. It was small wonder, therefore, that the Church forbade the "sinful" festivities of old. Bishop Jón Ögmundsson was particularly strict in this regard, determined as he was to impose the standards he had been taught overseas. Thus, he and Bishop Gissur Ísleifsson of Skálholt succeeded in eradicating the pagan names of the weekdays, *Týsdagur* (Tuesday), *Óðinsdagur* (Wednesday), and *Thórsdagur* (Thursday). There is no reason to believe, however, that the Church managed to put an end to all merriments in the country. For chieftains, they remained an important tool for establishing and maintaining their influence in society. The greater the feast, the greater the respect, as before, and the people of Iceland continued to drink, sing, dance, and sin.

During the eleventh and twelfth centuries, the founding period of the Catholic Church, an uneasy compromise therefore existed between established customs and the novel faith. For instance, while all adults were required to know the two central prayers, *Pater noster* and *Credo*, the penalty was the older but un-Christian punishment of three-year exile from society. For people who had almost ingrained notions of honor, revenge, and feuds, the doctrine of mercy and compassion must have seemed alien. Also the men of the church did not always practice what they preached. Tellingly, the first bishop, Ísleifur Gissurarson, was both married and a *godi*, and more often than not the priests were chieftains who simply calculated that by taking on this new role they could maintain their dominant status.

By the twelfth century, the Catholic Church had become a well-organized institution in many parts of Europe, a state within the state of kings or lords. With the Concordat of Worms in Germany in 1122, the papacy and the Holy Roman Empire (then the largest entity in Central Europe) agreed that the clergy should appoint bishops and abbots. It was also determined that these church leaders had an ecclesiastical role on the one hand and worldly powers that derived from the emperor on the other. This settlement soon spread to other parts of the Christian world, but it usually led to bitter disputes about power in society. In Iceland, that was certainly the case, and a paradoxical period lay ahead. It was not only a time of unrest and civil war but also a cultural pinnacle—an age when the Icelandic sagas and other classic treasures were composed.

CIVIL WAR AND SAGAS

As the twelfth century drew to a close, the increasing wealth of the Church became more evident. At Skálholt, a new cathedral was made of imported wood from Norway. More than 160 feet long, it was possibly among Europe's biggest timber structures at the time. At Hólar, a large cathedral also demonstrated the might of the Catholic Church. Apart from the tithe and other regular income, many people, rich and poor, made donations to parish churches, monasteries, or the bishoprics as they hoped for mercy and eternal life in heaven.

The might of the Church was not only demonstrated with the construction of cloisters, churches, and cathedrals. Inside, books were kept and soon written as well. The oldest written documents, which have survived in Iceland, date from the first decades of the twelfth century. Apart from the *Book of Settlements* and the *Book of Icelanders*, secular and Church laws were inscribed. Latin texts were also translated into Icelandic, and a treatise on Icelandic grammar was composed. The writer Ari the Learned has already been mentioned and another notable scholar was Sæmundur Sigfússon, an influential *godi* who was known as Sæmundur the Wise. His writings have not survived, but he was said to have composed in Latin stories of Norwegian kings and other tales.

Meanwhile, in the secular world, the balance of power was in flux. The old system of chieftain *godar*, maybe increasing in number to around 50–60 in the eleventh century, was waning as a few families sought to play a leading role in the country. Ever fewer chieftains held a number of chieftaincies in their own hands, and the local *things*, venues where the *godar* often attempted to resolve local disputes (and maintain their prestige), were losing their value. By the late twelfth century, they had been abolished. Instead, a single chieftain usurped judicial powers and offered protection to people in his region. Geographically, the balance of power also shifted. The old *godar* had been scattered, usually residing near the sea. A typical new leader lived near the center of a region, often at a crossroads where he could observe travels and move swiftly with a small force if needed.

Why did this change occur? First, it seems almost inevitable that some chieftains would gradually become stronger at the expense of others. Farmers may also have felt that regular feuds at the local *things* were tiresome and that it would be better to be subject to one strong leader. Furthermore, the Church intensified the process of centralization. Beginning in the first decades of the twelfth century, rampant civil strife wrecked Norwegian society, and church leaders there concluded that forceful rulers were needed to quell the unrest. That message found its way easily to Iceland.

It was another matter, however, whether the powerful chieftains would tolerate a totally independent Church in the country. The subjugation of faith to secular might, personified in chieftains who built their own churches and took up the priesthood if they so desired, was bound to lead to conflicts.

Late in the twelfth century, a process that scholars later dubbed the Church's "struggle for independence" began in earnest. While chieftain-priests still chose bishops and expected them to be docile, some of them disobeyed, inspired as they were by developments overseas. Most notably, bishops Thorlákur Thórhallsson at Skálholt and Gudmundur Arason at Hólar argued with the chieftains in the land about ownership of church property and the right to ordain priests. At first, Thorlákur was successful but he did not have his way against Jón Loftsson, a chieftain in the south, grandson of Sæmundur the Wise and probably the wealthiest man in the land at the time. Jón flatly refused to put churches and other riches under the bishop's tutelage. When Thorlákur died in 1193, Jón even succeeded in having his own son ordained as bishop at Skálholt although he was illegitimate, married, and a *godi* to boot. As for Bishop Gudmundur at Hólar, he repeatedly excommunicated his arch enemy, a chieftain called Kolbeinn Tumason, who in turn sentenced to exile those priests who followed the bishop. In 1208, Kolbeinn was killed in a fight with the bishop's followers. Other chieftains in the north expelled Gudmundur from Hólar, but he was allowed to return in old age and died in peace in 1237.

Upon Gudmundur's death, the archbishopric at Nidarós in Norway decided to ordain Norwegian bishops to both dioceses in Iceland, apparently having reached the conclusion that the chieftains in the country would never be guided by ecclesiastical thinking in the matter. Then, however, the struggle for control over the Church was entwined with a deeper conflict between the chieftain clans in the country.

By the early thirteenth century, political power in Iceland had become divided roughly between eight families. Borders were unstable, alliances insecure, and suspicion prevailed. Initially, the so-called Sturlunga family from the western part of the country was most influential. Around 1220, Snorri Sturluson became its most powerful member, and for the next couple of decades, he was probably the most influential individual in Iceland, entering twice into marriage to increase his influence and strategically marrying his daughters to leading chieftains in other families. Snorri was not only a great chieftain, however. Educated at the home of Jón Loftsson, he wrote the poetic textbook *Edda* and *Heimskringla,* the history of Norwegian kings from the primeval days of Odin to the late twelfth century. Although it is now considered unlikely, Snorri used to be credited for writing at least one of the famous family sagas, a literary genre that developed in the thirteenth century and deserves special consideration.

Overall, the Icelandic saga literature can be divided into a few categories: historical sagas, sagas of kings, sagas of bishops and hagiographies, family sagas, heroic sagas, and contemporary sagas.

The historical sagas are oldest, consisting of works like the *Book of Settlements* and the *Book of Icelanders,* which primarily aim to describe the settlement of Iceland. The kings' sagas contain tales about Norse kings, and the sagas of bishops describe the lives of those dignitaries in a hagiographic style, as was the case elsewhere in Christian Europe. Best known, however, and most widely read in Iceland through the centuries are the family sagas. These narratives describe the fate of individuals or families, feuds, travels, feats, and transgressions in early Iceland. Although they cannot be taken at face value, they were based on oral tradition to some degree, and general theories about settlement life can be built on their testimony. Thus, while it cannot be true that Egill, the son of the settler Skallagrímur, wrote masterful poetry at the age of three, as claimed in the *Saga of Egill,* that account indicates how oratory and lyrical talent were considered worthy of esteem. Likewise, the story of his first slaying, at the age of six, need not be taken for granted, but it can be used to demonstrate the degree of violence accepted or expected in society. And descriptions of a blind and feeble Egill in old age, at the mercy of women who mock him, support assumptions about the poor standing of the elderly in the social stratum.

In other words, the family sagas bring to life individuals who love, hate, long for, envy, or like each other. They are depressed or happy, popular or detested, contented or cold, ached and hungry. While the fictional essence of the tales must be reemphasized, as well as their time of writing, they help us to imagine that the first generations of people in Iceland shared these human traits just like all others up to the present day. It is the sources that are lacking, not the feelings. By the same token, the epic *Saga of Njáll,* with its descriptions of the wise Njáll (the Icelandic version of Niall), his proud wife Bergthóra, and other notable individuals from the first centuries of Icelandic settlement, signifies how the *Althing* worked and how disputes were solved, or not solved.

But why were the sagas written? As historian Helgi Thorláksson has surmised, in the early twelfth century, Ari the Learned's *Book of Icelanders* may have been recorded at the wish of the bishops at the time to demonstrate that the population fared best when secular and religious powers joined hands to maintain peace in the land.[1] Composed as it was during and after the

Concordat at Worms, this seems plausible. Similarly, some family sagas were possibly composed at the behest of chieftains and their aim was not to preserve for posterity a credible description of Icelandic society; rather, it seems likely that the chieftains wanted to prove their noble ancestry. This may also be the case with regard to the *Book of Settlements*. Moreover, it has been surmised that if Snorri Sturluson wrote the *Saga of Egill,* he did so to demonstrate how the people of Iceland had fared well even though they were not subject to royal rule.[2] Conversely, mythical tales about heroes and kings from presettlement Scandinavia, which were composed in the latter half of the thirteenth century, indicate that the chieftains in Iceland were then increasingly interested in a joint Nordic heritage. Those tales come under the category of heroic sagas and can be linked to another genre from the same time, the sagas of chivalry. At first, these consisted of translations of epic poems from France, but later Icelandic versions were composed as well. Here the rationale may simply have been a desire to follow the prevailing fashion abroad.

Some sagas may of course have been written simply because its authors felt the urge to compose. However, the question of motive is especially pertinent with regard to the contemporary sagas, narratives about the internal strife that marked Icelandic society for the larger part of the thirteenth century. Most significant is the *Saga of the Icelanders,* almost certainly written by Sturla Thórdarson, the nephew of Snorri Sturluson. Through these accounts and other sources like the sagas of kings and bishops, a rough description of tumultuous times can be given. Still, it must be kept in mind that the authors were not determined to give a balanced view. They were participants rather than observers.

What can be established with reasonable certainty is this: After decades of unrest, by the early thirteenth century, royal rule in Norway had consolidated, under the reign of the teenage king Hákon Hákonarson and the de facto ruler, his father-in-law, Earl Skúli Bárdarson. By this time, it had become an established fashion in Iceland that the sons of chieftains became courtiers at the Norwegian court. The young men were impressed by the relative grandeur abroad, and the Crown's means to influence matters in Iceland increased. For the last half-century, disputes about the price of goods had also led to lethal fights between Norwegian merchants and locals in Iceland. Consequently, Jón Loftsson and other chieftains had diverted their trade to merchants in the Orkney Islands who were not under the tutelage of the Norwegian king. Around 1220, Skúli the earl became so enraged when he heard of renewed attacks on merchants in Iceland that he threatened to dispatch a mighty force to Iceland. In Norway, he was dissuaded by Snorri Sturluson, who then resided at the court. Snorri had been a law-speaker at the *Althing* from 1215 and was no friend of those chieftains in south Iceland who traded with the Orkney merchants. Apparently, Snorri promised that he would use his powers in the country to make all the chieftain clans accept the authority of the Norwegian king. Back in Iceland, however, he did no such thing, and in 1235, King Hákon, an adult by then, accepted the offer of Sturla Sighvatsson, his courtier and Snorri's nephew, to further the royal cause in Iceland.

Bloody fights ensued. In 1238, Sturla and many of his family and followers were killed in a battle with their greatest foes, Gissur Thorvaldsson from the south and Kolbeinn Arnórsson from the north (the nephew of Kolbeinn Tumason). Snorri Sturluson remained a threat, however, and it seems likely that Earl Skúli had secretly made him an earl of Iceland, hoping as well to become the king of Norway. Intrigue abounded everywhere, and in 1241, things took a turn to the worse for Snorri, the great chieftain at the time and an eternal giant in Iceland's literary history. Gissur Thorvaldsson brought a force of more than 70 men to Snorri's estate in west Iceland and managed to have him killed. While that slaying is described in detail in the *Saga of the Icelanders*, the account cannot be believed in its entirety and serves as a clear warning not to believe all descriptions from the period. We know with certainty that Snorri died around the time, but not how.

In Norway, meanwhile, Earl Skúli rebelled against the king but was killed in a battle shortly afterward. King Hákon held sway and looked determined to bring Iceland under his rule, encouraged by the tendency of Icelandic chieftains to seek his support, and ardently backed by church leaders. Considering Snorri Sturluson a traitor, the king laid claim to all his wealth. Furthermore, some other chieftains gave their chieftaincies to King Hákon so that he became the largest *godi* in Iceland. With the benefit of hindsight, things seemed to be moving inexorably toward royal rule in the country. By this stage, the realm of the Norwegian Kingdom included the Faroe Islands, the Shetland and Orkney Islands, the Hebrides, and the Isle of Man. In 1261, the Norse chieftains in Greenland also pledged their allegiance to King Hákon, but five years later he yielded control of the Hebrides and the Isle of Man to the Kingdom of Scotland.

As for Iceland, the turmoil continued, and Gissur Thorvaldsson gradually gained the upper hand, surviving among other things an attack on his farm when his wife and three sons were burned to death. In 1258, King Hákon granted Gissur the title of earldom in Iceland. In the following years, Earl Gissur threatened and pleaded with other chieftains in Iceland but may have thought more about assuming power himself rather than forwarding the royal cause. The king redoubled his efforts, therefore, sending new emissaries to the island. Ultimately, he had his way. In 1262–1264, the leading chieftains in Iceland swore allegiance to the king of Norway. In retrospect, again, that conclusion seems inevitable in the long term. The people of Iceland relied on trade with Norwegian merchants. Their pathway to the outside world, the Christian universe, lay through Norway, which had become, for a brief period, a superpower in the northernmost parts of Europe. Put simply, consolidation and interdependence had to be favored over independence and isolation.

Furthermore, the unrest ended, at least temporarily. For decades, it had greatly disrupted the lives of poor farmers who had been ordered to follow chieftains into battles where rocks, wooden poles, and bare arms were the weapons most used. Victory was often achieved, it seems, by arson, deceit, and surprise attacks. The sanctuary of churches and clergy was not always respected, nor were women and children spared the violence.

The commoners of Iceland desired peace and must have been glad when it came. The leaders of the Church were pleased as well, and while some chieftains lost out, others simply looked for new ways to preserve their wealth and power. In that sense, the more things changed, the more they stayed the same. In other respects, a sea change had occurred. For better or worse, foreign rule had been introduced to the island.

FOREIGNERS AND ICELANDERS

Apparently, the chieftains, who in 1262–1264 pledged allegiance to the king of Norway, promised that all farmers in Iceland would pay the sovereign an annual tax. It amounted to one-sixth of the value of a cow, on average a heavy but not insurmountable taxation. Iceland would be a separate entity within the kingdom, but the inhabitants were to enjoy the same rights in Norway as the local subjects. The king was also to preserve peace in Iceland and ensure that enough merchant ships sailed each summer to the island.

This arrangement, revised in 1302, has only survived in replicas, the oldest one from the fifteenth century. While the original understanding may well have been different in some respects, it need not be doubted that in the latter half of the thirteenth century, the people of Iceland became subjects of the king of Norway. A new identity was also enhanced. Since the beginnings of the settlement period, most inhabitants of Iceland considered themselves separate from other peoples. Simultaneously, however, they shared an affinity with the Norse world, especially Norway. In Iceland, the law distinguished between Norsemen and other foreigners. Outside the Nordic region, however, an inhabitant of Iceland might call himself a Norseman or even a Norwegian. Furthermore, the Christianization of Iceland increased the notion of inseparability from other faithful subjects of God.

Conversely, the subjugation to the king of Norway fostered the feeling of separateness. From now on, we can safely speak of *Icelanders*. The division into *us* and *them* had been established, as has, for instance, been outlined by historian Sverrir Jakobsson. Also languages in Scandinavia began to develop faster and differently than the tongue used in Iceland. Before, the inhabitants spoke Norse. Then they spoke Icelandic.

With the transformation in 1262–1264, executive power was created, albeit a weak one, and the judiciary and the legislature were overhauled. Earl Gissur died in 1268 and with him vanished the earldom as well. Instead, in the fourteenth century, the office of governor was established, usually occupied at first by an Icelandic magnate. The old office of *godi* was eradicated, and the *Althing*'s nature changed. Its law council came to consist of 36 members, presided by two men (called lawmen) who replaced the law-speaker. The council could set new laws, subject to royal blessing, but this practice gradually came to an end. In essence, the *Althing* became a supreme court, adjudicating in cases from the country's districts and usually sitting for only a few days each year.

Royal rule was also fortified by the ratification of a new legal code for Iceland, first in 1271 and again a decade later. Although it abolished blood feuds, it contained much of the old law and remained in force for the next four centuries or so. Locally, enforcement was in the hands of sheriffs, a new body of officials who were initially as few as four for the whole country. Gradually (maybe as late as the fifteenth century), they reached more than 20 in number, each reigning in a single county. The sheriffs also appointed men to the *Althing*'s law council, and they held the important task of tax collection. With the governor and the lawmen, the sheriffs therefore formed a new aristocratic class of officials who partly maintained their separation from the general population through excessive intermarriage. "Political elites were reorganized," it has been argued, "and found new ways to legitimize their power."[3]

Simultaneously, constitutional changes occurred overseas. In 1319, Norway and Sweden entered into a royal union. It proved unstable, and in 1397, a more lasting arrangement was reached: the three kingdoms of Norway, Sweden, and Denmark were joined in the Kalmar Union, named after the city of Kalmar in southern Sweden today. Denmark was the dominant party in the association, but in the early sixteenth century, Sweden broke from the union. Norway became a dependency of Denmark.

All these changes served to increase the separateness of Iceland. While the Norwegian cities of Bergen and Trondheim had been relatively close, the Danish capital of Copenhagen seemed further away. The Icelanders were in no position to question, let alone resist, the foreign hold on their country. Even so, during the era of Norwegian rule, they had sometimes managed to resist increased taxation, and the chieftains had protested the appointment of Norwegians to official posts. Both then and afterward, the autonomy of officials in Iceland was quite strong. Communications were scarce and risky, the royal presence weak.

Meanwhile, the Catholic Church grew from strength to strength. In 1269, the archbishopric at Trondheim had ordained an Icelander to the see in Skálholt for the first time in decades. Once in Iceland this new bishop, Árni Thorláksson, immediately insisted that church property should be surrendered to the Church. Six years later, he got the *Althing* to confirm laws that ratified the property rights of the Church and its authority in moral matters. Unstable rule in Norway meant that the process was halted somewhat, but at the end of the thirteenth century, the Catholic Church gained a decisive victory: In 1297, a royal decree stipulated that most church farms should be handed over to the clergy. At that stage, there appeared to have been 330 parish churches in the country, each serving some 5 to 15 farms. In addition, there were at least a thousand other places of worship, small houses where a priest ministered around 12 times a year.

The change in ownership did not happen overnight, but the old custom of the chieftain church vanished. Instead, the bishoprics and the monasteries became the largest landowners in Iceland. In 1274, for instance, the monastery at Helgafell in western Iceland possessed 7 to 8 farms but 57 a century later, including many of the richest ones in the region. During the fourteenth and fifteenth centuries, the rule of clerical celibacy had also been imposed and the Church aimed to control human life from the cradle to the grave. Christian compassion was preached, or meant to be preached. At Christmas, Easter, and various days of saints, food and other necessities were distributed to the poor. Paupers and the sick got relief at the monasteries, and everyone could seek mercy for their sins as they were defined by the medieval Church. Atonements included fast or abstention of comforts, prayers, acts of charity, and pilgrimages. Since wrath was one of the cardinal sins, it could be said that the old right to hate and avenge had been abolished.

Lust was another sin, and the Church laid down explicit rules against sexual offences like adultery, incest, and same-sex intercourse. As before, however, the clerics did not necessarily live up to the standards that they set for others. Greed and corruption existed, and some of the bishops were more like warriors than men of faith. Nor did the general population begin to abstain from feasts and other merriments. Dances could turn into drinking binges so that priests and worldly leaders regularly complained about the vices of the common people. From the mid-thirteenth century, Icelandic-style ballads were extremely popular. Usually, these rhymes contained stories of love or gallantry, sometimes with comedy included. Ditties became widespread as well. Often they were sarcastic, directed against an enemy or even the authorities.

Women remained an oppressed half of the population although their lot improved somewhat. After the thirteenth century, chieftains could no longer keep mistresses and the Church was meant to confirm marriage only if both parties had given their consent voluntarily. Naturally, that may not always have been the case, and the husband was still master of the house. Domestic violence was not considered a valid cause for divorce, and women played a minimal role in the higher echelons of society. A notable exception might be the tale of Ólöf Loftsdóttir, the wife of a king's governor who was killed by English merchants in 1467. Allegedly, she gathered a force to avenge her slain husband and therefore lived up to the tradition of strong women who egged men on in the Icelandic family sagas. That tale must be considered fictional, still.

In the relatively few written sources of the thirteenth to sixteenth centuries, women hardly figure at all. Fortunately, however, archeological evidence can indicate how their lives were lived. From the thirteenth century, for instance, changes in housing structure may have made women's domestic chores a little lighter. Instead of a long chamber with an open fire, farmhouses developed into turf houses of similar size but with separate rooms for sleeping, working, and cooking in a stove. Thus, it became easier to store food and keep comfortable heat inside.

Infant mortality remained high, and people of both sexes suffered from a variety of illnesses. Arthritis was common, possibly acquired through centuries of labor in cold weather. Overconsumption of dried, smoked, or pickled food contributed to stomach aches and disorders. Then again, starvation was a more common cause of death. Smallpox and other infectious diseases were rampant. Some people fell victim to leprosy, and in the early sixteenth century, a syphilis epidemic seems to have struck the population.

Solace was hard to find, although the monasteries served as hospitals and pharmacies. Excavations at the Skriduklaustur monastery in eastern Iceland have revealed that medicinal plants were grown there. Knives, needles, and stones, which were believed to hold healing powers, were discovered as well. Often, however, the cure could be worse than the disease. Bloodletting was a popular remedy, and common wisdom even held that the ointment of urine could heel various ailments.

Presumably, the remoteness of Iceland was also more a curse than a blessing. The relative isolation was never complete so that a disease like measles could turn into an epidemic because people did not develop immunity to it, as gradually happened elsewhere in Europe. Likewise, whereas Iceland was spared the plague that ravaged through the continent in the mid-fourteenth century, it came with full force when it finally reached the country at the start of the fifteenth century. By then, there may have been around 60,000 people on the island, and some historians argue that at least half of the population died, probably a higher number than in most other European regions.

At the end of the fifteenth century, the plague swept through the island again. Callous as it sounds, after these two epidemics, the survivors may have led a better life than before since they enjoyed a larger share of the land. The Church also benefited because on their deathbed people often bequeathed their possessions to monasteries, bishoprics, or the parish. Naturally, however, the pain of losing loved ones must have hurt those who lived on, and the disease did not spare the clergy.

Elsewhere in Europe, by the beginning of the sixteenth century, the population began to increase slowly, despite almost continuous warfare, feudal oppression, and diseases. In Iceland, however, the number of inhabitants was probably unchanged, at some 50,000 to 60,000 people. Slavery came to an end in the twelfth century at the latest, but in terms of work, the life of farm laborers, tenants, and poor farmers was almost akin to that of slaves before. From this century, a system of big manors with surrounding tenant smallholdings was firmly in place. The great majority of farmers were tenants and, as before, all individuals had to belong to a certain farm. Vagrancy was forbidden although (and because) in hard times desperate people searched far and wide for food and mercy.

While cattle and sheep farming remained the predominant source of sustenance, fisheries grew in importance. This was another process that began in earnest during the twelfth century. By then, the islanders had realized that the best fishing season was in late winter when the cod spawned off southern and western Iceland. The strengthening of the Church also led to an increased demand for fish during Lent and other fasts. Seasonal hamlets emerged, primarily in the Westman Islands, off Snæfellsnes, and Reykjanes in the west and around Eyjafjördur in the north. Sleeping in stone huts, tenants and farmhands ventured out to sea in rowing boats, usually with hand line and hook. Although these fishermen learned to read into the weather, it was a hazardous effort. For men (it was primarily a male vocation, with a few notable exceptions), drowning must be added to the long list of common fatalities in Iceland.

From the fourteenth century or so, fish was the force for change in Iceland, but the ruling class resisted, aided in no small degree by epidemics and the general harshness of life. Had the population managed to grow as in most other parts of Europe, people might well have moved to the seaside, settled in fishing villages, and changed the structure of farm landlords and tenants. This, of course, cannot be stated for sure, but in pre-plague times, the prerequisites for a development in this direction can be detected. During the late thirteenth century, the large-scale export of stockfish (dried fish) from Iceland began, supplementing the trade in homespun cloth and the occasional sale of falcons to kings and dignitaries abroad, including the distant lands of the Middle East.

Some of the ships that were used in the emerging fish trade were owned by Icelanders, but the bulk belonged to Norwegian merchants. The fish was brought to Bergen, where the German Hanseatic League, the trading giant of central Europe, had its Norwegian headquarters. From there, it was taken to the continent.

After the middle of the fourteenth century, the plague in Europe put a decades-long halt to the fish export. Then the plague epidemic in Iceland disrupted the whole of the island's economy although fisheries continued to influence its development, albeit in a different manner. From the late thirteenth century, when the Kingdom of Norway stretched to Greenland in the west, its kings also claimed sovereignty over the North Atlantic. This right was upheld once Norway had come under Danish rule. Around the turn of the fifteenth century, however, English fishermen began to fish off Iceland. Within a few decades, more than 100 fishing boats were engaged in this activity each year. English merchants also sailed to Iceland on a new type of vessel, two-mast ships, which could carry hundreds of tons and had dozens of men in the crew. The merchants bought fish from the locals in return for necessities and consumer goods, to use the modern term. Temporary fishing and trading posts were established, mainly on the south coast.

The effects in Iceland were drastic. For one, the English sold iron-made horseshoes, which must have made communications much easier. Before, primitive horseshoes were used or none at all, making it necessary to change horses often and travel at slower pace. Furthermore, clothes, wine, and weapons were popular products as well as nails, glass, wax, silverware, sculptures, and other ornaments, whether religious or secular.

The outside world opened up more than before, but the trade could have negative overtones. Some of the foreigners kidnapped children or bought them for a pittance, selling them into servitude in England. Others stole stockfish or livestock, and contemporary reports also mention the burning down of churches and other misdemeanors. Prostitution appeared alongside the trading camps, and members of the nobility, not to mention royal officials, spoke with contempt about the debauchery that the foreigners brought to the country.

While those magnates who benefited most from the foreign trade must have been content, the stability of Icelandic society came under threat. Consequently, the Danish king forbade English fishing and trade in Iceland. Diplomatic wrangle and skirmishes at sea ensued, but in Iceland itself, the intruders usually had the upper hand. Once, the English even took the governor of the island with them to England. In effect, the Danish authorities were helpless in this distant part of the kingdom. Meanwhile, some local leaders in Iceland grew immensely rich by contemporary standards, trading in fish with the English and using the proceeds to amass farmland. They also purchased armory and weapons and fitted small bands of men, which they used to further their cause. The rule of law weakened, and poor farmers and tenants were caught in the middle as noblemen fought over land and other goods. While slayings were probably rare, robberies and physical violence disrupted the already challenging lives of the masses.

For a large part of the fifteenth century, two families, those of Loftur the Rich Guttormsson and Thorleifur Árnason, campaigned for mastery in the country. The office of governor was occupied by men on either side. Both families sought the support of the Danish king but must also have been tempted to benefit from the lucrative trade with the English, leading to accusations of treachery from the opposite camp. Although the scarcity of sources makes it difficult to reach solid conclusions, Icelandic society was in upheaval. The times were not as tumultuous as the civil war era of the Sturlungs and other clans in the thirteenth century. Yet the state was weak and an effective rule of law often absent.

Apparently, royal power strengthened in the latter half of the fifteenth century, and in the 1470s, the struggle over trade and fish took on a new dimension. German merchants, mainly based in Hamburg, ignored the dictates of the Hanseatic League and traded with the Icelanders. Then, in early 1490, Denmark and England reached a temporary peace. English fishing and trade were permitted, subject to levies. In the early 1520s, that treaty was renewed, but the fight over the lucrative Iceland trade continued. In 1528, English merchants robbed a German camp at Snæfellsnes, the following year they sank a German ship in Eyjafjördur, and in 1532, a force of Germans and Icelanders killed about 40 Englishmen in Grindavík and other posts on the south coast. A year after that, the kings of England and Denmark signed a peace treaty, together with the city council in Hamburg. The English had discovered rich fishing grounds off Newfoundland, and the Danish king always held a strong bargaining card—the threat to interrupt English voyages through the sound between Denmark and Sweden into the Baltic Sea, an important trading region.

In the following decades, the English presence in and off Iceland drew to a near-complete halt. Commerce with merchants from England continued into the sixteenth century, but the treaties and agreements about foreign trade in the country ensured that the landowning class had its way. In the summer of 1490, when the governor at the time notified the *Althing* of the Anglo-Danish peace treaty, its members reacted by reinforcing their resistance to change on the island. A law was passed, either at the initiative of the governor or the *Althing*, forbidding all foreigners to reside in Iceland over winter and banning all vagrancy or residence outside a farm.

As before, this quest for order and stability was understandable. But would it succeed? Nobody knew it then, but a watershed lay ahead. The age of volatility and insecurity was over. Furthermore, the Catholic Church, for centuries the only strong and lasting force in the country, was about to be destroyed. Instead, a solid state structure finally emerged.

HEROES AND VILLAINS

We have already seen that the Viking spirit has sometimes been used to define the alleged strengths and superiority of the Icelanders. Thus, it should not be surprising that the first centuries of settlement have also been looked at with similar admiration. As early as in the thirteenth century, there are references to much better days in Iceland during the previous centuries. In the seventeenth century, the scholar Arngrímur the Learned also reminded foreigners how the Icelandic sagas described real heroes who feared nothing and no one. Echoing similar claims in the *Book of Settlements*, Arngrímur aimed "to silence those who are apt to insult our nation by claiming that we are nothing but a band of villains."[4]

From the middle of the nineteenth century, when the struggle for independence and advent of modern historiography went hand in hand in Iceland, this notion of a golden age took a firm hold in the nation's collective memory. "Then there were heroes," wrote Jónas Hallgrímsson, arguably the country's foremost romantic poet, in one of his masterful descriptions of the first centuries of Icelandic settlement. The historians followed suit, providing an apparently credible record of rise and decline—prosperous times when the Icelanders were masters of their own land but destitute when they succumbed to foreign rule. This version of the past was enforced by an increased interest abroad in Icelandic manuscripts and literature, beginning as early as the mid-eighteenth century. In Britain, thinkers and writers like William Morris and Walter Scott became fascinated with the sagas, and J.R.R. Tolkien was later inspired in part by Nordic tales and mythology when he composed his magical works, *The Hobbit* and *The Lord of the Rings*. In Germany, Richard Wagner's operatic Ring Cycle drew on the sagas, and the scholar Konrad Maurer wrote extensively on the laws of the Icelandic Commonwealth, the name that came to be used for the free state of Iceland in the first centuries after settlement.

Foreign interest was a clear source of pride for the Icelanders, and the presentation of a previous golden age of freedom was an obvious tool in the campaign against Danish rule. In fact, it could hardly have been otherwise, and the Icelandic case was no different from developments in many other parts of Europe. Throughout the continent, the notion that people with the same language, history, or clear identity of some kind should enjoy their own, separate statehood, was gaining ground.

In this version of events, the decline of Iceland had a fairly clear starting point. The rise of the Church and its struggle for independence in the twelfth century was deemed to have weakened the Commonwealth, along with the emergence of greedy and corrupt chieftains. The ensuing civil strife and the subjugation to the king of Norway in the late thirteenth century were then demonstrated as a catastrophe, an avoidable loss of freedom that condemned the Icelanders to centuries of hardship and foreign tyranny. In the seventeenth century, Arngrímur the Learned already contended that according to the Old Covenant, as the agreement of 1262–1264 had then come to be known, the king of Denmark could not change the laws of Iceland. More importantly, during the nineteenth century, the undisputed leader of Iceland's independence movement, Jón Sigurdsson, wielded the Old Covenant as the main weapon in debates with the Danish authorities, arguing that since Icelandic chieftains had entered a personal agreement with the king of Norway, that arrangement became void when absolute monarchy was abolished in Denmark in the middle of the nineteenth century. Consequently, Earl Gissur and men of his ilk were roundly condemned as traitors to the national cause.

In the latter half of the twentieth century, however, many historians began to doubt the general image of a glorious age, followed with the lamentable loss of independence and foreign oppression. The positive portrayal of the so-called Commonwealth period was dismissed, and the fairer argument made instead that it was a period of lawlessness when starvation and misery could befall anytime. Similarly, revisionist historians rightly discarded the view that the old *Althing* was an assembly of free men, "the world's oldest parliament" as many Icelanders liked to claim.

Already before this revision of Icelandic history, faith in the credibility of the Icelandic sagas had begun to wane. They were still held in high esteem and treasured in their own right as literary gems. But the older view that they described real people and real events made way for the more plausible theory that they were works of fiction, although based in part on oral testimonies about individuals who certainly existed. Furthermore, contemporary scholars emphasize the fact that the sagas were written long after the events that they describe and that they have often survived only in fragments, which vary to a small or large degree. Thus, a modern version of, say, the *Saga of Njáll* can be based on more than 60 manuscripts as it is standardized and streamlined into a single coherent tale.

As for the demise and decline after the imposition of foreign rule, the new generation of historians downplayed the importance of the Old Covenant, even doubting that it was composed at all in the claimed form since the oldest copies date from the fifteenth century. Was it perhaps a forgery from that time, made by Icelandic officials to protect their standing within the Danish Kingdom? While that theory is controversial, Jón Sigurdsson's legal arguments have been criticized with more general conviction and also the belief that the people of thirteenth-century Iceland shared latter-day ideas of nationhood and independence.

Naturally, not all historians shared a single view of Iceland's past, and some have recently argued against the revisionist effort, complaining that source criticism and dismissal of nationalist feelings have been too severe. Also whatever the academic community may think and conclude, the revisionist approach of most Icelandic historians has not necessarily found support among the nation's politicians or the general public. Just like the Viking image of brave warriors and voyagers appeals to the common Icelandic psyche, so

to speak, a collective memory of glory days has generally been more alluring than descriptions of poverty, hunger, and misfortune. Today, this schism
between the academics and the nation at large, led by its statespersons, is
especially evident in the historical image provided for visitors to Iceland.
Throughout the island, tourists can visit Saga centers, where local heroes of
the old literature are in the foreground. The *Althing* will more often than not
be described as the world's oldest democratic convention, and reconstructions
of dwellings from the so-called Commonwealth period are sometimes based
more on modern imagination and exaggeration rather than a careful respect
to archeological remains and other evidence. A certain positive view of history is therefore constructed, both literally and figuratively. First there were
settlers, proud and free, cruelly betrayed by villains in their midst who paved
the way for Norwegian tyranny—and then entered the "evil Danes."

NOTES

1. Helgi Thorláksson, "Thorgils á Thingeyrum," [Thorgils from Thingeyrar],
Saga 46/1 (2008), 168–180 (here 172).

2. Jesse Byock, "Egilssaga og samfélagsminni," [The Saga of Egil and collective memory], *Íslenska söguthingid* I. Gudmundur J. Gudmundsson and Eiríkur
K. Björnsson (eds.), (Reykjavík: The Association of Icelandic Historians, 1997),
379–389 (here 387).

3. Henric Bagerius, *Mandom och mödom. Sexualitet, homosocialitet och aris-
tokratisk identitet på det senmedeltida Island* [Manhood and maidenhood:
sexuality, homosociality, and aristocratic identity in late medieval Iceland],
(Gothenburg: University of Gothenburg, 2009), 206.

4. Arngrímur Jónsson (transl. by Jakob Benediktsson), *Crymogæa* (Reykjavík:
Historical Society of Iceland, 1985 (original Latin print 1609)), 200.

3

Danish Iceland: State, Cold, and Stagnation (1550–1786)

REFORMATION AND SEVERITY

By the mid-sixteenth century, the Catholic Church was at the height of its material wealth in Iceland, owning nearly half of all farms in the country. The two sees of Skálholt and Hólar possessed most of the land (well more than 300 farms each), but the monasteries were powerful as well. Thus, 120 farms came under Videy, the richest monastery in Iceland (as compared with 57 a century before). During the fifteenth century, however, a grudging resentment against papal sovereignty could already be detected within the Christian world. In Iceland, priests began to choose their own bishops, and with resistance to the papacy boiling over abroad, it was only a matter of time until the effects would also be felt on the faraway island.

The Reformation is said to have begun in 1517 when Martin Luther, the German friar, publicly criticized the Church practice of selling indulgences. Luther's emphasis on each individual's direct relationship with God appealed to the general public and was particularly popular among the nobility and royalty. Although some of them may have been guided by religious ideals, power calculations mattered most, and soon after Luther's initial protests, many regions in the northern parts of Europe were in an open revolt against Rome.

In 1537, King Christian III of Denmark severed all ties with the papacy, confiscating Church property and vastly improving the state's finances. The new custom was of course meant to be adhered to in Iceland as well. Two years later, an agent of the governor of Iceland (who by then resided at Bessastadir, a farm near Reykjavík) stormed the neighboring monastery of Videy and put it under royal rule. The plan was obviously to seize more church property, but the agent was met with resistance. In the summer of 1539, he and his men were killed at Skálholt, and shortly later other royal officials were slain at Videy. Effectively, the administration in Iceland had been wiped out.

The power vacuum did not last long. In the summer of 1541, a Danish warship sailed to Iceland, and the authority of the Crown was restored, at least in the southern part of the country. In the north, however, the Catholic bishop at Hólar, Jón Arason, remained in power and was determined to uphold the old custom. He built fortifications at his see, and in 1549 he managed to capture a newly ordained bishop for Skálholt. In the following summer, Jón Arason traveled with a strong force south to Skálholt and Thingvellir, where he proclaimed to the *Althing* that both dioceses then came under his rule.

In the long term, Jón had to put his hopes on the ultimate downfall of the Lutheran Reformation or Protestantism as it came to be called. Until then, he would have to endure in Iceland, but in the fall of 1550, a group of men, faithful to the king, captured the bishop and two of his six sons. Fearing that their followers in the north might soon seek to release them, Jón Arason and his two sons were executed at Skálholt. By then, Jón had been the sole Catholic bishop in the Nordic region for almost a decade. His death was avenged, and for the second time in just over a decade, the royal presence was eliminated. As before, however, a Danish force was dispatched to restore order. Furthermore, the Lutheran custom held ground in the Danish Kingdom and elsewhere in Northern Europe. Jón Arason would never have succeeded in resisting the strong current from abroad.

The Catholic Church vanished as a force in society. The monasteries were abolished. Although the sick and deprived were still to be assisted, mostly through the continuance of the tithe, many proponents of Protestantism claimed that the emphasis on poor relief had encouraged idleness, a terrible sin. This attitude, coupled with the state's appropriation of church wealth and income, meant that the needy had to suffer. Some scholars contend that the change was drastic and sudden; others feel that the proponents of that view exaggerate both the capabilities of the Catholic Church and the negligence of Protestantism. Certainly people did not change their habits and beliefs overnight. The religious Reformation, which began in the mid-sixteenth century, was a process rather than a sudden transformation, just like the Christianization of Iceland in the eleventh century.

Unsurprisingly, some Icelanders also found it hard to adapt at once to stricter rules of conduct. With the onset of Protestantism, the Crown absorbed the ecclesiastical component of the judicial sphere, and the division between sin and crime vanished. Fines for adultery were increased and floggings introduced. Furthermore, the death penalty then awaited both parties if a man had a child with his mother, sister, daughter, stepmother, daughter-in-law, sister-in-law, or other close relations. The men were beheaded and the women were never spared, although they must (almost) always have been victims in the act, not instigators. The only difference was that they were put in a sack and drowned in a pond at Thingvellir. According to records of the *Althing*, 25 men and 25 women were executed for incest, the last ones in 1762. Infidelity was a more frequent misdemeanor, and extramarital childbirth was by far the most common offence. Heavy fines and floggings were then meted out, with the practice continuing into the 1800s.

Why this severity? In general, the established order wanted to have sexual relations and conception confined to married couples. While they could point to the scriptures, the main aim was to control population growth and maintain stability in society. Otherwise, it was argued, poverty would increase to the detriment of all. This was no peculiar feature of Icelandic society but rather the prevailing point of view in Europe.

In moral matters, the authorities tried to guide the masses through the use of the pulpit and also the press, the revolutionary invention of the time. Most notably, during a tenure that lasted over half a century (1571–1627), Bishop Gudbrandur Thorláksson at Hólar printed around 90 books, including the Bible, a collection of psalms, and a book of religious poetry. In a similar vein, in the seventeenth century, Pastor Hallgrímur Pétursson composed the *Passion Psalms*, describing the suffering and death of Jesus Christ, and in the early eighteenth century, a collection of fiery sermons by Bishop Jón Vídalín proved as popular.

The psalms and the sermons struck a chord with people but so did vulgar verses and other secular rhymes, carried orally from one generation to another. Some commoners even dared to coin offensive poems about officials, the clergy, or the king himself. Words of that kind could be the only means to express anger about misfortune, poverty, and injustice. However, the masses also used songs and dances to express their enjoyment, to have fun and to drink. Life was not all doom and gloom and feasts remained popular, to the dismay of the clergy and the ruling class. At the start of the eighteenth century, they finally managed to put an end to organized merriments (during one of the last events, 19 illegitimate children were said to have been conceived).

By the end of the century, the old group dances were all but forgotten, but the rhymes and the verses survived. So did the superstitious belief in elves, ghosts, and trolls that had not been that common in Catholic times when people instead put their faith in saints. This fear of the "hidden people" could make life miserable, especially for children and gullible adults. During the seventeenth century, witch hunts also swept through Iceland like most parts of Europe. Egged on by sermons about the power of the devil, people were tempted to link sickness or the death of livestock with sorcery. More than a hundred cases of such witchcraft were investigated, and 25 people lost their lives at the stake. Unlike elsewhere, all but two were men, probably because in Iceland the activity was connected to the writing of magic symbols, a feat that illiterate women could hardly accomplish.

By the early eighteenth century, witch hunts had ended, but the belief in elves and trolls remained an integral feature in the mind-set of ordinary people. Priestly homilies about heaven and hell may have served only to maintain the superstition. In short, many Icelanders probably felt that they lived in a world where otherworldly creatures existed as well. Also they were led to believe that while their true God would indeed be merciful to those who obeyed His word and the law of the land, He would be vengeful toward the wicked.

ABSOLUTISM, MONOPOLY, AND ARISTOCRACY

The passage from the Catholic faith to Protestantism did not only herald a change in religious and moral matters. A strong executive was finally established in Iceland, a *state* was formed.

In 1660, Denmark became a hereditary kingdom and the Danish nobility lost their political power. The structure of the state was overhauled and strengthened. This consolidation of royal rule, a general development in Europe at the time, was confirmed in Iceland two years later when more than a hundred Icelanders—the bishops, pastors, sheriffs, lawmen, and *Althing* representatives—pledged to observe the absolute rule of King Frederick III. Some of them may have lamented the change, not for nationalistic reasons but rather because they feared for their own privileges and wealth. Thus, they asked that they be allowed to keep the old laws of the land, including a promise that only Icelanders should be appointed sheriffs. That wish was almost always respected, if only because foreigners were not interested in the employment.

With the onset of absolutism, the *Althing* lost all influence on lawmaking, and the revamped authorities in Denmark intended to introduce a new set of laws for Iceland, as they did in Norway. Work began but was never finished. Instead the Norwegian code was introduced on the island, although parts of the old law remained in force well into the eighteenth century. In this sense, confusion reigned, but in most other aspects, the power system was clear. The highest court in Iceland remained at the *Althing*, albeit in revised form, and cases could be referred to the king and his Supreme Court in Copenhagen. Locally, county sheriffs served as prosecutors and judges as well as duty collectors, making their income from a share of the taxes and the fines they imposed. At first, a governor was the highest official in the land. He paid the king a certain rent but received instead the royal levies. In 1684, the position of the king's representative was renamed. That office was held by a Dane who resided in Copenhagen, with a subordinate in Iceland. Also the status of the island within the monarchy was redefined. Before, it had essentially been a tributary asset of the king of Norway and then Denmark. Then, Iceland became a province of the Danish Kingdom, admittedly with a separate legal system and other unique features because of its isolation.

Thus, the rise of absolutism abroad determined the power structure in Iceland. Likewise, the rise of mercantilism, the state control of trade, shaped the system of commerce. In 1602, the king granted certain merchants a monopoly on trade with Iceland, and in 1684 the country was divided into trading districts. The locals were forbidden to trade elsewhere so the merchants could determine prices and goods on offer. They mainly purchased fish, wool, and woolen products, providing instead grain, timber, tar, iron, and other essential goods along with sugar, alcohol, and similar luxuries.

In line with the trade monopolization, the Crown attempted to exclude other subjects from fisheries off Iceland and commerce with the locals. Thus, the construction of a fortress was planned at the Westman Islands to prevent British presence there, and at the end of the sixteenth century, a fishing limit was imposed around the islands. But of course the foreigners did not withdraw at once. In 1614, English pirates robbed goods from the people of the Westman Islands (admittedly they were caught and hung back home). By the seventeenth century, whalers had also begun to operate off Iceland, and in 1615 three whaling vessels from the Basque Country stranded at the Westfjords, the northwestern region of Iceland. Suspicion and fright incited the locals to slay around 30 of the foreigners while the majority managed to escape on a ship that they stole from the English. In 1627, however, the Icelanders were on the receiving end of violence and horror. A team of corsairs from the Barbary, the north coast of Africa, arrived on five ships and ransacked many coastal regions in Iceland. The inhabitants were as defenseless as the monks who had faced marauding Vikings in previous times. The attack on the Westman Islands was the most brutal. The assailants kidnapped more than 240 islanders, killed dozens, stole valuables, and burned down buildings. In all, almost 400 people were taken from Iceland and sold to slavery in Algiers. Ultimately, less than 30 managed to return to the country, the best known of them being Guðríður Símonardóttir, who married the priest and the poet Hallgrímur Pétursson.

The weakness of Danish rule in Iceland was obvious. The Crown could control the Icelanders, but the country was exposed to outside assaults. While Norwegian kings had earlier claimed the whole ocean between Greenland and Norway as their own waters, the Danish Kingdom was forced to retreat. In 1631, Britain and Denmark agreed on a fishing limit around Iceland, equaling four nautical miles (one nautical mile is about 1.2 miles). For the next of couple of centuries, the Danish Crown claimed a limit of 16 to 24 nautical miles. Its naval presence was lax, however, and fishermen from Britain continued to work the rich fishing grounds off Iceland, joined by the Dutch and the French as time went on. Furthermore, the locals still managed to trade with the foreigners. In the late seventeenth century, the fear of strict punishments, both for the inhabitants and the foreigners, probably put a near-complete end to that business. Sources are lacking, however, so it is difficult to reach solid conclusions.

The monopoly arrangement was certainly not unique to Iceland at the time and had its general benefits. The aim was to provide a secure outlet for the island's exports and an equally secure provision of necessary imports. However, the country's remoteness and the residence of merchants abroad meant that profits were not invested on the island itself. Despite a relative reduction in the price of fish abroad, the trade was generally lucrative for both the merchants and the Danish authorities. On the other hand, there simply were no Icelanders ready and willing to conduct the trade. There was no bourgeoisie in the country, and the wealthiest farmers seemed perfectly content with the stagnant state of affairs. In particular, they were pleased with stipulations forbidding merchants to reside in Iceland, which was still a prerequisite for the establishment of villages and economic diversification.

Near the end of the seventeenth century, a few tiny villages or clusters of cottages had nonetheless been formed, mostly in the region from the Westman Islands up to Snæfellsnes. We also know that by the late eighteenth century, commoners in these parts of Iceland gained their livelihood more, or as much, from fisheries than farming. In general, fishermen lived with their families in huts, sometimes keeping a single cow but purchasing meat and dairy products from farmers in the neighborhood. Seasonal fisheries also maintained their importance, with farmers and workers flocking to the seaside early in the year for the traditional fishing season and returning in springtime when haymaking and other agricultural work took over.

Predominantly, however, the population lived on farms. As before, each household was a self-sufficient unit, more or less. On average, 5 to 10 people lived together, the farmer with his wife and children and two laborers, a man and a woman. The farmer would own 4 to 6 cattle and 30 to 60 sheep. In wintertime, the male laborer, and sometimes the farmer as well, went to the hamlets by the sea and took part in the fishing season.

In the household, the farmer was king, but that was where his mastery ended. Around 1700, fewer than 100 individuals owned half of the roughly 4,000 farms in the country (some of them were split between two farmers or more). The church and the Crown held almost all other land so that, together, tenancy accounted for 94 percent of all landed property. Within that group, we can find both rich and poor, but, in general, there existed a mass of manual labor and impoverished tenants under the rule of a select few. Moreover, that elite class of landowners and administrators monopolized public positions by making sure that sheriffs, pastors in the most profitable parishes, and other officials originated from within their own rank. To take a late but telling example, when one Ólafur Stefánsson became governor in 1791, he also held two of the three vice governorships in the country, the other one occupied by his sister's son. The governor's half-brother was bishop at Hólar, his son-in-law bishop at Skálholt. Ólafur's son was also to become the country's treasurer and supreme judge.

Since the elite were mostly confined within a few families, intermarriages were common as before. The select group was so small, still, that they would also seek people from the lower echelons of society. Formally, this ruling class could not be distinguished from the rest of the populace, but their separateness was registered in genealogical compilations akin to the *Book of Settlements*. The most detailed record, composed in the mid-seventeenth century, has been called a *Who's Who* of its time.[1] The writer was Pastor Thórdur Jónsson and another notable dignitary was one Gísli Magnússon, son of Magnús Björnsson, a lawman and the richest person in the land. Gísli argued that the most significant families in the land should acquire noble status like the aristocracy in Denmark and elsewhere in Europe. While this did not come about, the upper-class dominance remained intact, and some of its members abandoned the traditional custom of patronymics for Danish-style family names. Thus, the children of Governor Ólafur Stefánsson took up the surname Stephensen and the children of Stefán Thórarinsson, an influential sheriff, became the Thorarensens. Both names still exist, as do a number of other surnames with similar origins.

The ruling class—or the de facto aristocracy of Iceland—was conservative in thought and behavior. Naturally, there were exceptions to that general rule. Gísli Magnússon was dubbed Gísli the Wise, in the same vein as other savants who have already been mentioned, Ari the Learned, Sæmundur the Wise, and Arngrímur the Learned. Unlike them, the well-educated Gísli was primarily an entrepreneur in thought, convinced that the Icelanders could benefit greatly from the island's natural resources. In the 1640s, he acquired a monopoly on the sale of sulfur from Iceland, a precious commodity that was needed for ammunition production. He also wanted to search for precious minerals, grow new vegetables, and improve fishing methods. But despite his enthusiasm, little actually happened. The export of sulfur took off only later and lasted, with intervals, until the nineteenth century.

Many contemporaries considered Gísli the Wise a naive dreamer. Such attitudes were rarely detected, however, when another dignitary, Skúli Magnússon, embarked on ambitious reforms in the mid-eighteenth century. In 1749, he became the first Icelander to hold the office of treasurer in the country. Supported by Danish officials and receiving financial assistance in Copenhagen, Skúli almost immediately got a small group of distinguished Icelanders, primarily sheriffs, to form a corporation that would revitalize Iceland's economy.

In Reykjavík, which at that time was only a farm with a church, a row of houses were built for wool processing and related industries. Almost 100 people worked for the corporation when the going was good. A number of Norwegian and Danish farmers came to Iceland in order to teach the locals grain production. The mining of sulfur was revived. In 1771, the first prison in Iceland was built in Reykjavík and Skúli Magnússon also had his official residence constructed in the style of a Danish manor, on the nearby island of Videy. The new corporation ran two decked vessels and thus introduced a progressive change in fisheries that had long been established abroad while the Icelanders were still stuck in their small rowing boats.

Initially, the corporation turned a healthy profit. Later, however, it ran into difficulties. At the start of the nineteenth century, the wool factories had been closed. The effort may have been too ambitious and the products too expensive for the European market. The foreign farmers had also left after a few years and grain was not harvested. The import of foreign sheep, another bold plan, led to the outbreak of scabies, a grueling sheep disease. Neither did a more modern fishing industry develop.

Still, the attempt to diversify and rejuvenate the Icelandic economy demonstrated that forward-thinking individuals could always be found among the ruling class in the country. Alongside the church, this elite ensured as well that objects of art were to be found on the island. Altarpieces, baptismal fonts, and other carvings were often elaborate and excellent. Paintings tended to be more primitive.

The general public could admire art in the churches. Privately owned pieces were the privilege of the richest part of the population. Still, it must be kept in mind that the distinction between the affluent few and the masses was not clear-cut. Some tenants were better off than others, and some pastors and sheriffs were poor. Commoners were also among those intellectuals who compiled historical annals, descriptions of Icelandic nature, or other accounts. Among the more remarkable ones must be an account of the Turkish raid, as the corsairs' attack on Iceland in 1627 came to be known, and the travel tale of Jón Ólafsson who, in the early seventeenth century, sailed from the Westfjords with English fishermen, served in the Danish fleet, and ventured as far as India.

Even so, the upper class of landowners and officials had a near-total monopoly on higher education. For the first centuries of Protestant Iceland, the state of instruction seems to have been similar as in the rest of Northern Europe. Children were meant to know Luther's catechism but probably only about half of the population learned to read (considerably fewer women than men). Still rarer was the skill to write. The only sites of formal schooling were the church seminaries at Skálholt and Hólar, and initially only a handful of Icelanders sought university education, almost solely at the University of Copenhagen. By the late eighteenth century, however, the majority of sheriffs in the country boasted a law degree from that university. For the Icelanders, Copenhagen had become a window to the wider world, the center of the state to which they belonged.

For foreigners, conversely, Iceland seemed to offer a view into a strange or forgotten world. More often than not, tales about the island included descriptions of monsters and natural anomalies like eternal darkness or the constant eruption of fire at sea or land. Most ominously, Mount Hekla in southern Iceland came to be known as a gateway to hell. The locals were also seen in a negative light, diminutive, barbarous, immoral, uneducated, and crude.

Accounts of this kind encouraged Arngrímur the Learned and other educated Icelanders to compose more truthful narratives of volcanoes, geysers, glaciers, and people who were poor but could nevertheless claim a glorious past. Indeed, the spirit of renaissance in Europe (which included an interest in the classical world and the roots of peoples and states) led scholars to the sagas and other Icelandic scripts. Subsequently, old manuscripts at Skálholt, Hólar, and farmsteads around the country were taken abroad, primarily to Copenhagen. The most prolific collector was Árni Magnússon, the son of a pastor and an archdeacon's daughter. During his theological studies at the University of Copenhagen in the late seventeenth century, Árni was instructed by the royal archivist to gather Icelandic documents, which he did with great enthusiasm, becoming the university's first professor of Danish antiquity. In 1728, however, disaster struck. A great fire engulfed Copenhagen, and many invaluable items perished, primarily printed books, various parchments, and Árni's notes. Still, he and his friends managed to rescue most of the manuscript collection. If not, the Icelanders would have lost forever a sizable portion of their national heritage.

Similarly, it could be said that the Icelandic language was under the threat of extinction. By the Reformation era, it had long become separated from the other Nordic tongues. Bishop Thorláksson, Arngrímur the Learned, and other intellectuals encouraged the use of Icelandic (or Latin) in printed works, and the general population conversed in Icelandic. However, in the following centuries, many official documents were either in Danish or Danified Icelandic so that, by the late eighteenth century, the fear seemed real that the old language would gradually perish. Even more ominously, however, the question justifiably rose of whether people could actually survive on this cold, distant, and treacherous land.

THE LITTLE ICE AGE, EPIDEMICS, AND ERUPTIONS

Around 1300, climate changes occurred in Northern Europe. After a series of volcanic eruptions in Iceland and elsewhere, ash clouds obstructed sunlight, which led to an increased spread of pack ice in the Northern Hemisphere and a general drop in temperature by 1 to 2 degrees. At least this is the most likely explanation. What is certain is that the so-called little ice age set in, lasting until the mid-nineteenth century or so, with the coolest period in the sixteenth and seventeenth centuries. In Iceland, where cold weather could easily cause famine and misery, the change arguably had a huge impact on people's living conditions. Actually, a natural alteration of this kind may even have affected their lives more than all modifications and revolutions in the human fields of power, religion, and societal structure.

The drop in temperature led to a decrease in cattle farming and the end of grain harvesting, probably in the fifteenth or sixteenth century, although the import of cheap grain must also have played a role in that regard. Farmsteads in or near highlands had to be abandoned because of the cooler climate. Glacial encroachment even destroyed some farms and closed established tracks. Glaciers may have advanced some 5 to 10 miles during the little ice age and the snow line (demarcating where snow or ice covers the ground throughout the year) moved from some 3,500 feet in the mid-sixteenth century to 2,500 feet by the nineteenth century. Likewise, pack ice drifted to the shores of Iceland more often than before or since, disrupting fishing and sea communications.

Volcanic eruptions could also cause death and destruction. Thus, ash from the notorious and active Mount Hekla repeatedly ruined farms and pastures in its vicinity, and in the late fourteenth century, a terrific eruption underneath Vatnajökull, Iceland's largest glacier, put an end to all habitation in a nearby region. Throughout the centuries, volcanic ash fall killed livestock and damaged farmlands. Repeatedly, earthquakes demolished dwellings, and in the mountainous parts of the country, avalanches threatened in wintertime.

Moreover, epidemics continued to ravage through Icelandic society. Diseases like influenza and leprosy were a regular threat and melancholy became a recognized ailment—in annals from the fifteenth to eighteenth centuries, some 260 suicides or attempted suicides are recorded. And while the plague did not strike again after the fifteenth century, an outbreak of smallpox proved as devastating. Beginning in 1707, it lasted for two years. According to a national census at the start of the century (the first ever in Iceland), some 50,000 people lived on the island at the time. After the outbreak, only around 35,000 to 40,000 were left. In addition, young people were primarily hit so that the birthrate dropped considerably in the following decades as well.

After the abolition of monasteries during the Reformation, refuges for the sick and frail were hard to find. True, four hospitals for lepers had been established, but they were small and the conditions notoriously bad. As before, sick people were sometimes taken care of by family and friends. Others were forced to wander and beg. Cruelty was not necessarily to blame, but rather the stark fact that poor households could not sustain those who did not contribute and were only a burden to others.

Furthermore, infant mortality remained higher than the average in other parts of Western Europe, at least during the eighteenth century, when the death rate dropped abroad. Midwives in Iceland knew little about childbirth and breast-feeding was uncommon. Instead, toddlers were fed on undiluted milk, even cream, and this contributed to exceptionally high mortality levels as historian Ólöf Gardarsdóttir has concluded.[2] Also neonatal tetanus was a particular menace to the newborn in Iceland. As late as the mid-nineteenth century, about a third of all infants on the island died from this painful disease, as compared with 15 to 20 percent in Denmark. In the Westman Islands, with some 200 inhabitants, the ratio was 60 to 80 percent, primarily because of an unusually unhygienic practice of cord cutting, even by Icelandic standards, and the lack of clean water.

In general, common cures could also be worse than the disease in question. Sometimes, human and animal urine or feces was a recommended ointment and bloodletting remained popular even if it never worked. A near-total disregard for cleanliness, lasting longer in Iceland than in many other parts of Europe, contributed as well to bad health and untimely death. Judging from nineteenth-century practice, people may have washed shirts and other outer clothing once or twice a month, but underwear far less frequently. Bedsheets were possibly cleaned once a year. Children were bathed every now and then, but grown-ups would hardly wash themselves with the exception of their faces before going to church on Sundays. Women combed their hair regularly, men rarely, if ever.

Farmhouses must often have felt disgusting by modern standards. Built of stones, turf, and timber as in settlement times, they were dark and leaky, cold or stifling. The foul air of sweat, animals, food remains, and a variety of products was definitely unhealthy. The general diet was plain. Meat and fish were still preserved and eaten dried, smoked, or pickled. On the positive side, the average Icelander probably enjoyed more meat than the masses elsewhere in

Europe. Dairy products were also consumed, but fruits and vegetables hardly existed, with the exception of berries and sorrels. It was only in 1758 that the first potatoes were grown in Iceland, but for the remainder of the century, the general population did not take to this nutritious novelty. Lastly, the scarcity of grain meant that bread was fairly uncommon in the country.

Food was prepared in wooden or metal pots, and eaten in wooden bowls held in the lap, by the use of a spoon made of animal horn or wood. Drink was usually consumed from a tall wooden tankard. In the early seventeenth century, English merchants introduced the Icelanders to schnapps, which soon turned popular. Tobacco was also imported, and in the following century, the inhabitants became avid drinkers of coffee. Sugar was another delicacy to lift people's spirits. Despite diseases, the constant presence of death, and abject poverty, it must not be forgotten that daily life could be pleasant and sprinkled with sources of contentment. Indeed, in good years, pastors and officials regularly complained about the exuberant indulgencies of the masses, as demonstrated by the fact that people would not attend mass unless they could expect *brennivín* (burning water, the Icelandic term for schnapps). And while the loss of a child was devastating for parents—maybe more so for the mother than the father—the almost unexpected joy of watching an offspring grow up was presumably as rich as it can be in modern society. Even so, children were meant to work like adults from a young age, and if they misbehaved, physical punishment was usually administered.

Life was rough, and hunger continued to hurt the islanders with frightening regularity. According to annals and other written sources, at least a fifth of the seventeenth and eighteenth centuries were considered years of famine. And then, in the summer of 1783, Iceland suffered a terrible calamity. That summer, a massive volcanic eruption began next to the mountain Laki in the southern part of the Icelandic interior. For the next eight months, lava, ash, and poisonous gases spewed from a long fissure in the land. Harvesting collapsed, fields were ruined, and to make matters worse, in 1784, a huge earthquake shook southern Iceland. In the first years after the initial eruption, most of the country's livestock perished. Devastatingly, cattle may have decreased by half, horses by 60 percent, and sheep by as much as 80 percent. People fared little better. If records are correct, the inhabitants had numbered nearly 49,000 before the calamity, but in 1786 only about 38,000 remained. Most of the deceased died from starvation.

Volcanic ashes reached Europe and North America. In Britain, it has been suggested that more than 20,000 people died, a number equal to around 100,000 people today, making the calamity the worst natural disaster in recent British history. On the European continent, the haze of dust certainly contributed to a series of poor harvests that, in turn, were among the causes of the French Revolution in 1789. Nature, it is tempting to argue, had rarely affected the lives of humans in such sudden and tremendous manner. In Iceland, it even seemed that the attempt to survive on this remote northern island was over. Danish and Icelandic officials—including the forward-thinking Skúli Magnússon—seemed exasperated, suggesting that survivors from the worst hit areas of Iceland be transferred to Denmark. Subsequently, some even wondered whether the whole nation should not be resettled in, say, the sparsely populated moors of Jutland, the Danish mainland adjacent to Germany. Iceland was in shatters, as two Icelandic historians wrote in the late twentieth century.[3] But what was to blame? Was it just the harshness of nature? And was there really no hope ahead?

DARK DAYS, EVIL DANES?

We know that the Icelanders endured the devastation. They were not relocated in the moors of Denmark. Moreover, they managed to form their own state and become, for the latter part of the twentieth century, one of the most affluent nations on earth. It could be said, therefore, that they survived not only natural calamities but also the oppression that came with foreign rule—absolutism and trade monopoly to name the most obvious negatives.

This has certainly been the prevalent view in recent times. It has been mentioned previously that the leaders in Iceland's independence struggle during the nineteenth and early twentieth centuries saw civil strife and the subjugation to the Norwegian king in 1262–1264 as turning points, the beginnings of a centuries-long misery. Similarly, the national leader Jón Sigurdsson called Catholic bishop Jón Arason the last Icelander, emphasizing that his fight against the Danish-instigated Reformation was a nationalistic struggle. It also became a commonly accepted fact that when Icelandic officials pledged their allegiance to the absolute rule of the Danish monarch in 1662, at least one of them shed a tear and only gave in when the Danish governor pointed out the presence of warships mooring in the vicinity. Another popular story involved Skúli Magnússon and the trade monopoly. "Measure correctly, boy!" a Danish merchant is to have sneered at him when he was a young assistant, indicating that he should cheat on farmers when they brought in their wool and other products. When plagues, epidemics, famine, a little ice age, earthquakes, volcanic eruptions, and other natural disasters were added to a long list of adverse events, there was little wonder that students of Icelandic history were bound to feel that life in the country from the fourteenth century to the end of the eighteenth century was absolutely miserable. Hardly anywhere did the so-called dark ages seem as dark and long-lasting as in Iceland.

Caveats are in order, however. Although climate changes can hardly be disputed, in recent decades many historians have begun to doubt whether life necessarily became worse for the general population with the onset of foreign rule. The argument goes that not only had the first centuries of settlement been glorified by ignoring hardship and turning lawlessness and the rule of the few into a legend about democracy and justice, but that the benefits of a state structure, established in the sixteenth and seventeenth centuries, were overlooked as well. Thus, it has been maintained that the introduction of a fairly effective bureaucracy under the Danish monarchy may just as well have improved the lot of common people, freeing them from the whims and tyranny of local overlords.

Likewise, although Bishop Jón Arason partly portrayed his struggle against Lutheranism in nationalistic terms, he saw himself primarily as the obedient representative of the pope and the Catholic Church. As for the trade monopoly, as early as in the late nineteenth century, Jón Jónsson Adils, the country's leading historian and a dedicated admirer of the glorious ages during the first centuries of settlement, was willing to admit that it was not a peculiar product of Danish wickedness but rather the prevailing arrangement of the times. The same could of course be said about absolutism, and the stories of Icelanders shedding tears when they promised to obey absolute royal rule only emerged long after the event. According to contemporary sources, that occasion was marked by much drinking and merriment.

In modern Icelandic historiography, the nationalistic image of misery under foreign rule has therefore come under considerable criticism. "Where is this general decline?" historian Axel Kristinsson asked at the start of the twenty-first century, noting that deterioration could be detected in some fields but certainly not in others. Overall, he argued, people must have been at least as well-off during the seventeenth century than some 400 to 500 years before.[4] In comparison with other Europeans, the Icelanders were spared warfare and conscription, so burdensome in many parts of the continent, and taxation was lower in Iceland than in other parts of the Danish Kingdom. Furthermore, international researchers in geosciences have used archeological remains in Iceland and Greenland—where the Norse population vanished in the late Middle Ages—to support the theory that the Icelanders were able to adapt wisely to climate deterioration and major changes in the economy of Europe. Quite contrary to the notion of decline, therefore, the argument goes that the inhabitants of Iceland "developed trade in wool and fish to overcome difficult times and built a successful economy."[5]

Yet there is one underlying fact that must seem to convey an image of stagnation and, yes, decline. At the end of the eighteenth century, the number of inhabitants was about the same as it had been in the initial settlement period. From around 1300, however, elsewhere in Europe, the population had doubled on average, despite almost continuous conflicts, epidemics, and emigration to the New World.

A few arguments need to be considered here: First, it has been suggested (in line with the population growth theories that the English scholar Thomas Malthus put forward at the start of the nineteenth century) that adverse agricultural conditions in Iceland determined that the number of inhabitants could not grow beyond the maximum level of 50,000 to 60,000. Another contention holds, however, that the country could easily have sustained at least 300,000 people. Nature was not responsible for the population stagnation, therefore. To begin with, it may well be that the initial group of settlers was simply too small and vulnerable. Shocks like epidemics and volcanic eruptions could therefore be more devastating than similar events in larger societies. The smallness of the population may also have meant that there was little incentive to seek new ways of sustenance. After each catastrophe, there was plenty of land for the survivors to cultivate. Furthermore, the societal restrictions on marriage and childbirth must have held the number of people in check.

As we have seen, the ruling class of monarchy, clergy, officials, and landowners favored conservatism and the status quo, and that attitude seems to have permeated the general population. During the eighteenth century, for instance, the scholar and the poet Eggert Ólafsson complained of an aversion to progress in the country, an almost ingrown inertia in Icelanders, strengthened by their fatalism, admiration of a long-gone glorious age, and a feeling of helplessness against a hostile nature and remote rulers. "In the minds of many Icelanders," it is argued in a recent overview of the nation's history, "the universe may have been gigantic but often their experience of it only encompassed their own parish."[6]

Salvation could only lie in a general revolution and the dismissal of myths. The Icelanders had to reject the prevailing belief through the centuries that their country was unlike others, savage, primitive, and uncivilized. A societal transformation would also be needed; the landless 96 percent would have to wrest power and wealth from the elite few. And, finally, foreign rule would have to be improved or overthrown. The Danish overlords were not evil, but they could be inept or unresponsive. That, for instance, caused the famine in the mid-1780s more than the Laki eruption itself, a learned Danish observer contended.

During the nineteenth century, the dawn of modern Iceland, revolutionary developments could be detected on all these fronts. Some myths prevailed, however, and remain even to this day. The leaders of Iceland's struggle for increased independence, primarily of a privileged class in the country, nourished the false notion that all Icelanders shared the same sufferings and must hold together a single goal—the abolition of foreign rule. And despite the revisionist historiography, in contemporary Iceland, the average person will still view the thirteenth through eighteenth centuries as a period of long, un-interrupted misery, mainly attributable to the evils of an alien power. That is also the image that foreign visitors and Iceland enthusiasts can glean from many exhibitions, brochures, and guidebooks. The themes of glory, decline, and resurrection are simply too irresistible to be eradicated from the collective memory, tourist promotion, and political propaganda in Iceland.

NOTES

1. Davíd Ólafsson, "Ættartölusafnrit séra Thórdar Jónssonar í Hítardal," [The genealogy collection of Pastor Thordur Jónsson from Hítardalur; book review], *Saga* 47/1 (2009), 226–232 (here 228).

2. Ólöf Gardarsdóttir, "Ljósmædur, brjóstamjólk og hreinlæti," [Midwives, breast milk, and cleanliness], *Saga* 42/2 (2004), 95–128 (here 127).

3. Björn Thorsteinsson and Bergsteinn Jónsson, *Íslandssaga til okkar daga,* [History of Iceland to the present day] (Reykjavík: Historical Society of Iceland, 1991), 255.

4. Axel Kristinsson, "Besta öldin og sú versta?" [The best century and the worst century?], Erla Hulda Halldórsdóttir (ed.), *Annad íslenska söguthingid* I (Reykjavík: University of Iceland Historical Institute, the Association of Icelandic Historians, Historical Society of Iceland, 2002), 108–120 (here 118).

5. "Scientists Turn to Archeology for Clues to Adapting to Climate Changes," February 19, 2012, http://popular-archaeology.com/issue/decem ber-2011/article/scientists-turn-to-archaeology-for-clues-to-adapting-to-climate-changes.

6. Árni Daníel Júlíusson and Jón Ólafur Ísberg, *Íslandssagan í máli og myndum* [Iceland historical atlas] (Reykjavík: Mál og menning 2005), 126.

4

Iceland Emerging: Optimism, Confidence, and Old Meets New (1786–1902)

DAWN

In 1786, the 38,000 Icelanders who had survived the Laki eruption and other calamities could not have realized that better days lay ahead. There would be no more plagues or epidemics, no more natural disasters of such devastating nature. Furthermore, the old society, under foreign rule and stagnant in many ways for centuries, was fading away. In its place, an independent state was emerging.

Naturally, the change was not sudden, and this division into periods and chapters is modern-day, artificial, and arbitrary. Still, around 1786, a great change clearly occurred. That year, six trading posts in Iceland were granted a municipal charter by the Danish authorities: Reykjavík, Grundarfjördur, Ísafjördur, Akureyri, Eskifjördur, and the Westman Islands. The plan was to encourage commerce and the growth of towns in the country. Moreover, the monopoly arrangement was abolished. With a decree that took effect in 1788, all subjects of the Danish king were permitted to engage in trade on the island. In reality, there was hardly any competition among merchants who usually enjoyed a local monopoly where they established themselves. Moreover, within a few decades, the charter privilege was rescinded for all sites except

Reykjavík. There, however, a town was developing. Urbanization, a prerequisite for material advancement in almost all societies at the time, was beginning in Iceland, albeit on a small scale.

Since the big earthquake of 1784 had destroyed many houses at Skálholt,
the seat for that diocese was moved to Reykjavík. Then, in 1801, the Hólar
district was abolished, making Iceland one see with a bishop residing in
Reykjavík. The schools at the old bishoprics were also closed and a new one
established, again in Reykjavík. Insufficient funds, pitiful housing, and the
schoolmasters' incompetence led to its shutdown in 1804. A year later, the
school was reconvened at the nearby Bessastadir, under new management
and better conditions. Already in 1766, the office of national surgeon had
been established, with offices in the close vicinity of Reykjavík, and by the
early nineteenth century, the country's sole printing press was located on the
island of Videy.

Institutions and officials were being drawn to Reykjavík or its surroundings. Most significantly, in a historical and nationalistic context, in 1800, the
old *Althing* was terminated by royal decree. Having served almost solely as
a court of appeal for the previous centuries, the abolition had little political
or bureaucratic effect, but in the following year, a new provincial court was
established in Reykjavík.

Despite all these changes, the town remained tiny. At the start of the nineteenth century, it had 307 registered residents who lived in scattered huts and
houses and a cluster of buildings alongside two streets. Gradually, Danish
merchants increased their presence in Reykjavík. It became the undisputed
center of Iceland's commerce and trade with Copenhagen, which was still the
island's main window to the outside world. Establishments and associations
also appeared. In 1818, a library was opened, and we know that in the 1820s
the Reykjavík Club, an association for the town's upper crust, ordered from
Denmark 25 dance songs for its music box. In 1837, a café was established,
and by the 1860s, the population had grown to some 1,500 people. There were
more streets and more houses. Yet foreign visitors to Iceland were generally
not impressed with the town. In the mid-nineteenth century, one of them compared the forlorn stone-and-turf dwellings on its outskirts to rabbit holes. Another traveler considered the prevailing stench of rotten fish so disgusting that
it reminded him of a Chinese quarter in a Californian mining town. Prejudices
abounded, but the fact remains that it was easy to brand Reykjavík as a poor
squalid site, not worthy of being called a nation's capital. Sewage floated in
open streams, and the streets were muddy and hardly traversable on rainy
days. Most of the tourists, who greatly increased in number throughout the
century (at least 130 tales of travels to Iceland in the latter half of the century
have been published), were upper-class gentlemen and ladies who easily noticed the smell and the dirt, the poverty and the drunkenness. Similarly, some

tourists made fun, politely or not, of the small Reykjavík elite of both sexes who tried to act cosmopolitan but failed, lagging behind the current fashion and barely able to speak international languages.

Thus, the negative descriptions of Iceland and the Icelanders, so prevalent in previous centuries, could still be heard. The people were said to be diminutive, filthy, and immoral in sexual matters, the country a cold, barren rock on the edge of the inhabitable world. Increasingly, however, more positive reflections appeared as well. It may be restated how interest in the Nordic heritage grew in the nineteenth century, especially in Scandinavia, Britain, France, and the German-speaking parts of continental Europe. Furthermore, instead of broken French or English, some foreign visitors noticed a high rate of literacy in Latin-speaking parish priests and farmers who knew the old sagas by heart. Indeed, Iceland came to be known as the Saga Island. *exotic*

Often, the rugged nature of Iceland was also admired and awed. Negative aspects of industrialization like smoke and noise in overcrowded cities enhanced romantic ideals about the pristine and sublime North. And no longer was Mount Hekla deemed to be the gateway to hell. Instead, the French writer Jules Verne immortalized another volcano, Snæfellsjökull, making its crater the starting point in his famous novel, *Journey to the Center of the Earth* (first published in 1864).

The Icelandic officials and intellectuals who conversed with foreigners or followed their writings were likely to welcome the acclaim about Iceland's pure nature and precious heritage. Nonetheless, some of them argued that the past held nothing worthy of acclaim. Thus, Magnús Stephensen (son of Governor Ólafur Stephensen and the first chief justice of Iceland's provincial court, which was founded in 1801) heartily welcomed the abolition of the old *Althing* and complained about the Icelanders' hero-worship of fictional characters in the sagas. Instead, he argued, they should look forward and seek inspiration abroad, from more prosperous and enlightened nations. Unsurprisingly, Stephensen was Iceland's primary advocate of the Enlightenment, the drive for societal reform, religious tolerance, and rational thinking, which prominent intellectuals like Voltaire, Rousseau, Benjamin Franklin, and Thomas Jefferson spearheaded in the eighteenth century.

In 1796, Magnús Stephensen began the publication of a news magazine that soon had around 1,000 subscribers, around 2 percent of the population. There certainly was demand for enlightened information. The journal was in Icelandic but in Stephensen's time, another Icelandic official recommended the adoption of Danish in the country, arguing that the loss of the mother tongue would in fact be beneficial since the islanders had fared best when they shared a language with the other Nordic nations. In Reykjavík, Danish was at least equal to Icelandic as the language of trade and administration, and it was the language used in the Club.

language — connecting to crit on Jonas' poems!

Similarly, in the first decades of the nineteenth century, foreign consumer goods began to change and internationalize the daily life of Icelanders. Thus, in the period from 1819 to 1840, the import of coffee grew from 5 to 44 tons. The availability of overseas literature also increased (the *Grimm's Fairy Tales* were translated and published, for instance) and foreign dances like waltz, reel, polka, and mazurka gradually replaced the styles of old. At last, the Icelanders also began to grow vegetables on a significant scale, prodded on by Danish officials and those few fellow countrymen who had studied or lived abroad. In the first two decades of the nineteenth century, the number of vegetable gardens in Iceland grew from around 270 to almost 3,500.

But was modernization and advancement tied, then, to foreign imports and customs, the growth of Danish Reykjavík, and the demise of old institutions like the *Althing*, not to mention the Icelandic language? During the first decades of the nineteenth century, some Icelandic intellectuals argued on the contrary that the disreputable town of Reykjavík was primarily a non-Icelandic Danified slum, the exact opposite of progress and prosperity. In their minds, also, the abolition of the ancient parliament, founded by free settlers nearly 1,000 years before, had been devastating. And while prosperity was certainly needed, the argument went that Icelandic customs should be cultivated, not discarded.

In other words, the rise of nationalism could be detected in Iceland. Separation, not integration, would rescue the nation from the long centuries of poverty and stagnation.

FIGHTING DANISH RULE

Throughout the fight against foreign subjugation, words were the strongest weapons in the Icelanders' armory. Nobody died in the Icelandic struggle for independence. Still, the nineteenth century certainly began with a challenge to Danish rule in Iceland. It was not a long-lasting affair, however, and the locals were hardly involved. In essence, it was a tragicomic occurrence rather than a serious threat to the established order of things. Then again, the episode is rightly embedded in the traditional history of Iceland for it demonstrated the fragile nature of Danish sovereignty on this faraway island.

Near the end of the eighteenth century, a number of British notables were suggesting that Britain should increase its influence in Iceland, possibly by a wholesale annexation. A prominent advocate of this idea was Sir Joseph Banks, a widely traveled naturalist who had visited the country. Moreover, he was the president of the Royal Society and an influential player in London's governing circles. But despite the long history of trade and fishing off Iceland, the British government was never seriously interested in the proposition of acquiring the island. Nonetheless, the onset of the so-called

Napoleonic wars at the turn of the nineteenth century demonstrated that it was firmly in the British sphere of influence. In 1807, Denmark sided with France, which prompted Britain to seek the capture of all merchant vessels sailing between Copenhagen and Iceland. Thus, in the autumn, nearly half of the 41 ships that had sailed to Iceland in the summer were arrested and diverted to Britain. In the following year, an English adventurer also went to Iceland and stole a trunk containing all royal dues in the country. Although the British authorities forced him to return the funds, the actual weakness of Danish rule was exposed.

In the summer of 1809, it seemed to have been undermined yet further. A British merchant was then determined to purchase much-needed fats in Iceland for his soap factory. In this he had the tacit consent of the Royal Navy and was to be assisted by one Jørgen Jørgensen, a Dane who had been taken as prisoner of war but sympathized with the British cause in the ongoing conflict in Europe. After a brief stay in Iceland, they realized that the governor, Count F. C. Trampe, was unwilling to lift a ban on all trade with non-Danish subjects. The response was swift. A small team of armed Britons put Trampe under house arrest, and as the soap merchant conducted his trade, Jørgensen declared an end to Danish rule on the island, proclaiming himself Iceland's protector and supreme commander. That position he promised to hold only briefly, however, or until the Icelanders could resurrect the old *Althing* and run their own independent country (under a new flag that was to have three dried white codfish on blue background).

Unfortunately for Jørgensen, this usurpation of power did not have the blessing of the British government. In late summer, a Royal Navy warship arrived in Iceland, and order was reestablished. Then, in 1814, Denmark had to surrender its control of Norway to Sweden. The notion that the Atlantic islands of Greenland, Iceland, and the Faroe Islands would also be included in the transformation did not even seem to arise, even though they had all been part of the Norwegian Kingdom. Thus, the union between Iceland and Norway, which had lasted more than half a millennium, came to a quiet end.

Presumably, the Icelandic nation would not have cared that much whether a change in foreign rule had actually come about. During the eventful summer of 1809, some sheriffs and other Icelandic administrators demonstrated cautious support for Jørgen Jørgensen's undertakings. Mostly, however, they stood on the sidelines and were quite happy to continue with their business as usual as winter set in. In the same way, while the general population disliked Danish merchants and Danish officials, they demonstrated no visible interest in the radical agenda of independence and liberty. This was partly because they had no means to do so but also because they could not imagine that anything of the kind could really be done. The Icelanders had of course heard about the two big revolutions in the United States of America and France, but in Iceland circumstances were radically different. The overthrow of perceived oppressors was inconceivable.

Even so, changes abroad had to have their effect on the island. So it had been when the Christian faith spread to northern Europe, royal power was consolidated in Norway and absolutism and Reformation changed the power structure in Denmark, to name a few vital developments. Similarly, when the so-called Romantic Era began around the end of the eighteenth century, it was only a matter of time when it would have its effect in Iceland. Partly a response to the scientific emphasis of the Enlightenment, the new romantics were more emotional and passionate in their thinking. In the field of politics, the notion of the nation-state (the belief that all nations were unique and should exist in their own separate states) therefore took hold.

The rise of nationalism included the protection of languages. In 1816, the still-functioning Icelandic Literature Society was formed. Somewhat ironically, it was founded in Copenhagen, although it had a branch in Iceland, and the main instigator was Rasmus Christian Rask, a Danish linguist and admirer of Icelandic culture. In a more political context, the first Icelandic stir could be detected around 1830. A revolutionary change of kings in France led to an upsurge throughout the continent. At the time, the two duchies of Schleswig and Holstein belonged to the Danish Kingdom although they were primarily populated by Germans. The gentry and other parts of the ruling class in the duchies then demanded increased political rights. Rumblings were also heard in Denmark. In Copenhagen, the king retreated and four diets or advisory assemblies were formed: for Schleswig, Holstein, Jutland, and the island-part of Denmark (Funen, Zealand, and the numerous other islands). Representation was restricted to wealthy landowners and farmers, even affluent tenants. Iceland and the Faroe Islands were to be included in the diet for the Danish islands.

While some officials in Iceland obediently welcomed that intention, among the growing body of Icelandic university students and intellectuals in Copenhagen, the complaint could be heard that Iceland should have its own assembly. Most prominently, the law student Baldvin Einarsson argued that the old *Althing* should be restored. Moreover, he stressed that the Icelandic nation had to wake up and realize its full potential. His twofold inspiration was obvious: On the one hand, there were the sagas and the perception of Iceland's glorious past during the period of freedom and prosperity. On the other hand, the international romantic wave of nationalism had reached Icelandic minds.

In 1833, the young Baldvin passed away, but others took up the torch. Two years after his death, four Icelandic students in Copenhagen—including the poet Jónas Hallgrímsson—founded a journal that was meant to stimulate an engrained feeling of national identity among the supposedly dormant Icelanders. Like Baldvin, these intellectuals insisted that the Icelanders must resurrect their assembly at Thingvellir. Initially, the authorities in Copenhagen did not accede to such wishes, appointing instead two conservative officials for each sitting of the Danish islands diet. In 1839, however, a more liberal king, Christian XIII, ascended to the throne in Denmark, and the designs for an Icelandic assembly gained ground. In 1845, it convened for the first time, in Reykjavík and not at Thingvellir. The romantic nationalists were disappointed about the location, but the body of officials and the more pragmatically minded leaders in the Icelandic camp were convinced that the assembly could work properly only if it was situated in Reykjavík. A suitable building was also at hand, a new building for the grammar school, which was relocated again to the town from Bessastadir.

The new assembly still took up the old name of the *Althing*. It consisted of six royally appointed representatives and 20 elected members from as many constituencies. Since sufficient property was a requirement for eligibility, less than 5 percent of the population could stand or vote in the first parliamentary elections. Tellingly, in the Westman Islands, nobody could demonstrate enough affluence so the constituency was not represented in the *Althing* until 1859, when the rules were relaxed. It need hardly be mentioned, also, that the franchise was restricted to men.

The *Althing* sat every second year. Although its members could make appeals to the king and the authorities in Copenhagen, it was only an advisory body without judicial powers. Indeed, clear dissatisfaction could already be detected a few years after the first convention of the *Althing*. Again, however, the stimulus also came from abroad. In 1848, a new revolution began in France, sweeping through the European continent. At the start of the year, King Christian XIII had died, and it was his son and successor, Frederick VII, who faced popular demands for political reforms. Fortunately, he proved to be as broad-minded and pragmatic as his father. The king readily renounced the royal claim to absolute power, and a more liberal government was formed. The bureaucracy was modernized as well, and a separate department for Icelandic affairs was created for the first time. Furthermore, the king agreed that the Icelanders themselves should be allowed to make their own recommendations about the status of their island in the Danish realm. A special national assembly was to be convened for this purpose. Then, in 1849, a new constitution took effect for the whole kingdom, including Iceland.

By then, the scholar Jón Sigurdsson had come to the fore as a distinct leader in the struggle against Danish rule. Born in the Westfjords of Iceland in 1811 to a priest and his wife, Jón went to Copenhagen to study philology but soon got immersed in politics. By the early 1840s, he had emerged as the strongest voice of those Icelanders who wanted increased autonomy from Denmark.

The national assembly, which gathered in the Reykjavík School auditorium in the summer of 1851, enhanced Jón Sigurdsson's reputation yet further. Led by him, the great majority of the assembly's 40 representatives argued that while Iceland should remain in a royal union with Denmark, it should enjoy home rule and a fully fledged parliament with legislative and fiscal powers. But the meeting did not go as well as the Icelandic members hoped. Although only three years had passed since the tumultuous events of 1848, the tide had turned. The revolutionary fervor had passed and the Danish authorities, having quelled separatist unrest in Schleswig and Holstein, were in no mood to accept Icelandic claims for extensive autonomy. A Danish warship even moored outside Reykjavík, with soldiers ready to intervene and make arrests if needed.

That fear was unfounded. The Icelanders were not in a rebellious mood, least of all the level-headed Jón Sigurdsson. Still, he protested loudly when the Danish governor, Count J.D. Trampe (a relative of governor Trampe at the start of the century) declared that the Icelandic proposals were out of order and that the assembly was herewith dissolved. "We all protest!" the other representatives are to have said in unison, and those words become instantaneously famous around the country. The constitutional status of Iceland remained unchanged, however, and a stalemate ensued.

Although there was never any reason to fear violent unrest in Iceland, the political impasse could not last indefinitely. In 1864, Denmark and Prussia, a rising power on the European continent, were engaged in a brief war over Schleswig and Holstein. Prussia won and gained possession of the two duchies. In desperation, some Danish dignitaries supposedly wondered whether Iceland could be offered in return for the control of the northern part of Schleswig, with its heavy Danish population. Nothing of the kind was seriously suggested, and it might even be argued that for the authorities in Copenhagen, Iceland was treasured as a symbol of Danish standing on the international scene, a miniature jewel in the crown, to paraphrase a common British description of India within the British Empire. Still, Iceland would not be best described as a Danish colony but rather a dependency within the Kingdom of Denmark.

It must be kept in mind as well that Jón Sigurdsson and other proponents of Iceland's case never foresaw an immediate and complete separation from the Danish Kingdom. A compromise of some kind always seemed attainable, therefore. In the late 1860s, a new governor in Iceland, Hilmar Finsen (a Dane of Icelandic descent), was instrumental in forging what seemed to be an acceptable solution. Iceland would remain firmly within the Danish realm, with a cabinet minister in Copenhagen responsible for Icelandic affairs, but a legislative assembly with full control over the island's internal interests would be established. A small administrative body would also be formed in Iceland, with an annual imbursement from Denmark.

Moderate elements on both sides seemed agreeable to this arrangement. However, the more radical or suspicious members of the Icelandic *Althing* and tightfisted Danish officials and politicians alternated in thwarting its progress. The deadlock was broken only in early 1871 when the Danish parliament passed a law on Iceland's status within the kingdom. Although it did not differ that much from the proposals that had been debated thoroughly the previous years, the Icelandic camp was then chagrined by the opening assertion that Iceland was an inseparable part of the Danish realm, albeit with certain special rights. Furthermore, the unilateral method was condemned, and a majority of the *Althing* declared the new arrangement unlawful. That, of course, did not change the actual situation. Neither did the *Althing*'s displeasure manage to alter another unilateral act in Copenhagen in 1873, a modification of the post of governor, which gave him (it was as inconceivable as before that the position would go to a woman) increased authority. Hilmar Finsen was the first official to hold the post and proved more popular than an incorrigible Danish bureaucrat could have been. Still, the administrative change had been made abroad, and the *Althing* remained as powerless as before, mostly able to appeal and hope, not decide and act.

In 1874, a novel constitutional move was made. The year was deemed to be the one-thousandth anniversary of settlement in Iceland, and the Danish king, Christian IX, agreed to the *Althing*'s suggestion that the occasion be celebrated by granting the country its own constitution. Parliament was granted legislative authority in internal affairs and limited powers of appropriation. The number of representatives was increased to 36, six of them royally appointed. These members were divided into an upper and a lower house in the *Althing*. A ministry for Icelandic affairs was formed and headed by the Danish Minister of Justice. King Christian IX also visited Iceland, the first sovereign to do so in the island's history, and was henceforth revered by most of his Icelandic subjects. Even so, the constitution, which was mostly based on the Danish version from 1849, had only been bestowed on the Icelanders, and Iceland remained an inseparable part of the Danish Kingdom. Moreover, the minister for Icelandic affairs was not chosen by the *Althing*, and the king could veto its bills, a means he often used in the following decades.

Consequently, Icelandic politicians and nationalists kept fighting. In 1879, Jón Sigurdsson passed away peacefully, having spent most of his adult life in Copenhagen in the salary of the Danish state, as an archivist, editor, and collector of antiquarian sources about Icelandic history. Earlier, when discussing the Old Covenant of 1262–1264, we had indeed seen how Jón used that arrangement to support the claim that when the Danish king relinquished his absolute powers in 1849, the constitutional ties between Iceland and Denmark were disbanded as well.

Although Jón resided in Copenhagen, he sailed to Iceland to attend the *Al-thing* and was almost always assigned to preside over its sessions. Thus, he became known as President Jón, and foreign visitors to Iceland noticed that his portrait was prominent in almost every farmhouse around the country. Although some of his views were disputed and he was even considered too cautious at times, he immediately became a national hero in the collective memory of Icelanders, similar to George Washington in the United States or Simon Bolívar in many parts of Latin America.

After Sigurdsson's death, no Icelander could assume his leading role. Members of the *Althing* wanted increased rights for the country but quarreled among themselves about precise details. Moreover, acquiescence in Denmark seemed in any case out of the question. From the 1880s, the Danish Leftist Party always gained a majority in parliamentary elections, but the Conservatives continued to hold the reign, ruling by decrees and aided by the king who regularly wielded his power to veto legislation. Since the conservative regime proved unwilling to accede to Icelandic wishes for home rule, by 1901, a narrow majority in the Icelandic parliament grudgingly accepted a compromise whereby a minister for Iceland would be an Icelander, accountable to the *Althing* but resident in Copenhagen.

This way out of the deadlock was the work of Valtýr Gudmundsson, a shrewd politician and scholar of humble origins who then seemed destined to become the first Icelander to wield ministerial powers. For Valtýr, however, fate turned cruel. After a landslide electoral victory in Denmark later in 1901, the Leftist Party finally managed to form a government. Parliamentary democracy was there to stay. Standing for liberalism and democracy, the new rulers in Copenhagen were perfectly willing to grant the Icelanders increased rights. This the king and the minister for Icelandic affairs confirmed in early 1902. In the *Althing* elections that summer, the opponents to Gudmundsson's scheme, who had by then formed the Home Rule Party, therefore won a clear majority. Their leader was Hannes Hafstein, a charismatic lawyer, sheriff, and renowned patriotic poet—an equal of Jónas Hallgrímsson according to his keenest admirers. After this turn of events, Hafstein looked destined to become the first Icelandic minister for Iceland, with a ministry and staff in Reykjavík.

Finally, after half a century of struggle against Danish rule, a decisive triumph had been secured. Home rule beckoned. Naturally, it was vital to have executive power in the country itself and not in the hands of a Danish minister with little interest in Icelandic affairs. The hard-fought victories of previous decades—the resurrection of the *Althing,* gradually increased legislative powers, a separate constitution—were also important and noteworthy in a historical context. Nevertheless, successes in the political and constitutional struggle were by no means the sole prerequisite in the development of an independent state in Iceland. Arguably, it was not the most important factor at all because modifications of the superstructure would have been futile if the foundation remained unchanged. It may even be surmised whether the emphasis on constitutional advancements delayed actual advancements in economic and political terms. The struggle had become "nothing but some negative formalism," one Icelandic nationalist complained in 1871. Furthermore, what kind of freedom seemed closer at hand in 1902 than it had been in the first decades of the nineteenth century? Who were to benefit? Who were being liberated and who were as suppressed as before?

COD OR SHEEP? THE COLLAPSE OF THE OLD ORDER

The Icelandic struggle for independence rarely included demands about increased personal freedom. Although the franchise was expanded in the late 1850s, for the rest of the century, only 8 to 10 percent of the population were allowed to take part in parliamentary elections. This privileged class consisted primarily of farmers who paid communal taxes, officials, academics, and the few merchants and burghers in Reykjavík and smaller communities like Hafnarfjördur, Ísafjördur, Akureyri, and Seydisfjördur. Within the *Althing*, there was little interest to allow others to take part in politics, and the argument went that only those who contributed financially to society should be involved in its management.

Voter turnout was also low, always less than 50 percent. Often there was no doubt that the sitting representative or a successor of his choosing would be reelected, so eligible voters may have reasoned that there was no need to waste a day or two to reach the polling station, as was the case in some of the large constituencies. Moreover, around the middle of the nineteenth century, the Icelanders—including the elite—had little or no experience of cooperation in associations. Few knew the rules of order for meetings or how to construct speeches. Indeed, one delegate at the famed national assembly of 1851 found it utterly chaotic and attributed the disappointing outcome partly to that fact.

Regularly, the members of the Icelandic *Althing* also turned out to be more conservative than the authorities in Copenhagen. In 1853, the *Althing* was temporarily allowed to reject Danish laws that granted Jews the right to settle in the kingdom. Similarly, it turned down calls for religious freedom although the constitution of 1849 was meant to guarantee that entitlement. Some believers inevitably suffered. Around the middle of the century, a small number of Icelandic Mormons were engaged in missionary work in the country. They were persecuted, however, and ultimately banned from offering baptism to the few who were willing to convert. Likewise, two Catholic priests from France tried to spread their faith but were unsuccessful, at least to some extent because of the negative reaction they caused among officials and, it seems, the public at large.

Although there were always notable exceptions, conservative attitudes appeared to permeate daily life. On the typical farm, pastime was controlled by the master of the house. It was he who decided what should be read in the evenings when people gathered together in the open chamber that doubled as a living room and a shared bedroom. By and large, the word of God was chosen or the sagas and other old tales. Reading in private was difficult, at least during the dark winters, because the farmer controlled the provision of light, and illumination was expensive. Usually, it was provided by fish oil lamps. Candles were rarer.

In general, children were loved, or appreciated at any rate. Yet they were still meant to contribute to the household, and if they were deemed to have misbehaved, physical punishment was considered just and necessary. During the nineteenth century, both sexes were generally taught to read at home and many learned to write. Still, boys were encouraged more, and further education continued to be out of girls' reach. They were meant to become wives and housekeepers, obedient, industrious, and aware of their limits. Undoubtedly, many women were content with that fate or at least resigned to it. Others wondered whether the subjugation was fair. This they did mostly in silence, though, and they were unable to do anything about it.

As before, the elite were fixed on order and stability. If tenants found themselves forced to ask the authorities in their district for help, more often than not the family in question was dissolved. Usually, children would be dispersed to other farms where they could be welcomed and appreciated. Sometimes, however, they were accepted only because of the small allowance that the district authorities provided. Miserable treatment could then await the young ones. And while fines for childbirths out of wedlock were abolished in 1812, intellectual nationalists like the aforementioned Baldvin Einarsson later warned against the dissolution of the traditional agricultural society. In the mid-nineteenth century, moreover, affluent farmers asked the newly reinstated *Althing* to prohibit people who seemed unlikely to be able to sustain a family to enter into marriage. In 1865, a majority in the parliament subsequently agreed to restrictions in that vein, also limiting matrimony to men over the age of 25 and women of 20 years or more. The move was rejected by the Danish authorities, however.

Although people fell in love and could live happily ever after, romance was still not considered an essential or preferable requirement for marriage. That institution served a societal function, to maintain the population in a controlled manner. By the middle of the nineteenth century, some 35 to 40 percent of Icelanders over the age of 15 belonged to the group of workers who were not in a position to run their own farm, marry, and have children. In the words of historian Helgi Skúli Kjartansson, they were socially infertile.[1] Also regulations that forbade vagrancy and compelled laborers to sign up annually for work on a farm were in force. Free labor was not an accepted concept.

But the system seemed to be bursting at the seams. Illegitimate births increased, and a slow but steady growth in the population meant that the countryside appeared to be at the risk of overcrowding. While that may sound incredible for a nation of some 60,000 people in a country of 40,000 square miles, the limited amount of habitable land must be kept in mind. Around 1860, new farms and cottages had spread deep into high valleys and cold uplands. Yet workers found it ever more difficult to find employment in farming. Seasonal fisheries helped somewhat, but by this stage, only 3 percent of the population lived in Reykjavík and the smaller towns and villages around the coastline.

The protectors of the old society—the bulk of wealthy farmers, officials, and *Althing* members—would have liked to maintain this state of affairs. Looking back, however, historians have noticed a revolutionary change in Iceland around 1870. A new society was emerging. Seen in a positive light, a period of increased freedom, prosperity, and diversification had begun. Already in 1855, full freedom of trade had been achieved, not the least because of Jón Sigurdsson's agitation, and trade with Britain and Norway increased. Even so, Danish merchants remained dominant, and attempts by a few Icelandic entrepreneurs to engage in trade failed or lasted only for a short period. Likewise, trading companies initially fell through. In 1882, however, farmers in the northeastern part of Iceland formed the country's first cooperative society. Others followed, mostly in the north of Iceland at first, and in 1902, the Union of Icelandic Cooperatives was founded.

Farmers were getting organized, and they began to modernize. By the end of the nineteenth century, the cultivation of grassland increased considerably. Moorlands were dried and hayfields expanded. About the same time, the sale of live sheep to Britain also provided a sudden and unexpected improvement in the fortunes of Icelandic farmers. Icelandic ponies were sold as well since this sturdy type could be used in the narrow shafts of coalmines. The British buyers paid in cash, and this animal trade became one of the motivators in the formation of cooperative and trading associations in the last decades of the nineteenth century.

The windfall proved short-lived, however. Near the end of the century, improvements in freezing methods abroad made the export of live sheep from Iceland uncompetitive. Fears about the spread of scabies in Britain also played a role. And more substantially, the underlying problem remained that there simply were not enough opportunities for people in the countryside, especially the young generation who wanted to stand on their own feet. They still had to find a way out.

One escape route led them to the New World. In 1855, the first Icelanders sailed to North America, a small group of Mormons who settled in Utah. In the next decades, a few dozens of their brethren followed, and in the early 1870s, some 30 Icelanders emigrated to Brazil. In both locations, people of Icelandic origin can still be found.

A great exodus had begun. In the years from 1870 to the outbreak of World War I in 1914, some 17,000 people left Iceland for North America. Although more than 2,000 returned, this was a considerable part of the population—at the start of the period, there were almost 70,000 Icelanders and their numbers had grown to 87,000 by the end. Women comprised over half of the migrants, an unusually high proportion in a European context, but further proof of the fact that lack of employment and progression in the agricultural society convinced many Icelanders to leave the island for good. In that sense, women were even worse off than men. For both sexes, other reasons mattered as well, though: adventurism and the sales skills of foreign agents, a great volcanic eruption in the northeast in 1875, and harsh winters for most of the 1880s.

While some of the newcomers settled in the U.S. states of Wisconsin and North Dakota, most went to Canada. Out of those, a few ventured as far as Alberta and even to British Columbia. The great majority, however, put down roots in Manitoba, most notably in New Iceland, a settlement by Lake Winnipeg, where places still have Icelandic-sounding names like Hecla Island and the town of Gimli (the name of a heavenly abode in Norse mythology). Initially, many lived in abject poverty. The Icelanders were unused to the continental climate of freezing cold winters and hot summers; they missed the mountains back home and the open sea. Nevertheless, most of those who had left everything, often including close family, claimed that they did not regret the move and spoke derogatively of the old society with its greed, class division, and injustice.

Gradually, the Icelanders managed to establish themselves in their new milieu, and many came to hold a romantic view of the land of their forefathers and foremothers. In Iceland, however, the prevailing opinion, at least among intellectuals and politicians, was that those who left had betrayed their homeland. But they had to admit as well that everything was in a state of flux on the island. The period of exodus not only entailed the migration of people from Iceland to North America. Icelanders also continued to move from the countryside to Reykjavík and the towns by the coastline. In 1890, the number of people living there had risen to 12 percent, a fourfold increase in three decades, which steadily continued so that in 1901, Reykjavík had 6,682 inhabitants, Akureyri 1,370, and Ísafjördur 1,220. A few other towns had more than 500 residents: Hafnarfjördur, Akranes, Ólafsvík, Seydisfjördur, and Eyrarbakki.

In a sense, the migrants were abandoning the sheep and turning their attention to cod. Fisheries were becoming an independent industry, not a supplement to farming as had been the norm in times past. The effort itself changed little. Fishermen went to sea at dawn in a rowing boat with their fishing nets or lines, and returned ashore the same day. Cod remained the prime catch, closely followed by haddock. The whole fish was exploited, including the head, the liver, and the stomach. Once on land, the fish was dried or salted. For a while, shark fishing was also a lucrative activity, especially in the Eyjafjördur region in the north. Shark liver oil was used for streetlighting in European cities, but increased use of kerosene put a near end to that business.

Throughout the century, the number of rowing boats in Iceland increased from some 2,000 to more than 3,500. In the first decades of the nineteenth century, a few innovative Icelanders also began to run decked sailing vessels, which, due to their bigger size, were more profitable and able to bring greater catches on a regular basis. In the 1850s, some 25 ships of this kind were in operation in Iceland, most of them from the Westfjords and around Eyjafjördur. At the turn of the nineteenth century, there were almost 170 decked sailing vessels in the country, and Reykjavík had become the main fishing port.

In the last two decades of the nineteenth century, fishing accounted for some 60 percent of Icelandic exports. The other 40 percent consisted of agricultural products, including live sheep and horses. Fisheries formed the basis for the growth of Reykjavík and the coastal towns. Alongside increased trade, they led in 1885 to the adoption of the Icelandic *króna* (crown), a separate currency for Iceland. At the same time, a small state-run bank was founded (beginning its operations the following year). The emergence of new laws also demonstrated the arrival of a new economic environment. As the century drew to a close, the *Althing* passed laws on bankruptcy, collaterals, bills of exchange, lien, and other legal measures.

The 1880s witnessed a worldwide economic slump that affected Iceland, but overall, the country's economic lot seemed to be improving. Despite regular fluctuations in catches and prices on foreign markets, forward-looking Icelanders therefore concluded that fishing rather than farming alone could produce a basis for modernization and prosperity. But much more needed to be done, and what was worse, the foreigners seemed to be reaping most from the rich waters around Iceland.

Foreign fishing off the country had not abated. For a large part of the nineteenth century, the French were especially prominent. In 1830, for instance, they came on 60 vessels, and some three decades later, they were around 260. On board were more than 4,000 fishermen. Around this time, the French authorities had also asked for permission to establish a fish-processing camp in the Westfjords with living quarters for more than 500 people. The *Althing* was against the idea, however, and the French fishing effort gradually diminished in the following decades. Instead, the Norwegians arrived on the scene. Around 1870, fishermen from Norway began to catch herring off the northern and eastern coasts of Iceland. Some towns flourished and got a Norwegian look about them, for instance, Seydisfjördur in the east. In the 1880s, permission was also granted for a Norwegian whaling station in the Westfjords. For a while, Norwegian magnates operated eight whaling stations in that region and later five on Iceland's east coast. In the early twentieth century, the relentless effort had led to stock depletion, and a total ban by the authorities in 1915 spelled the end of whaling off Iceland.

Throughout the centuries, herring had not been deemed suitable for human consumption in Iceland. Gradually, however, the Icelanders got involved in this fishing effort, either salting the catches and selling abroad or using herring as bait for the cod fishery. They also got employment and some tax income from the foreign fisheries. Still, the Norwegians took almost all the profit of their whaling and herring catches back to their home country.

The same could also be said about steam trawling, the most revolutionary novelty in fisheries off Iceland. Around 1890, German and primarily British trawlers arrived on the fishing grounds off the south coast, around the Westman Islands and in Faxa Bay in the southwest. These vessels, powered by steam engines, dragged the trawl (fishing net) along the ocean floor to catch demersal fish like cod, haddock, and halibut. Usually, the catches were far greater than what Icelandic fishermen got on their small rowing boats or the decked sailing vessels. By the end of the century, steam trawling was definitely the future in fisheries.

Despite a gradual accumulation of capital in Iceland through increased fishing, trade, and the sale of live sheep and horses, the new productive method seemed beyond the Icelanders' reach. Furthermore, the local fishermen who had to compete with the relatively gigantic steam trawlers complained that trawling destroyed the fishing grounds. It was certainly true that, in the long run, the increased effort could lead to depletion. During the 1890s, the *Althing* therefore wanted to protect the fishermen and the fishing grounds. But Britain had become a naval and world power, championing the freedom of the high seas and narrow territorial waters. In 1901, the authorities in London and Copenhagen agreed on the imposition of a three-mile limit around Iceland (and the Faroe Islands). Although the Icelanders initially stomached this arrangement, they grew to dislike it. A struggle for the fishing grounds lay ahead.

Soon Icelandic entrepreneurs would begin to operate steam trawlers but another breakthrough first occurred: in 1902, in Ísafjördur on the Westfjords, an engine was for the first time installed in an Icelandic rowing boat. It was a small, two-horsepower engine, but it was immediately clear that oars belonged to the past. In the latter half of the nineteenth century, communications also continued to improve. In 1858, steam-powered post ships had begun to sail to the island, bringing tourists and news on a regular basis. In 1878, the first lighthouse was constructed, with many to follow, and in the 1880s, scheduled voyages around Iceland were introduced. In 1893, the office of national engineer was established, and in the 1890s, Ölfusá and Thjórsá, the two main rivers in the large agricultural region in the south, were bridged. There were no cars in the country, still, and innovative Icelanders failed in their campaign to build railways from Reykjavík to the southern lowland and north to Akureyri. No tracks were laid at the time, but fervent debates about the possibility demonstrated a growing sense of optimism and bold thinking in the country.

Thus, as the twentieth century began, the Icelanders were getting more confident about what they could achieve in the country. It can be hard, admittedly, to measure such sentiments. If, however, we accept that assumption, we may also ask what came first: Was the increased feeling of confidence and optimism a cause or consequence of economic and political progress? It seems most sensible to conclude that all these features were closely interwoven. Indeed, it has been argued that the struggle against Danish rule was, to use a modern-day term, a self-reinforcement course for the Icelanders or a common realization that they could stand on their own feet and utilize their own natural resources. As the economy progressed, so did the self-confidence.

In general, the Icelanders were also getting healthier, happier, and freer. Near the end of the twentieth century, a woman in old age said that of all the revolutionary changes she had experienced, the introduction of rubber boots was most memorable. In Iceland, that watershed was probably reached in 1902, the year when the first newspaper advertisement for such boots appeared. While the skin footwear of past ages did provide some protection, it is tempting to say that the inhabitants of Iceland, that rainy island, could for the first time walk outside on dry feet.

The physical condition of Icelanders was definitely improving. In 1876, a medical school was founded but, more importantly, in that decade, the old habit of giving newborns milk or cream was finally shaken off and the practice of breast-feeding increased. By the start of the twentieth century, infant mortality in Iceland had become lower than in most other European countries. On the other hand, epidemics like measles and diphtheria regularly wreaked havoc and the health service was minimal. At the start of the twentieth century, there were five hospitals in the country and one doctor for every 2,400 inhabitants. Diseases that are easily treatable today could spell disaster, and prejudices abounded as well. Thus, like elsewhere in the Western world, the mentally ill were apt to face horrific treatments like solitary confinement, ice baths, or beatings.

On the positive side, arguably, a powerful abstinence movement came into being in the 1880s, with around 4,500 members at the turn of the nineteenth century. Assembly halls were built, members gained valuable experience in communal work, and drunkenness decreased, although it remained a significant predicament in Icelandic society. In the last decades of the nineteenth century, the first labor and employer unions were also formed, weak at first but mounting proof of the power of unity.

Likewise, the emergence of mass media demonstrated increased interest in public affairs. There were still no newspapers in the country, but weeklies and other periodicals began to appear. Translated low-class literature like crime or romantic novels received wide popularity, as expected, and the import of paraffin lamps, a new invention, transformed access to light in households. In almost all aspects, personal liberty was on the rise. In letters, diaries, and even autobiographies, more individuals than ever before expressed their feelings, experiences, and memories. Freedom of religion could also be exercised. In 1896, the sisters of St. Joseph established a school and a hospital in Reykjavík. In 1903, Catholic priests came to Iceland and gradually a tiny congregation was formed. Within the state Lutheran church, meanwhile, service attendances decreased, and ministers held less authority over their congregation.

People wanted to think for themselves. By the same token, love could better be expressed and enjoyed than before. Scholars have contended that in the Western world, the Industrial Revolution of the eighteenth to nineteenth centuries changed personal relationships and the institution of marriage, as the family ceased to be primarily a unit of production and sustenance. Instead, with more free time and prosperity, people of both sexes thought less about practical issues when they looked for a life partner. Private testimonies indicate that similar developments occurred in Iceland in the late nineteenth century. Romance became a bigger reason for marriage than sounder justifications like the apparent industriousness, thoughtfulness, or piety of the hoped-for spouse.

Similarly, calls for gender equality could finally be heard. As for individual women, the path breaker was the young Bríet Bjarnhédinsdóttir, who began to write and lecture in the 1880s about women's rights. In 1894, she was a prime mover in the formation of the Icelandic Women's Association, and the following year, she launched a magazine dedicated to women's rights. Another notable campaigner was Thorbjörg Sveinsdóttir, a fiery individual who refused to accept the ingrained inequality of men and women.

It was of course an uphill struggle. Women were still without the vote, and although women's colleges were founded, the focus was on sewing, cooking, and similar duties. Higher education remained the preserve of men. The male rulers of the home and society as a whole seemed to fear genuinely that were women to abandon their duties of motherhood and housekeeping, chaos would result. Many women were equally concerned, unsure about their position and suspicious of all radicalism. Furthermore, class divisions and deep differences still defined Icelandic society. There remained a huge gap between the few wealthy and the poor masses. In the 1890s, to take the most telling example, only around 20 percent of farmers owned their land. Tenancy was still the norm.

By and large, however, progress and optimism were in the air as the Icelanders celebrated the birth of a new century. Incidentally, this they did in 1901, poking fun at those foreigners who thought that the nineteenth century had run its course at the end of 1899. The inhabitants of Iceland, so poor, isolated, and even derided for centuries, had grown confident enough to know better. The future was theirs to take. The poets wrote ode after ode to Iceland and, apparently, the motherland had also decided to bless her subjects: At the end of the nineteenth century, Icelandic glaciers reached their maximum spread since settlement. Temperatures then rose, however, and the glaciers began a steady retreat. The little ice age was over.

"THE STRUGGLE FOR INDEPENDENCE IS OVER"

The national awakening, the revival, the rebirth: at the start of the twentieth century, these words came to be used to describe the struggle for increased independence from Denmark. It was a struggle that was not completed but had, nonetheless, become part of Iceland's history.

In the nineteenth-century Europe, the emergence of history as a systematic academic discipline coincided with the rise of nationalism. Predominantly, historians at universities, archives, or other institutions were also eager nationalists, determined that their efforts would bolster the national cause. The archivist and scholar Jón Sigurdsson worked in this vein and so did Iceland's first professional historians, men like Jón Jónsson Adils, who received popularity in the early twentieth century for his books and public lectures on Icelandic history. We have already seen how he and his few colleagues at the time divided the island's past into the glorious age of settlement and freedom until the thirteenth century when the long, miserable period of foreign rule set in. Ultimately, the story went, the nation had to wake up and realize that freedom and prosperity went hand in hand with independence from distant rulers. Thus, the historians of the modern period repeated the arguments of well-known individuals in the nineteenth century like Baldvin Einarsson, Jónas Hallgrímsson, and, of course, Jón Sigurdsson. In an international context, they also echoed the Czech scholar František Palacký, traditionally known in his homeland as the father of the nation, and the Prussian School of historians, which influenced the process of German unification by glorifying a common, Germanic past.

In Iceland, as elsewhere, the nation was defined as an innate, almost dei-
fied entity. Moreover, class divisions and conflicting interests within a nation
were ignored or downplayed in the name of unity. Another prominent feature
was the emphasis on the great man in history. Thus, the first generation of
Icelandic historians focused on individual heroes, beginning with the settler
Ingólfur Arnarson and moving to recent notables where the often-mentioned
Jón Sigurdsson rose above all others. History, in their minds, was made by
great men, and the masses simply followed their lead.

All this was understandable, almost inevitable, in the context of the times.
It is more questionable, however, that the nationalistic look on developments in the nineteenth century was hardly challenged until the 1960s, or
even later. One reason was that there were very few professional historians
in the country and the political body still expected a healthy dose of patriot-
ism in their works. Some politicians wrote history textbooks or treaties themselves, most notably Jónas Jónsson, whose overview of Icelandic history was
used in Icelandic schools for almost 70 years since its first publication in 1915.

For politicians, the public, and, indeed, most historians, the vision of a national revival under the leadership of brilliant heroes was simply too alluring,
just like the image of a golden age and foreign-inflicted decline. Then again,
the lot of the Icelanders did actually improve in the nineteenth century, as has
been established. But why? That was the true question. Beginning in the 1960s,
scholars began—cautiously at first—to reject the relatively simple explanation
of a general awakening championed by outstanding leaders. Jón Sigurdsson
and other individuals were not idolized as before, and more emphasis was put
on general developments abroad, in particular the revolutionary years of 1830
and 1848 as well as the growth of liberalism and the ultimate victory of parliamentary democracy in Denmark in 1901. Historians also noticed advances in
fisheries and farming, and the influx of foreign capital. Finally, they pointed
out the discrepancy between the demands for increased independence from
Denmark and the resistance to change in Icelandic society. Thus, for progressive historians in contemporary Iceland, the term *national awakening* is rather
a misnomer. For them, the members of the *Althing* were conservative in thinking and conduct, members of an elite class who looked determined to protect
their superior position in society. With all this in mind, historian Gudmundur
Hálfdanarson stated at the end of the twentieth century that the "struggle for
independence is over," paraphrasing a comment by his French counterpart,
François Furet, that the French Revolution was over. In both cases, the argument went that the long-gone events should be considered on their own merits, not within the context of current political debates.

Most recently, some historians have wondered whether the revisionism
has gone too far. Thus, they have been more willing to sympathize with the

argument that, despite class interests and conflicts, the Icelanders were more or less united in their aspirations about increased freedom from foreign rule. Also this goal may indeed have been a necessary prerequisite for material advancement rather than its consequence. Furthermore, the new critical version of Iceland's struggle for independence has found little support among the public or the majority of politicians. Iceland's struggle for independence may be over in the academic world, but outside its walls it is well alive.

NOTE

1. See Gísli Ágúst Gunnlaugsson, *Saga og samfélag* [History and society] (Reykjavík: University of Iceland Historical Institute, 1997), 15.

5

Iceland on Its Own: Progress, Class, and Fragility (1902–1940)

HOME RULE AND SOVEREIGNTY

It is worth recounting why the year 1902 can be used as a breakpoint in Icelandic history. In terms of everyday life, this was probably when Icelanders began to use rubber boots, a small but revolutionary comfort that people recalled fondly in old age. As for the economic foundation of subsistence, in 1902, an engine was installed for the first time in a fishing boat, and Iceland's Industrial Revolution had begun, as we shall see. This year also saw the formation of the Union of Icelandic Cooperatives, a cartel that soon rose to prominence in the island's economy. On the political level, finally, it was in 1902 that the Danish king and the new liberal regime in Denmark accepted the concept of a minister for Iceland residing in Reykjavík. Later that same year, the Home Rule Party won a majority in elections to the *Althing* and its leader, the charming Hannes Hafstein, seemed certain to become the first Icelandic minister.

All these events were important, both then and in a historical perspective. Yet we could easily move the turning point. For instance, 1901 was the first year of the new century and also the year when parliamentary democracy at last broke through in Denmark, with its knock-on effects for Iceland. Similarly,

1903 can be proposed. That year, discriminating rules were used for the last time to prevent girls from entering the Reykjavík School. Also the law on home rule for Iceland was passed and confirmed by the king.

And then there was the eventful year of 1904. It was then that the Bank of Iceland was launched, a private bank that injected foreign capital into the fishing industry with immediate results. The first all-Icelandic trawling company was formed, a technical college was founded and the first car was brought to Iceland—a flawed model that constantly broke down, admittedly, and had few roads to traverse in any case. The introduction of horse-drawn carriages around 1900 was more influential at the time.

Last but not least, it was in 1904 that home rule began in effect in Iceland. On February 1, Hannes Hafstein began his term as minister for Iceland. Indeed, in popular and academic works on Icelandic history, a dividing line at the start of the twentieth century is usually drawn in 1904, not 1902. Why one or the other? The main difference lies in the usage of symbolically important events in Iceland's economic history and everyday life (rubber boots and the first engine in a fishing boat) or the highlighting of a political achievement two years later.

While the onset of home rule in 1904 was undeniably a historic moment, the struggle for independence had of course not ended. If anything, political rows deepened in the country. The opponents of Hafstein and his Home Rule Party were divided into two political groups. The larger one consisted mainly of those who had, before the shift in Danish politics in 1901, been content with the idea of an Icelandic minister based in Copenhagen but then turned more nationalistic than Hafstein and his men. The smaller group went even further, insisting that the Icelanders could only accept personal union with Denmark; in all other aspects, they must achieve complete independence. Moreover, the two opposing parties condemned the fact that the Icelandic minister was considered to be part of the Danish cabinet. In 1905, a regime change in Denmark demonstrated that this was a mere formality since Hafstein was unaffected. As before, however, formalities and exact constitutional descriptions could be the subject of prolonged political debates in Iceland.

In the summer of 1907, the most radical champions of Icelandic independence convened about 400 people at Thingvellir to demand increased rights from Denmark. The gathering also consecrated a new flag for Iceland that the poet and the entrepreneur Einar Benediktsson had designed—a white cross on blue background and similar in form to the other Nordic flags. Later that summer, King Frederick VIII, who had succeeded his father the year before, visited Iceland and was widely acclaimed for his words about the two states in the royal union. Thus, he seemed to imply that the law from 1871, which was still intact and described Iceland as an inseparable part of the Danish Kingdom with certain special rights, was outdated.

In early 1908, talks in Copenhagen between members of the Icelandic and Danish parliaments led to a draft agreement on a treaty defining Iceland's position within the kingdom. In the main, it defined the country as free and independent, and the negotiators on both sides were content—except one. Skúli Thoroddsen, a member of the small radical faction in the Icelandic *Althing*, argued that Iceland must be described as a free and autonomous state, thus highlighting a separate statehood within a personal union. In Iceland, parliamentary elections lay ahead, and it seemed obvious that the supporters of the treaty would maintain their majority. As it turned out, however, the opponents won a resounding victory. In the spirit of the day, those who wanted most in dealings with Denmark were destined to be more popular than the advocates of moderation. Furthermore, for the first time, voting was done through secret ballots unlike before when voters had to state publicly whom they chose. This gave many the freedom and joy to reject the sitting representative.

When the *Althing* convened in the following year, 1909, Hannes Hafstein lost a vote of confidence. The previous parties in opposition had by then merged into a new party, the Independence Party. They then chose a new minister, Björn Jónsson, leaving Skúli Thoroddsen bitter and gradually fading away from political life. Björn, aged and failing, soon got embroiled in disputes with many of his supporters and, after a brief interlude by another member of his party, in 1912 Hannes Hafstein again took up the reins. That year, Hafstein, Björn Jónsson, and some of his supporters formed a new party, the Union Party, which supported a modified version of the abortive treaty from 1908. The Danish authorities proposed changes to it, however, which the Unionists deemed to be unacceptable to the Icelanders. In that, they were correct. Compromises would have to be presented delicately and the sensitive atmosphere was best demonstrated in 1913. The captain of a Danish warship mooring outside Reykjavík then confiscated the blue and white flag, which an Icelander carried on his boat. Although the flag was not legal, this was a tactless move that caused an outrage. Immediately, blue and white flags flew at full mast in every corner of the town.

By royal decree two years later, in 1915, the Icelanders got their own flag, but only for use in Iceland and on its territorial sea. It was not the blue and white version, however, since that was deemed to be too similar to the Greek flag but the red, white, and blue flag, which has since been the standard of Iceland.

Thus, during World War I, the Icelanders were edging toward ever greater autonomy within the Danish Kingdom. Britain's embargo on trade with Germany and its allies affected Iceland, and exports to Denmark dropped as well, even though the rulers in Copenhagen declared neutrality like the other Nordic states. In actual fact, the British authorities controlled all trade and communications in the North Atlantic and from 1916 to the end of the war, most of Iceland's trade was with Britain and the United States. While the war brought shortages and economic hardship, it also demonstrated that Iceland could easily survive without extensive ties with the old colonial masters.

The war's end also benefited the Icelandic independence cause. Loud demands for all nations' right to self-determination, pronounced most famously by U.S. President Woodrow Wilson, were of course heard in Iceland—and Denmark. Apart from the principle itself, the Icelanders were aided by the fact that the authorities in Copenhagen sensed a way to get back the Dane-populated northern Schleswig, which they had lost to Prussia (now Germany) in the war of 1864. With that in mind, the Danish rulers could hardly ignore Icelandic wishes for self-determination.

In July 1918, Danish and Icelandic representatives reached agreement on a Union Treaty, which stated unequivocally that Iceland was a free and sovereign state, albeit in a personal union with Denmark. On December 1 that year, after a plebiscite that was resolutely in favor, the treaty took effect. The Danish king remained the Icelandic head of state, and the authorities in Copenhagen continued to handle Iceland's foreign affairs. At the same time, the Icelandic authorities declared eternal neutrality, and the country was without military forces of any kind. Moreover, Iceland did not join the League of Nations, and diplomats of other countries, for instance, the United States, were not sure whether it should be considered completely independent. To all intents and purposes, still, sovereignty had been achieved, and in 25 years the treaty could be denounced. Then the Icelanders could sever all ties with Denmark if they so wished.

As the years went on, that seemed the most obvious outcome. In 1920, a Supreme Court was established in Iceland, in accordance with stipulations in the Union Treaty, and in 1926, coast guard duties were taken over from Denmark. Foreign fishing had intensified from the initial years in the late nineteenth century and stock depletion had become a real worry. Worldwide, however, Britain defended the principle of a narrow three-mile limit of the territorial sea, and the Icelandic authorities were naturally unable to contest that position.

The actual power of the new microstate was minimal, but in 1930, the budding, if fragile, sense of independence received a great boost. That year, the Icelanders celebrated the thousandth anniversary of the *Althing*. Foreign dignitaries came to Thingvellir, speaking appraisingly about the world's oldest parliament, and the U.S. government presented a gift from the American people, a statue of Leifur "the Lucky" Eiríksson, who was often described in those days as "the first American."

Iceland, it seemed to the Icelanders, was becoming a nation among nations, and they even held their own colonial ambitions as they were freeing themselves from Danish rule: in 1930, when a dispute over the rights to the east coast of Greenland was before the Permanent Court of International

Justice at The Hague, the *Althing* wanted to advance Icelandic claims to the whole of Greenland. Although this was never an issue of great importance, it demonstrated increased confidence and, it must be added, a self-righteous sense of superiority over the Greenlandic Inuit. A similar kind of duplicity appeared when the Icelandic authorities sold salted fish to Italy in abundance, gladly ignoring the League of Nations trade embargo, which was imposed after the Italian invasion of Abyssinia in 1935. But the self-interest was of course understandable. The new state was struggling to stand on its own feet.

CLASS, IDEALS, AND RADICALISM

At the start of the twentieth century, Iceland was among Europe's poorest countries. It was also a class-riddled country. The discrimination began at school level, the most common entrance to organized society. With the passing of a law on compulsory education in 1907, all children between the ages of 10 and 14 were meant to attend school for at least six months a year. Before that age, they were supposed to be taught at home, either by family or itinerant teachers. While this was a step forward, some school instructors obviously favored pupils from "good families," at least if we are to believe reminisces of children from the time.

Those who were born into extreme poverty and misery usually suffered most in early life. In 1901, almost 10 percent of children in Reykjavík were put into foster care, sometimes because one or both parents drank and ignored their offspring, and sometimes because the youngsters themselves had been found guilty of thievery or mischief. Parental poverty was the main reason, however, especially in the case of widows or divorced women who simply could not care for their young ones.

The notion that the authorities should do their utmost to help the less privileged in society was still a fair way off. Malice was not necessarily to blame. The emergent state of Iceland had meager financial means, and practically in every town or district, there were well-to-do individuals who tried to help those in need. Also in 1905, a law on poor assistance was passed. It was flimsy, however, and it can hardly seem surprising that certain individuals and groups started to fight more forcefully for their rights.

Women could still be labeled as a specific, subjugated body of people. Higher education was the preserve of a few, fortunate girls, almost always of affluent parents, and no woman held a notable public position. Yet at the beginning of the new century, increased wealth and diversification in the Icelandic economy benefited young girls who aspired to something more. They were able to study languages, nursing, teaching, sewing, and so on. The Icelandic Women's Association remained active, and "respectable" ladies (often

the wives, sisters, or daughters of Icelandic and Danish officials and merchants) founded various charities.

Political rights were also within reach. In 1908, when women had won both
the right to vote and run in municipal elections, the Women's List received
more support in Reykjavík than all other parties. Women also acquired seats
in the town councils of Akureyri and Seydisfjördur. In 1915, female suffrage
was secured through constitutional change in Iceland and Denmark, around
the same time as in other Nordic and many Western European countries. In
1922, Ingibjörg Bjarnason became the first female member of the *Althing*. That
same year, however, there was no woman left on the Reykjavík city council,
and women did not grow from strength to strength on the political scene. For
more than 60 years, three was the maximum number of women representatives in the *Althing*.

One reason for the long setback was the recurrent conflict within the
women's movement about their proper role in society. Some wanted equality
on all levels, a gender-blind society, but others felt that the struggle should
focus on offering women better opportunities to become good wives and
mothers. That vision was also championed by the male part of the population
who, while supporting female suffrage, felt that the running of society could not
be done by the "weaker sex," sentimental and impressionable as they were.

But who should actually run society, make decisions? The constitutional
change of 1915 granted not only women the vote but also workers of both
sexes. A minimal payment of local taxes was no longer a prerequisite. Moreover, the first decades of the twentieth century were the heyday of plebiscites
in Iceland. The vote on the Union Treaty in 1918 has already been mentioned,
and in a plebiscite two years before, the Icelanders had resolutely rejected a
proposal on compulsory civic work. Conversely, in 1908, more than 60 percent of those who took part in a referendum accepted a complete prohibition of alcohol, which took effect in 1915. Alcohol abuse was to be eradicated
and drinking certainly diminished, although bootlegging became a profitable
business.

The two propositions on civic duty and prohibition demonstrated a desire
among the elite of politicians, officials, and opinion-makers to improve Icelandic society. Although the voters were not willing to work for nothing, a
majority accepted a ban on drinking and therefore seemed to share this will.
Arguably, they wanted to create better individuals. The "true Icelander," as
historian Sigrídur Matthíasdóttir has argued, was strong in mind and body,
conscientious, religious, and dedicated to the fatherland. Christian associations like the YMCA (and YWCA) were established in Iceland in 1899 and
flourished in the first years of the new century. More significantly, the secular
Icelandic Youth Association set its mark on society. Founded at Thingvellir
in 1907, this national organization of local leagues constructed sports fields,

community centers, and even outdoor swimming pools. It organized public meetings and debating courses, published a journal, and soon boasted thousands of eager members.

The spirit of optimism and progress, kindled a few decades before, lived on. The association's stated aim was to cultivate the people and the country and the slogan was simple: "All for Iceland." In the latter half of the twentieth century, when people were apt to lament selfishness, materialism, and class conflicts in the country, they spoke wistfully of the dawn-of-the-century-generation with their unifying dreams and aspirations.

The noble sentiments clearly existed, but some Icelandic youths felt like failures because they did not live up to the image of the healthy, robust, and erudite Icelander—maybe in the same way that the importance of protecting one's honor could agonize the males of mediaeval Iceland. Women were suppressed, but men could also be hurt by a gendered view of what was to be expected of them.

Moreover, disunity and conflicting interests still marked Icelandic society, as we have already seen. The new century heralded the rise of class struggle, labor unions, and party politics. In 1913, the first substantial strikes took place, and three years later, seven trade unions formed the Icelandic Confederation of Labor, a nationwide organization that still exists. The year 1916 also saw the formation of two political parties. First, the Icelandic Labor Party was founded as the political wing of the labor confederation. Proclaiming the social democratic platform of the time about a classless society after the peaceful overthrow of capitalism, the party was initially small. In 1920, it won a single seat in parliamentary elections and did not increase its presence until 1927. Then, the party got five candidates elected, having received almost a fifth of the vote. At this stage, however, the *Althing* consisted of 42 members so the Labor seats were disproportionally few.

Most members of parliament were elected in single- or two-seat constituencies, but the countryside was overrepresented, at the cost of Reykjavík and other towns. The primary beneficiary was the Progressive Party, the other party formed in 1916. Initially a loose group of farmers who had been elected to the *Althing*, the Progressives grew stronger in the 1920s and their key man (although not party leader until 1934) was Jónas Jónsson, already mentioned as an author of textbooks on Icelandic history. Jónsson was in fact influential in the formation of both the Progressive Party and the Labor Party in 1916. In 1927–1932, when the Progressives were in government, he was the minister of justice and the most conspicuous member of the cabinet, industrious, intolerant, and actually considered mentally unstable by his strongest enemies.

The first government of Iceland had been formed in 1917, replacing the practice of a single minister for the country. Until 1939, there were never more than three members in the cabinet, and the Progressives were most often in

power, alone or in a coalition with other parties. They gathered their support in the rural constituencies, and the electoral discrepancy, which so aided
them, became most glaring in 1931. That year the Progressive Party received
35 percent of the vote but 23 seats, a majority in the joint *Althing* (although not
in both the lower and upper house). By contrast, the 43 percent support for
the Independence Party resulted in only 15 seats. In 1934, the imbalance was
slightly reduced, but the countryside was still overrepresented at the cost of
Reykjavík and the coastal towns around the island.

By that stage, the so-called four-party system had been established in the
country. In 1929, the new Independence Party was formed, with roots in the
bygone era when the independence struggle was in full swing. Although it
espoused individual freedom and economic liberalism, it was not a clear-cut
conservative party and proved to be popular among all sections of society.
From its inception to the early twenty-first century, the Independence Party
always gained the largest share of the vote in parliamentary elections.

The final piece in the four-party puzzle was created in 1930 when the Labor
Party split and the Communist Party of Iceland was founded, proclaiming
world revolution and the violent overthrow of capitalist society. The party
was not represented in the *Althing* until 1937, and the Icelandic communists
rose to prominence on the political field only when they founded a new party
the following year, the Socialist Party, in collaboration with a leftist faction
of the Labor Party. The leadership of this new organization kept clandestine
links with Moscow but espoused a national fight, an Iceland completely free
from Denmark and imperial tycoons. Meanwhile, the Labor social democrats,
who secretly accepted donations from their colleagues in Scandinavia, were
hurt by accusations that they were unpatriotic and weak in their struggle for
the working class.

Still, the Labor Party carried through some imperative reforms, especially
in the late 1930s. In 1934, the Progressives and the Labor Party formed a coalition, which became known as the Regime of the Toiling Classes. In the economic field, its lasting legacy was the imposition of regulations and controls,
which probably prolonged the effects of the Great Depression in Iceland. On a
more positive note, at least for the less fortunate sections of the general public,
a groundbreaking law on social security was passed in 1936. Primarily providing old age, disability, and health insurance, the scheme was initially weak
but a sign of things to come. The origins of a Scandinavian-style welfare state
could be detected.

Despite this progress, the 1930s were marked by radicalism, pay disputes,
and upheavals. The Great Depression had hit Iceland as the price for fish
dropped on foreign markets and practically all nations increased customs
on imports. Unemployment rose, especially in Reykjavík, where it reached
as much as 20 percent in the autumn of 1932. The unions demanded state

assistance and higher pay, but the employers protested that they had no lee-way. In November 1932, a violent fight in Reykjavík, which was incited by the communists but supported by the general labor force, left the tiny police force of the capital—around 30 officers—incapacitated. Some of them were se-riously injured. Although the communists received instructions and financial assistance from the Soviet Union, they were far too feeble to carry through a revolution in Iceland, a doomed folly that would have been quelled, with as-sistance from Britain or Denmark if need be.

Likewise, fascism was not a serious political force in the 1930s. An extreme nationalist party was formed, but it enjoyed negligible support. Even so, many Icelanders admired the ascent of Nazi Germany, where order seemed to pre-vail. The rising power still provided an important market for fish products, and the German interest in the sagas was cherished. Theories about eugenics and the Aryan race also found considerable support in Iceland. In 1938, a few years later than in other Nordic countries, sterilization surgeries were legal-ized. Sometimes medical reasons justified such operations, but in other cases mentally disabled persons were mercilessly deemed unfit to bear children. Actually, the medical community had wanted to go even further than the law allowed by practicing involuntary sterilization of "undesirable elements" in society. That unenviable group included alcoholics and women of "disrespect-ful reputation" who had already borne many children. Also the few Jewish immigrants who arrived in the country were mostly unwelcome and some were even expelled. The Icelandic race had to be protected. Such was the pre-vailing mood.

In a similar vein, some esteemed intellectuals spoke disparagingly of de-mocracy, in particular party politics and representative government. One of them even compared politicians to lice, which crawled on the creature of progress. Instead, and rather paradoxically, he favored a rule based on his glorified view of the chieftain dominance during the ancient settlement era.

Admittedly, it was easy to criticize the system of governance in the coun-try. Inside the *Althing*, the warring factions fought so ferociously that those who harbored beliefs about a single national interest were bound to lose faith. Nepotism was also rampant. In the first decades of the twentieth century, a small administrative body had expanded from the less than dozen officials, which had constituted the Icelandic ministry offices when Hannes Hafstein took on his high post in 1904. Within the growing bureaucracy, family connec-tions or support for the right political party often mattered more than quali-fications. As for the labor unions, they regularly tried to exclude unaffiliated members from work.

In Iceland's class politics, there were no clear heroes or villains, and the party struggle, single events, and views of individuals need to be seen in a wider context. The economic base shaped the political superstructure.

ICELAND'S INDUSTRIAL REVOLUTION

In the broadest of terms, the Industrial Revolution, which began in Britain in the eighteenth century and soon spread to continental Europe and North America, was characterized by the use of coal- and steam-powered engines in factories where various goods were produced. Closely connected was the spread of railways in the nineteenth century. Iceland's industrial revolution revolved around fish, however. It had little to do with coal and nothing at all with railways.

The timings vary as well. Abroad, the origins of the revolutionary change are traced to the late eighteenth century. James Watt's invention of an effective steam engine in 1769 is often mentioned in that regard. In Iceland, the epoch-making installation of an engine in a fishing boat in 1902 could be used as a symbolic beginning. Also in that year, the first dockyard was set up in the country, and soon small workshops opened up to service the mechanized shipping industry. Ten years later, there were more than 400 motor-powered boats in the country and gradually the rowing boats faded away.

The beginnings of trawling companies in Iceland were equally important. There, foreign capital provided a vital impetus. When the Bank of Iceland was founded in 1904, Icelandic citizens were offered an option to buy shares in it, but the total sum purchased only equaled 2 to 3 percent of the legally required amount of stocks. The rest came from abroad, primarily Denmark, although Icelanders always held a majority on the bank's board. Immediately, loans were offered to purchase and run trawlers. In the same year, the first Icelandic trawling company was formed, operating an old Scottish trawler from Hafnarfjördur. In 1907, a new trawler, owned by five skippers and a merchant, arrived in its hometown of Reykjavík. Given the grand name *Jón forseti* (President Jón), it heralded brighter days of prosperity and innovation. By 1912, 20 trawlers were run from Iceland, and in the 1930s there were more than 40. The newer vessels were bigger than the initial trawlers, which were usually between 200 and 300 gross tons (roughly double the size of Christopher Columbus's *Santa Maria*).

Two of the largest trawling companies were based in Reykjavík. One of them was owned by the Denmark-born Thor Jensen, who had moved to Iceland as a young man and, after initial reverses, established a fisheries empire. In Hafnarfjördur, Ísafjördur, and a few other trawling towns, wealthy trawler owners could be found as well. Successful trawler skippers got rich by Icelandic standards, and men longed for a place on a trawler. A good trip could be worth a lot.

The trawlers went to sea all year round, more or less. Cod was the primary catch. On board the vessels, living and working conditions were initially atrocious. All deckhands slept and ate and changed clothes in one area, the forecastle, and there were no toilet facilities. In the first decades, no laws on rest time existed, and men often worked for many days on end. In 1921, after strong objections by the trawler owners and conservative elements in the *Althing*, a law was passed that granted the crews a six-hour break for each 24 hours.

Work on a trawler or other fishing vessels was always a hazardous occupation. During a winter storm off the Westfjords in February 1925, three trawlers were lost with all hands. In total, 68 men died, making the tragedy the single worst accident at sea in recent Icelandic history. Three years later, *Jón forseti* ran aground, a fate that hit vessels with alarming regularity. In that calamity, 15 men lost their lives although 10 were rescued. In the first three decades of the twentieth century, more than 60 people on average drowned at sea each year in Iceland, around three times more than that in neighboring countries. Very few fishermen knew how to swim, and swimming lessons were not made compulsory in schools until 1940. By that stage, other security measures had improved somewhat. The loss of *Jón forseti* and other misfortunes at the time led to the formation of the National Lifesaving Association in 1928. Emergency shelters were built and the inclusion of lifeboats and other rescue equipment on vessels became more common. Furthermore, in the 1930s, lighthouses had been built on most locations where they were needed.

On land, the industrial revolution in the fishing industry was mainly manifested in the construction of herring factories. The small town of Siglufjördur in northern Iceland became the center of a new booming industry, located as it was close to the most profitable herring grounds at the time. In 1911, two herring factories were built in the town, both owned by Norwegian entrepreneurs. During the next decades, more factories were added, not only in Siglufjördur but also elsewhere in the northern part of Iceland and in the Westfjords. Usually, they were in foreign ownership, another example of how vital foreign investment was for the development of a modern fishing industry. Then, in the 1930s, the Icelandic state began to run its own factories and immediately became the dominant party in the field. Most of the profits were not transferred abroad, as before.

In the factories, the herring was melted and turned into fish oil and meal. The remnants were usually disposed of into the sea, and when the factories were running, most people agreed that the unavoidable stench was disgusting. So profitable could the process be, however, that it was referred to as the smell of money. Financially, it was still a risky business. Herring catches varied wildly from year to year, as did the prices on foreign markets that were mostly found in Denmark, Sweden, Germany, and Eastern Europe. The same element of risk followed the salting of herring, another mode of processing that grew in importance. Most notoriously, many herring salters went bankrupt when prices dropped dramatically in the early 1920s.

In general, fisheries continued to be a gendered line of work. Women prepared and salted fish on land but hardly took part in fishing trips, although there were notable exceptions to that rule. Their work was hard but that was not reflected in the wages, which were universally lower than what men got for their labor; during the interwar years, women in trade unions received contractually around 60 percent of men's wages. Women's most significant contribution was probably in the herring industry. Salting herring and putting it in barrels for export abroad were a female occupation. During the summer herring season, women flocked to Siglufjördur and other towns on the north coast, often earning more money than they could over the year for clerical work or domestic chores in Reykjavík.

During the 1930s, the Icelandic authorities began to control and organize the sale of herring and other fish products abroad. This upset many businessmen in the industry—there were hardly any businesswomen in the field. However, some management was probably necessary, if only to avoid bankruptcies through desperate underbids in difficult markets. The late 1930s also saw the first freezing plants were fish was quick-frozen. This was another technical innovation that, after World War II, was to revolutionize the Icelandic fishing industry.

While mechanization and technical innovations were most visible in the fisheries sector, grandiose plans appeared that would have transformed other fields of the economy and society—and indeed the Icelandic landscape. When King Frederick VIII visited the country in the summer of 1907, he and Minister Hannes Hafstein rode with their entourage to Gullfoss, the imposing waterfall in Hvítá River. Sipping champagne, they hailed the endless power that could be harnessed by the construction of a hydroelectric power plant there. The visionary Einar Benediktsson (mentioned before as the designer of the popular blue-and-white flag for Iceland) had great plans about the usage of Gullfoss and other waterfalls, including Dettifoss in the north, Europe's most powerful cascade. Rail tracks would inevitably follow, from the coast to fertilizer factories or other industries that needed large amounts of electricity.

Benediktsson has become the embodiment of these ambitious designs. Others were also interested, still, including the Icelandic authorities and overseas financiers, mainly from Norway, Denmark, and Britain. The onset of World War I interrupted everyone's designs, and although a company that Benediktsson spearheaded was granted a license in 1927 to build a hydropower station by Thjórsá, nothing came of it. Decades would pass until the hydropower of Iceland was exploited on a major scale. On the other hand, Reykjavík city council constructed smaller hydroelectric plants to provide energy for the growing town, in 1921 by a relatively small stream close to Reykjavík and in 1937 in the river that flows from the lake at Thingvellir.

It has been argued that, unlike Norway, where big hydropower stations were constructed, Iceland missed a golden opportunity to prosper and diversify its economy in the first decades of the twentieth century. Presumably, the construction of rail tracks would also have accelerated the rate of urbanization and had other positive effects. Timidity and suspicion of foreign investment, which would have been vital, are then blamed for the alleged shortsightedness. In reality, the plans by Einar Benediktsson and others were impractical. The proposed power stations were fairly far inland, making the cost of railway lines relatively high, for instance. Iceland was also farther away than Norway from continental markets for fertilizer and other possible products. Quite apart from these considerations, some people resisted the proposed projects on environmental grounds, and in contemporary Iceland, there is certainly more relief than regret that natural wonders and tourist attractions like Gullfoss and Dettifoss were not spoiled.

Thus, people have admired the constant campaigns by Sigríður Tómasdóttir, a woman who grew up near Gullfoss, to prevent the construction of a power plant there. The passionate Tómasdóttir did not determine the ultimate outcome, however, and she was always in a minority. For most Icelanders, nature and its resources were to be exploited, not protected. Tellingly, some of the island's summits were first conquered by foreign visitors, and it was only in 1927 that the Icelandic Tourist Association was formed, offering organized travels into the interior and other scenic excursions.

Put simply, geysers, waterfalls, gorges, and mountains were not considered beautiful by the average Icelander. The splendor of the land was determined by its usefulness, in particular with regard to farming. Good hayfields and wide meadows continued to be the definition of good farmland. Then again, the agricultural sector underwent radical changes as well. To begin with, independence was achieved on the farms, as it were. Regulations that compelled laborers to work on a designated farm were abolished at the end of the nineteenth century, and while only a quarter of farmers owned the land they ran in 1901, by 1922, this ratio of freeholders had risen to almost a half.

The mechanization of work—Iceland's industrialization—was also felt in the countryside. After World War I, small bulldozers were imported to the country. Ditches were made and wetlands drained. By the end of the century, some 20,000 miles of drains had been dug and vast moors turned into fields. Sheep farming remained most common, and the ancient cycle of lambing time in spring, haymaking in summer, and gathering sheep from grazing lands in the interior in the autumn was unchanged. Around 1930, however, the first tractors came and revolutionized work in the hayfields, although the change was not sudden and horses were still widely used. Likewise, technical advances eased the milking of cows and simultaneously that labor ceased to be the preserve of women.

There was progress but setbacks and side effects inevitably followed. In 1931, minks were introduced to Iceland, with the intention of breeding them in closed cages. Alas, a few animals soon escaped and multiplied in nature. Preying on birds and even sheep, the minks were quickly considered a total pest and prizes were offered for their capture. Naturally, the draining of wetlands affected the Icelandic fauna as well. Various types of birds lost their essential habitat, some became almost extinct. Although the big waterfalls were not utilized and rail tracks did not appear, it may be suggested that humans began to change the nature and landscape of Iceland faster than their predecessors had done for more than a thousand years—or since the first settlers burned wood and cleared woodlands with great gusto.

Was it progress? The fate of useless birds was generally of little concern and nobody could really lament the loss of wetlands. On the contrary, this was a period of optimism in Icelandic agriculture. Favorable loans were offered to farmers. New farmhouses were built, often out of concrete and replacing previous buildings of turf, stone, and a timber front. Most spectacularly, the Danish-born entrepreneur and fishing magnate Thor Jensen used his wealth to build a state-of-the art dairy farm near Reykjavík. With 250 milking cows, the ranch stood out in the country, but this image of big capitalism quickly came under fire. In 1934, the Progressive and Labor Party coalition, the Regime of the Toiling Classes, passed a new law that regulated the production, pricing, and distribution of dairy products. Jensen's innovation was doomed, to the joy of his adversaries.

Small was considered beautiful. The Progressive Party, led ideologically by the fiery Jónas Jónsson, held an idyllic vision of small self-sufficient homesteads in every corner of the country as the crux of its economy and culture. Many farmers and families shared that dream and worked happily to make it a reality. Others contended, however, that people longed to escape from the soul-destroying monotonousness of life and labor on secluded farms. Writing on those lines, the young author Halldór Laxness reaped the wrath of the country folk, not to mention when he added some harsh words about their miserable housing and the general lack of cleanliness.

Hard facts and statistics can be used to support Laxness's view rather than Jónas Jónsson's. Despite innovations in agriculture and governmental support between the wars, the flight from the countryside continued as ever before. In 1910, more than a third of Icelanders lived in Reykjavík and other towns. By 1940, that ratio had jumped to two-thirds, and almost 40 percent of the population lived in the capital and surrounding regions. By then, almost a quarter of houses in the countryside were still made of turf. In towns and villages by the seaside, the juncture of old and new, urban and rural, manifested itself in the custom of fishermen and their families owning a cow and a few sheep that provided food and income. In the depopulating countryside, self-sustenance made way for increased division of labor and provision of foodstuffs for those "on the gravel" as the people of Reykjavík and the bigger towns were referred to disparagingly.

Reykjavík, in particular, grew and developed by the year. In 1902, the first sewer was laid and gradually the disposal of sewage was resolved satisfactorily. In 1909, the introduction of the town's waterworks vastly improved living conditions. Office buildings and stores were built in the town center. Beyond that, scattered huts and houses made way or were integrated into organized quarters. The new homes that arose in previous fields, hillocks, or moors were modern and solid, often made of stone or timber with corrugated iron. Living conditions could still be poor, however, with big families having to share a single room or two in basements or attics. Then again, a few blocks of flats were built to meet increasing demands for relative cheap accommodation, including a building with some 70 apartments that were sold to workers at favorable rates. Finished in 1931, it stood by the Ring Road, a street that circled practically the whole town. By this stage, almost 30,000 people lived in Reykjavík. Only a few years later, in 1940, the population had multiplied to nearly 39,000. The growing capital remained the country's main conduit for relations with the outside world. More foreign goods arrived than ever before, and not only goods, fortunately. Inspirational ideas also arrived from abroad, a broadly defined vastness in the eyes of all islanders. So while changes in the political system and the economic understructure were certainly important, even revolutionary, the revolution of the mind may have been even more critical.

THE END OF ISOLATION AND THE REVOLUTION OF THE MIND

Technological advances and increased affluence continued to decrease Iceland's isolation. In 1906, an underwater telegraph cable was laid from Scotland via the Faroe Islands to Seydisfjördur on the country's east coast. Simultaneously, a cable for telegraphs and telephone conversations connected Seydisfjördur to Reykjavík, through Akureyri in the north. Domestic and international communications changed dramatically. By 1912, there were 300 phone numbers in Reykjavík, in 1928 more than 2,400. Telephones were less common in rural areas, and it was only in 1935 that calls could be made to other countries. Initially, the cost was tremendous, almost the equivalent of the price of a sheep for a three-minute conversation.

Icelanders marveled at the new technology, just like other peoples had done or would do. Likewise, the dawn of the age of aviation in Iceland must have seemed most remarkable. In 1919, the first flight took place in the country. For the next two years, a small two-winged aircraft took people on short excursions from a grassy field near Reykjavík. In 1928, passenger journeys were provided by a new airline company that struggled from the start and ceased operations three years later. More encouragingly, planes were also employed in the search for shoals of herring at sea, an innovation that prevailed and could provide invaluable results for the fishing fleet. In 1938, ultimately, passenger flights really took off in Iceland, after the foundation of another company the previous year, which offered trips and postal transport between Reykjavík and Akureyri and other towns.

Aviation also seemed capable of reducing Iceland's isolation—for better or worse. In 1930 and again the following year, the citizens of Reykjavík stared in awe at the German airship *Graf Zeppelin* as it hovered above the town, en route to the United States. In 1933, 24 Italian air force planes visited Reykjavík. During the 1930s, transatlantic commercial flights were not viable, but technical advances would surely change that in the near future. A stepping stone in Iceland might then be needed, and in 1936, Pan-American Airways were granted permission to construct a wireless station in Reykjavík. Around this time, the German state-run airline company Lufthansa also became interested in facilities in Iceland.

Flights were more for the future, still. Around the country, the gradual improvement of roads continued. In the summer of 1929, a car could make the 275-mile journey between Reykjavík and Akureyri for the first time. With few bridges and many rivers, not to mention mountain passes, the drive took two days. Improvements were made in the 1930s and hundreds of cars had by then been imported to the country. Scheduled bus trips were introduced and inland travel progressed.

Coastal shipping traffic increased as well and the sea-lanes remained the country's main links to the outside world. The construction of Reykjavík harbor, which began in 1913 and was finished four years later, transformed the loading and unloading of vessels. The town's old timber piers had become hopelessly out of date, and the installation of a large crane in 1927, considered the most sophisticated in the Nordic region, was another important step, if only because it was so imposing in the Reykjavík landscape.

The ships also came and went under a new flag. Having had to rely on foreign, primarily Danish, shipping companies, the foundation of the Icelandic Steamship Company in 1914 was greeted with universal pride and joy in the country. Thousands of Icelanders purchased shares in the company, a positive change from the lack of interest and capacity when capital was requested for the establishment of the Bank of Iceland a mere decade before. Moreover, the Western Icelanders, as the immigrants in North America had come to be known, gave the new shipping company enthusiastic support and had representatives on its board. In 1915, the first two vessels arrived, *Gullfoss* and *Godafoss,* and the practice of naming the ships after Iceland's waterfalls has remained ever since. Despite the war, the company prospered, partly through trips to North America. In 1921, grand headquarters were built in the heart of Reykjavík. The five-story building was the first one in Iceland equipped with an elevator. Thus, increased communications created wealth for the company.

Naturally, the society at large benefited as well. Although the disparity between an affluent minority and poorer masses persisted, a modern consumer society was in the making. It was largely based on foreign goods. Merchants, officials, and other members of a growing bourgeoisie were influenced by prevailing currents abroad and others followed. As early as 1910, more than half of the calories consumed came from imported grain food. In September 1914, when war had just broken out, more than 1,200 housewives in Reykjavík signed a petition protesting huge increases in the price of bread. During the interwar years, the import of coffee, tea, tobacco, and sugar increased considerably. In fact, the Icelanders consumed more sugar per capita than most other nations.

Consequently, teeth were in bad shape, but, overall, the well-being of the Icelanders steadily improved. So did the treatment of sick people, although prejudices still abounded. At the start of the twentieth century, there were still more than 60 leprosy patients in Iceland, isolated in a special hospital that had been built near Reykjavík a few years before. In 1943, the building burned down, but by then the spread of leprosy had long been halted and the last patient died in 1979. In 1907, the first mental institution was opened. Initially meant to house 50 patients, it was overcrowded from the start, and in 1929 an extension was constructed. Although more modern and humane therapies were introduced, the older torture-like methods of beatings, forced starvation, and submersion were applied at times. Furthermore, public attitudes toward the mentally ill were typified by trepidation or apathy at best. Views on venereal diseases were often similar. Most outrageously, 11- to 13-year-old girls were known to be expelled from school because they got infected after rape by older men. With the emergent bourgeoisie came the petit bourgeois mentality.

Compassion and assistance also increased, however. In the late nineteenth century, tuberculosis had begun to spread seriously in Iceland. In 1910, a hospital for the sufferers of this infectious disease was founded, again in the vicinity of Reykjavík. It was at the time one of the country's biggest buildings, with rooms for more than 80 patients, and another sanatorium of this kind were later opened near Akureyri. The need seemed definite. Between 1911 and 1925, around a fifth of all deaths in Iceland could be traced to tuberculosis, and it was only after the middle of the century that it ceased to be a fatal threat. As for other diseases, the single most deadly menace was the outbreak in late 1918 of the Spanish Flu. This influenza epidemic killed some 500 people, or more than 0.5 percent of the population, most of them in Reykjavík. And to make matters worse, in October there was a huge eruption in the Katla volcano underneath Mýrdalsjökull glacier. While no persons died, hundreds of cattle perished and some farms were ruined or damaged for years because of ash and melted ice that rushed down the glacier. Also massive gush of volcanic ash pushed the southernmost tip of Iceland some two miles outward. Ocean waves later changed the coastline again. For many Icelanders, 1918 therefore brought sad memories of misery rather than joy over the establishment of a sovereign state.

Apart from the infirmary that Catholic nuns operated in Reykjavík, by the start of the century, there was a hospital in Akureyri and smaller hospices in a few towns and villages. In 1930, a big step forward was made with the opening of the National Hospital, a grand building by the capital's Ring Road, which was largely financed through the enthusiastic campaign of women's organizations and charities. They were also instrumental in the establishment of home nursing and infant and maternity services.

On the negative side, prosperity came at a cost. More smoking raised the number of cancer victims. Ample food, office work, and lack of exercise led to an increase in cardiac and arterial diseases. Still, the general situation was getting better by the year. Whereas one child out of every nine died in its first year of life at the start of the century, by 1940 only one infant in 27 passed away. A set of new laws on sustenance and foster care in the late 1920s and early 1930s put more emphasis on children's interests. In 1939, only 0.5 percent of children in Reykjavík were put into foster care.

The average life expectancy had also increased, between 1901 and 1940 from 50 to 65 years for both sexes combined, although women could always hope to life longer than men. In the 1920s, the first proper old people's home was opened in Reykjavík, a sign of greater support for the elderly. Furthermore, a healthier and longer life could arguably be richer on many levels. Personal freedom increased in the first decades of the twentieth century. In 1923, new laws on marriage made breakups easier than before, and in the 1930s, contraceptives contributed to a slight reduction in the number of children for each married couple. Undoubtedly, they also increased the possibilities of pre- or even extramarital intercourse. The age of kisses had arrived, read an advertisement for a kiss-friendly toothpaste during these years. On the other hand, the authorities and the society at large frowned upon all discussions about sex education. Abortions were made legal in 1935, although almost solely for medical reasons. Getting pregnant outside marriage remained a shock for many young women and a cause for consternation.

In 1935, after a nationwide referendum, prohibition was abolished with the exception of beer, which remained banned. As early as 1922, the sale of wine had been permitted, after threats from the Spanish government to cease all imports of salted fish—*bacalao*—unless Spanish wines could be sold to Iceland. By the early 1930s, widespread home brewing and misuse of spirits for medical use had diminished the effects of the prohibition, so much so that some conventions by the Icelandic Youth Association had become notorious for excessive drinking.

Individual desires had outdone a drive by the authorities and a sizable part of the intelligentsia to control people's behavior and longings. Some individuals used drink to destroy their own lives and often that of their family as well; alcoholism remained a burden in society. While that can of course be construed as a negative aspect of individual choice—which the opponents of the lifting of prohibition certainly did—others could drink wisely. The freedom to choose was rising in most aspects of society. In the field of religion, for instance, the Lutheran state church faced a growing demand by people to practice their faith as they wanted instead of accepting unquestioningly the sermons of ministers. In particular, spiritualism, the strong conviction of afterlife, gained ground in Iceland. Among its adherents were esteemed intellectuals and, although it may seem odd, many men of the church. People attended sessions where mediums claimed to establish contact with deceased individuals on the other side. Catholicism was another option, although it was nowhere near as popular as the spiritualist movement. In 1929, however, a Catholic cathedral was consecrated in Reykjavík, much larger than other churches in the country at the time.

The media offered various views and news. By the start of the twentieth century, many papers and journals were published, two of the largest ones appearing once or twice a week with nearly 3,000 subscribers each. In 1910, the first daily arrived, and three years later another newspaper arrived, *Morgunbladid*, or The Morning News. It later established close links with the Independence Party, and the other parties soon established their own newspapers.

Although higher education remained the preserve of a select minority, more Icelanders than before could choose to study what they desired. On June 17, 1911 (Jón Sigurdsson's one-hundredth anniversary), the University of Iceland was founded with the merger of Iceland's Medical School, the recently founded Law School, and the country's Lutheran Seminary. Icelandic studies were also taught, but science departments were lacking, primarily because of inadequate funds and expertise. Around 20 men graduated each year, and every now and then a woman as well, the first one in 1917. In the 1930s, fisheries studies were established, but students who wanted to seek further education in the various fields of science had to go abroad. Copenhagen was the primary destination, as before. Increasingly, however, young Icelanders registered at universities elsewhere, mainly in Germany.

In 1936, compulsory education was lengthened so that it started at the age of 7, not 10 as before, and ended when the pupils had reached 14 years. Still, in the most rural areas, children were not required to attend school on a regular basis. In 1930, a high school was founded in Akureyri. Still, the school in Reykjavík kept its dominance at college level. Secondary schools were also set up in various towns and in the countryside. Many of these changes took place when Jónas Jónsson was in government, in 1927–1932. He realized that the strengthening of the rural regions required more than new farmhouses, barns, and sheds. The fact that he was the author of patriotic textbooks on Icelandic history also seems quite logical in this connection. Jónas Jónsson, the Progressives, and, indeed, many intellectuals and politicians across the political spectrum wanted to preserve the old Icelandic way of life.

At the same time, wave after wave of foreign customs and inventions crashed on the people, especially in Reykjavík and the coastal towns. More people began to dress according to the latest fashion abroad. In 1906, the first movie theater opened in the capital, with a second one in 1912. Together the two—named The Old Cinema and The New Cinema—fulfilled the needs of Icelanders for visual entertainment of this kind until the outbreak of World War II. In 1916, a store for musical instruments was established, and in 1926, the Hamburg Philharmonic Orchestra visited Reykjavík. For the first time, Icelanders could hear live symphony.

In the late 1920s, a small private radio station was operated for a while in Reykjavík, and in 1930, the Icelandic State Radio began broadcasting. It was greeted with great interest. Although an insistence on absolute neutrality meant that political reporting primarily consisted of reciting speeches made in the *Althing,* farmers and fishermen were interested in items about fishing catches or haymaking around the country. Story serials proved very popular and classical music was played. In the mid-1920s, Icelanders became acquainted with jazz, the new phenomenon abroad, but in its infancy, Icelandic State Radio owned only a dozen or so jazz records—and played them sparingly. Even so, foreign currents had definitely arrived. In 1925, the young writer Halldór Laxness commented that, almost in an instant, Reykjavík had acquired the essential contents of a proper city, "not only a university and a movie theater, but also football [soccer] and homosexuality."[1]

Admittedly, this was irony. Reykjavík was not a city in the proper sense of the word. It was true, still, that in 1912, the first soccer tournament was held in Iceland. Three male teams competed, two from Reykjavík and the third one from the Westman Islands. For decades, soccer was considered fit only for men, as was the case with most other sports, gymnastics and skiing excluded. A few sportsmen competed at the interwar Olympic Games, none reaching a podium except (although the definition of an Icelander is then stretched), the Winnipeg Falcons. At the 1920 Olympics, this hockey team of Western Icelanders represented Canada and won a gold medal.

While Halldór Laxness may have referred favorably or impartially to gays and, by implication, lesbians, same-sex encounters or relationships were far

from being accepted by society at large. Still, writings about them were beginning to appear. Laxness himself was among those Icelandic writers who
introduced or experimented with modern influences in literature, expression-
ism and surrealism in particular. Becoming a devout Catholic and then, more
lastingly, an apparently convinced communist, he sought external inspiration
while writing mostly about daily life in Iceland throughout the centuries to
the present day. Halldór Laxness gained popularity in the 1930s, and the old
sagas continued to be read, not least because they were scrutinized by Iceland's emergent academia. Simultaneously, however, light literature became
trendy. Translated novels with exotic titles like *The Terrible Secret* or *The Half-
Breed Girl* were probably read more widely than the *Saga of Njáll* or the *Saga of
Grettir* the strong. In the world of art, painters were stimulated by the nature
and the literary treasures. Also, however, they learned from artists abroad:
the expressionists, the cubists, the impressionists, and the futurists.

But what was this mixture of inspirations creating? Something new and
fresh or just some wishy-washy hodgepodge, not Icelandic and certainly not
pure? In the 1920s and 1930s, a sizable number of foreign visitors to Iceland
lamented the modernization of a previously unspoiled gem. Unfortunately,
they complained, the Icelanders wanted to tear down the turf houses, throw
away their national costumes, and listen to foreign music instead of honor-
ing their precious past. With more ominous undertones, the German envoy
in Reykjavík, the staunch Nazi Werner Gerlach, described his bitter disap-
pointment when he realized that the "typical Icelandic woman," was not a
"proud, clean, blonde-haired wife and mother, but a slut with shaved eye-
lashes, bright-red lips, curled hair and red nails."[2]

This criticism the envoy kept for himself, and for the Icelanders, mockery
could in any case seem as bad as the harshest of condemnations. During
the 1930s, Icelandic filmmakers emerged and started making documenta-
ries about Iceland, not the least to counter portrayals that were considered
false and degrading. In a sense, they followed in the footsteps of Ari and
Arngrímur the Learned, who composed their works in order to refute foreign
insinuations about Iceland and its inhabitants.

Then again, many Icelanders agreed that alien influences were indeed cor-
rupting the national culture. It should not come as a surprise that among them
was Jónas Jónsson. He complained that light literature like *The Terrible Secret*
only increased the lethargy of common people, and his derision of progressive
currents in the arts knew no bounds. Respectable men (and women) also condemned the intrusion of jazz and deemed the women's fashion of the 1920s
and 1930s as fitting for "prostitutes and sluts."

In essence, a fight over Iceland's future was being waged. Gone was the
general enthusiasm of the dawn-of-the-century-generation. All but gone was
Danish rule, the common uniting foe. Instead we had a "revolution of the

mind," as historian Ólafur Ásgeirsson later put it.[3] Yes, left and right were important markers in the political struggle, but another dividing line was equally clear—the rift between those who supported or opposed industrialization, urbanization, and internationalization.

Moreover, while the standard of living and personal freedom had definitely increased, by the late 1930s, it was easy to foresee gloomy days ahead. From the beginning of the century, the country had experienced rapid economic growth: 3.2 percent in 1901–1913 and 2.2 percent in 1913–1950 as compared to 1.8 and 1.3 percent for 16 other European countries. But this expansion had primarily been based on catching up, by the application of foreign innovations in the fishing industry. Also since fish exports accounted for around 90 percent of exports in 1930s (the remaining 10 percent being agricultural products), the Icelanders were especially susceptible to fluctuations in production and prices, just like other nations with a one-crop economy. The closure of markets because of the Spanish Civil War was particularly harmful. By the end of the 1930s, the young Icelandic state struggled to fulfill its financial commitments abroad. The possible combination of bad fishing seasons and poor sales in the next few years might obviously prove devastating. A national insolvency was not out of the question.

At the same time, Icelandic statesmen were inevitably concerned by the rise of the Soviet Union and Nazi Germany, as well as the growing war scare in Europe. Secretly, influential members of the Independence Party even wondered whether the security of Iceland might be best guaranteed by a continuation of the personal union with Denmark after 1943, when the Union Treaty from 1918 could be denounced.

In March 1939, when hostilities seemed imminent, the Progressives, the Labor Party, and the Independence Party formed a National Coalition, a regime that was deemed worthy of that name although the Socialists were not included. That summer, the impending war on the European continent came closer to Iceland's shores with the request by the German Lufthansa for flying facilities in the country. Although it was based on alleged commercial needs, the political and military connotations were obvious to all. Previously, the Icelandic government had acquiesced in German demands and instructed left-wing newspapers to tone down their Nazi denunciations. Then, Prime Minister Hermann Jónasson of the Progressive Party turned down the airline's request, acquiring a short moment of worldwide attention. The country's eternal neutrality was to be protected and honored. Then, however, war broke out. As ever, Iceland's fate would be determined elsewhere.

NOTES

1. Halldór Kiljan Laxness, "Af menningarástandi," [About the cultural situation], *Vördur* July 11, 1925.

2. Thór Whitehead, *Stríd fyrir ströndum. Ísland í sídari heimsstyrjöld II* [War next to the shores. Iceland during World War II] (Reykjavík: Almenna bókafélagid, 1985), 17.

3. Ólafur Ásgeirsson, *Idnbylting hugarfarsins. Átök um atvinnuthróun á Íslandi 1900–1940* [The revolution of the mind. Conflicts over Iceland's industrial development 1900–1940] (Reykjavík: Menningarsjódur, 1988), 148–152.

6

American Iceland: Internationalization, Welfare, and Love (1940–1994)

THE GOOD WAR

While the first decades of the twentieth century were marked by fast changes in all spheres of life, during World War II, that transformation continued at an almost frenzied pace. In a few years, "old" Iceland was no more. In its place, a much richer country appeared, populated by people who were less inhibited and better off, especially those who had been underprivileged, ignored, or chastised before. The state was a proud member of the international community and strategically important in the Cold War struggle between East and West.

World War II changed everything. Admittedly, the German invasion of Poland and the outbreak of hostilities in September 1939 did not have an immediate impact on Iceland. In fact, the ruling National Coalition was intent on maintaining profitable sales of fish products to Nazi Germany as if nothing had happened. In November, however, the Soviet invasion of Finland brought the war closer to Iceland's shores. To begin with, the Icelanders felt an affinity with the Finns, a Nordic nation, and the assault led to a split in the newly formed Socialist Party where the pro-Moscow leadership barely kept the upper hand. Also the war was clearly spreading, and the British authorities secretly notified the government in Reykjavík that they wanted to put up defenses in Iceland if the Nazis were to invade Denmark, a highly credible scenario.

The British signal was not welcomed. A request for U.S. military protection was even mentioned instead, but that idea had not been given serious consideration when German forces overran Denmark on April 9, 1940. King Christian X stayed in Copenhagen, and a Danish government remained in power although real authority was clearly in German hands. Almost immediately, the government of Iceland notified the rulers in London that, while previous offers of assistance were acknowledged, the Icelanders still wanted to shield themselves behind the 1918 declaration on eternal neutrality. At the same time, the *Althing* resolved that since the king was unable to fulfill his duties for Iceland, royal powers would temporarily be vested in the Icelandic government, which would also take over the conduction of the country's foreign affairs.

For one month, supreme authority over Icelandic affairs was in Icelandic hands, for the first time since the late thirteenth century. In the early hours of May 10, however, four British warships arrived and moored off Reykjavík. Troops rushed ashore, took over the radio headquarters, the main post office, and the telephone exchange. They also arrested a number of Germans, including the envoy Gerlach as he was busy burning secret documents. At the same time, a newly appointed British minister to Iceland notified the government that the British authorities had found themselves forced to occupy the country, thus staving off a Nazi invasion.

Apart from that official justification, the British navy needed a base in Iceland to protect its vessels from submarine attacks and to strengthen an embargo on Germany. Although the government in Reykjavík protested formally the occupation and the violation of the country's neutrality, Icelandic statesmen grudgingly accepted the British presence. After all, they really had no other choice. Their feelings were best summed up by Ólafur Thors, the eloquent leader of the Independence Party and a minister in the National Coalition when he said that the Icelanders would of course have preferred to have no foreign troops on their soil, but since it had to happen, they were glad that they were British, not German.

Was the fear of Nazi aggression real? We know that Adolf Hitler was enraged when he heard about the occupation because he had spoken of the need for German bases on Iceland. After the British occupation, an invasion of Iceland was planned for the summer of 1940. While military strategists in Berlin agreed that the island could be taken in a surprise attack, representatives of the navy and air force insisted that it would be practically impossible to maintain a German presence there. Just like in the Napoleonic wars and World War I, Britain's Royal Navy ruled the North

Atlantic waves. A German invasion never took place. Still, the capricious Hitler might well have ordered one, overruling all military objections as he was known to do.

Quite understandably, the British forces were constantly on the lookout for an attack. They grew in numbers, from some 2,000 troops to more than 25,000 in 1941, including Canadian and Norwegian units. The forces were mostly based in Reykjavík, where an airfield, which had been under construction, was hastily finished. A naval base was also established in Hvalfjördur in Faxa Bay and soldiers set up camp in Akureyri in the north, Seydisfjördur in the east, and on a few other locations.

Meanwhile, the war waged on. Until the summer of 1941, the U.S. authorities had not been that interested in the fate of Iceland. By then, however, President Franklin Delano Roosevelt was determined to increase assistance to Britain in the deadly fight against Nazi Germany. Part of that would involve the protection of cargo ships with goods across the Atlantic. Facilities in Iceland were therefore needed, whatever the Icelanders might say. On the one hand, the Icelandic authorities were willing to accept the arrival of U.S. forces and an end to the formally unlawful "occupation" by Britain. On the other, they also wanted to preserve their adherence to eternal neutrality in the hostilities. A subtle solution was found: a defense treaty whereby the United States took over the protection of Iceland, which remained a neutral state. Furthermore, the United States pledged to remove their forces once the war was over, honor the sovereignty of Iceland, and ensure the economic well-being of the country during the war. Simultaneously, the London government agreed to similar commitments, and although British units remained on the island, their presence was reduced.

In July 1941, the first American troops arrived and their numbers soon swelled to the maximum number of 47,000. Work on a big airstrip began near the fishing town of Keflavík to the west of Reykjavík and other military installations. After the German invasion of the Soviet Union in the summer of 1941 and the United States' entry into the war at the end of that year, the delivery of supplies to the Soviets was an important part of the war effort. Hvalfjördur became a key assembly point for massive convoys en route to Murmansk and other Soviet ports in the Arctic. U.S. and British airplanes took off from Iceland, searching for German vessels and submarines. Although single German planes made sporadic air attacks on Icelandic towns, no fatalities resulted, and Reykjavík was never hit. Still, altogether about 230 Icelandic lives were lost because of the war. A few people were killed by the troops on land, either through fateful misunderstandings or a refusal to obey military orders. But the vast majority lost their lives on cargo ships and fishing vessels that struck mines or suffered attacks by submarines and fighter planes. While the total number of war losses looks minimal next to the colossal death figures in

Eastern Europe and even the British casualties, Iceland lost more people, per capita, than the United States.

The military presence also had its negative effects on society, at least in the minds of the Icelandic authorities and a sizable part of the population. Right from the start, the public adhered to official appeals that the foreign forces should be met with neither hostility nor undue friendliness. Afterward, most soldiers kept poor memories of the Icelanders, having found them to be aloof and even pro-Nazi, a sentiment that was sometimes enhanced by the unfortunate fact that the emblem of the Icelandic Steamship Company, proudly displayed on its headquarters in Reykjavík, was an innocent version of the ancient Swastika.

In fairness, the large majority of Icelanders did not support Nazi Germany, if only because of its aggression in Denmark and Norway. Moreover, the sudden arrival of thousands of soldiers was bound to have a tremendous impact. The newcomers were mostly young, and although they were under military discipline, they liked to enjoy themselves when opportunity offered. Naturally that included encounters with Icelandic women. Those exchanges could range from chatting, dancing, mutually agreed one-night stands, love, engagements, and happy marriages to infidelity, unwanted pregnancies, broken promises and broken hearts, prostitution, rape, and sex with underage girls.

A "situation" had arisen, Icelandic officials wrote in 1941. According to a ministry of justice report, around 20 percent of women in Reykjavík were then in close contact with the foreign forces, as it was put. This figure was undoubtedly exaggerated, and the problem—the situation—was mainly in the minds of Icelandic men and the older generation. Partly, the concern stemmed from plain envy and a minority complex embedded in young Icelanders who suddenly had to compete for the hearts of Icelandic girls with uniform-clad soldiers. Later in life, the women recalled how the foreigners were polite and respectful while the Icelandic boys were drunken and rude when they made their clumsy advances.

On the other hand, many of the soldiers who were stationed in Iceland during World War II remembered the women of Iceland as cold or shy and absolutely determined to stay away from them. Spurred on by official attitudes and the great majority of the intelligentsia, the society as a whole saw sexual relations and romance between Icelandic women and foreign men as a threat to the Icelandic nation and the Icelandic race. While the context of the times must be kept in mind, the most outrageous example of this anxiety was the secret insistence by the government of Iceland that no "colored" troops be sent to the island. And although some 300 women married soldiers and moved abroad, that of course had no real effect on the future of the Icelandic population.

Almost overnight, Reykjavík was transformed and the lifestyle of many as well. Restaurants, clubs, and cafés sprung up. The Icelanders learned to like fish and chips, hamburgers, and chewing gum. In 1942, they also sipped Coca Cola for the first time. A third cinema opened, and movie attendance more than tripled during the war, not only because of the foreign soldiers. Jazz music was increasingly heard, especially swing, and the old imported dances like polka and waltz made way for foxtrot, tango, samba, conga, and calypso.

In other words, the consumption of foreign—especially American—goods and ideas increased drastically. Even the language came under threat. Icelandic had undergone few changes, at least in writing, since the days of the Sagas. It had withstood centuries of creeping Danification and was sacred in the opinion of Icelandic intellectuals and statesmen. Then, however, the youth suddenly started saying "bye, bye" and "okay," and Hollywood heroes were idolized, not Grettir the Strong or the wise Njáll. Previous assaults on Icelandic culture seemed to pale next to the American influx.

And yet it was called "the good war." True, the enemy inflicted losses at sea, and there were societal conflicts with the foreign forces. But since the casualties were few, in comparison with most other nations, the description seems reasonable. Also the introduction of clubs, swing music, and Coca Cola enriched people's lives, especially the younger generation, and for streetwise girls, the situation could be pure fun and excitement.

Apart from all this, the war was principally good because it led to a true transformation in Iceland's economic fortunes. It is worth recalling that at the end of the 1930s, on the eve of the hostilities, the Icelandic state was near bankruptcy. Abroad, prices for fish were unsatisfactory, and vital markets had shrunk or closed. Unemployment had increased, especially in Reykjavík. The arrival of foreign forces put an end to these tribulations. The airports at Reykjavík and Keflavík were built and improved. Nissen huts (prefabricated barracks of corrugated iron with a semicircular roof) were constructed. Various services had to be provided. Hence, there was ample work for everyone, so much so in fact that farmers found it hard to seek laborers and some fishermen preferred the better-paid and usually easier employment on land. Sluggishness was even a commonly accepted feature of working for the military authorities.

The marketing problem vanished as well. At the home front, British trawlers and trawlermen were needed in the war effort so they stopped working the distant fishing grounds. That gap was filled by the Icelanders, who gained from the desperate need for foodstuffs in Britain. In 1940, the price for fish exports from Iceland had quadrupled from the year before. Also in conjunction with the U.S. Lend-Lease program of assistance to friendly states and the United States-Icelandic defense treaty of 1941, the Washington administration agreed to pay for the ever-growing fishing exports to Britain. Ordinary Icelanders benefited as U.S. products could be purchased for U.S. dollars. Farmers sought jeeps, a vehicle that became extremely popular and useful in the countryside. Housewives eyed laundry machines, refrigerators, and electric mixers. Teenagers dreamed about gramophones. More than ever, common people could spend money on so-called luxury items. Besides, fishing companies and the Icelandic treasury accumulated great currency reserves, with the general understanding that these profits would be used after the war to strengthen the economy, in particular the fisheries sector.

Understandably, the sudden riches affected labor relations and the political landscape. In 1942, a series of strikes were organized by the trade unions, which grew stronger by the year. Great wage rises resulted, and the working week (the time when the standard rate is paid) was reduced from 60 hours to 48. Meanwhile, support for the Socialists intensified, mainly at the cost of the social democratic Labor Party, which lacked charismatic leaders. Conversely, the Socialist Party enjoyed the writing skills of Halldór Laxness and the great oratory of Einar Olgeirsson, its main spokesman, and one of party organ's editors. So fiery was Olgeirsson in his condemnation of the British forces that in April 1941, he was arrested with a few other comrades and imprisoned in Britain. That summer, however, the German invasion of the Soviet Union transformed the fighting lines in Icelandic politics. The pro-Moscow Socialists, with the released Olgeirsson in the forefront, became ardent supporters of the war effort. Among the public, memories of the reprehensible Soviet invasion of Finland faded, and in 1942, the Socialists were the primary beneficiaries of a constituency change that increased the number of MPs in the *Althing* to 52 and granted Reykjavík more seats than before.

As before, attempts to redress the electoral imbalance that favored the rural regions were fiercely contested by the Progressives. This time, the agreed reforms led to a breach of trust between the Independence Party leader Ólafur Thors and his Progressive counterpart, Prime Minister Hermann Jónasson. The National Coalition came to an end, and after a short-lived minority government by the Independents, a government crisis ensued. The crux of the problem lay in the fact that no political party received a majority in the *Althing,* and mistrust or ideological differences made coalition formation next to impossible. What could be done?

In 1941, the *Althing* had established the office of regent and granted it the powers that had constitutionally been vested in the king in Copenhagen. Sveinn Björnsson, Iceland's minister to Denmark during the interwar years (and son of Minister Björn Jónsson, who ruled in 1909–1911), became the first and only man to hold this post. At the end of 1942, he solved the cabinet crisis by establishing a government on his own. It was to remain in power until a regime that enjoyed a majority support in the *Althing* could be formed.

The move was controversial but probably wise because a strong government was needed. Inflation was running out of hand. Although wages rose radically during the war and purchasing power almost doubled, the price of goods spiraled as well. A vicious circle seemed in the making. For the next two years, the extra-parliamentary regime was in power but resigned in late 1944, having had its latest price-control proposals rejected by the *Althing*.

By then, the final victory in the long struggle against Danish rule in Iceland had finally been achieved. As early as in the first years of the war, the argument was raised that since Denmark was subject to hostile occupation, the Icelanders were in full right to declare independence. Deterred by the British and U.S. authorities who feared adverse reaction in Copenhagen and possible propaganda usage by Nazi Germany, the *Althing* agreed to wait at least until the required 25 years had passed from the signing of the Union Treaty in 1918. In Iceland, a small minority of mainly social democrats and intellectuals continued to argue that, since Denmark was occupied, talks on the inevitable conclusion, full Icelandic independence, should be postponed until the end of the war. Within parliament and in society at large, this appeal for fairness fell on deaf ears. At Thingvellir on June 17, 1944, the birthday of Jón Sigurdsson, Iceland was declared an independent republic. Sveinn Björnsson was elected president. In Denmark, King Christian X, Danish politicians, and a majority of the public were hurt—some even angry—that the Icelanders had acted unilaterally. All knew, still, that nothing could or should be done.

The actual change was minimal; the real successes had been achieved with the terminable Union Treaty of 1918 and the absorption of royal power in 1940. Still, the historical, emotional, and symbolic weight was immense. At long last, freedom was attained. For most Icelanders, a new era of prosperity, independence, and pride lay ahead, akin to the "glorious" days of the Commonwealth in the first centuries of Icelandic settlement.

POLITICS, NATURE, ECONOMY

On the joyous day of June 17, 1944, victory against the Axis powers remained to be achieved. The new republic did not declare war on Nazi Germany, maintaining the formal claim to neutrality despite the United States-Icelandic defense treaty of 1941. Having no army, the Icelandic attitude was reasonable. Yet the noninvolvement meant that Iceland could not be a founding member of the United Nations (UN) in 1945, after the end of World War II. Membership was granted the following year but was this microstate capable of real self-sufficiency on the international scene? It was the smallest state within the UN, a nation of less than 130,000 people who huddled together on a rugged island in the North Atlantic and, despite the wartime riches, relied on fish for their survival. Around this time, the British historian Alfred Cobban mocked the notion that entities like Iceland claimed full independence. Similarly, the world-famous biologist Julian Huxley deemed it debatable, due to the harsh natural conditions, whether a cultured society could be maintained in Iceland.[1]

When the cruel history of previous centuries was described earlier, the query was aired whether nature decided more about people's lives in Iceland than human actions. Speculations about evacuations after the Laki eruption of 1783 can also be recalled, as well as the mass emigration to North America a century later. Was Iceland still on the edge of the inhabitable world, despite its "industrial revolution" and constant technological advances in the modern era?

Time would tell whether the Icelanders had mastered their rough environs. The war had definitely given their young republic a strong impulse. In October 1944, a government that enjoyed a majority support in the *Althing* was finally formed. The two forceful leaders, Ólafur Thors of the Independence Party and the socialist Einar Olgeirsson, were influential in the formation of the so-called Innovation Regime, a coalition of their parties and the Labor Party. Political foes agreed to join hands, therefore, and to use the huge war profits to invigorate the Icelandic economy. They certainly had money to spend: At the end of 1944, Iceland's foreign currency reserves amounted to $85 million, a colossal figure in relation to both previous circumstances and the smallness of the population.

In agriculture, favorable loans were offered for the purchase of tractors and bulldozers, and a fertilizer factory was designed, starting production in the early 1950s. Fisheries were mainly in focus, however. New fishing boats were made in Iceland and abroad, and trawlers were ordered from Britain. In February 1947, people flocked to Reykjavík harbor to welcome the first new trawler, the aptly named *Ingólfur Arnarson*. Altogether, more than 40 new trawlers were purchased in the late 1940s, and the trawlermen could then enjoy the revolutionary comfort of proper sleeping facilities and flushing toilets instead of a bucket by the railing. A number of herring factories were built as well, primarily by the state but also for Reykjavík city council and individual entrepreneurs. A whaling company was formed, running its growing operations from Hvalfjördur and thus ensuring that the hustle and bustle from the war years did not vanish completely from that region.

The use of the ocean's resources was undergoing a revolutionary change, akin to the watershed of trawling and mechanization half-a-century before. The desire to energize the fishing industry was both determined and sensible. The rapidness was regrettable, however. In late 1947, less than a million USD were left in the state coffers and the investment in the herring industry turned out to be disastrous. After a series of good seasons during the war, this fickle fish all but vanished from Icelandic waters just as the new factories were complete. Thus, the Innovation Regime gained a mixed reputation, praised for the cross-political cooperation, admittedly without the Progressive Party, but criticized for its reckless spending.

The coalition lasted until early 1947, a surprisingly long tenure in light of the inherent ideological divisions. In its place, a regime of all parties except the Socialists ultimately took over in early 1947, introducing stringent economic restrictions. With a few notable exceptions, governments followed similar economic policies from then on and until the 1990s. Knowing the track record but not the composition of coalitions, an outside observer would find it next to impossible to guess which party was in power at any given moment.

At the obvious risk of oversimplification, it could be said that the Icelandic economy relied, for better or worse, on fishing and the sale of fish in Europe, the United States, the Soviet Union, and even African countries like Nigeria, which provided a valuable outlet for stockfish (air-dried and unsalted fish). The economy was characterized by higher inflation than in almost all other Western countries, regular devaluations of the Icelandic *króna*, publicly run industries and state-run companies alongside free enterprise, and the mighty Union of Icelandic Cooperatives, which was dominant in many regions and towns. Also Iceland had a public banking sector and a complex system of governmental funds, which were used to aid and control the economy. Interest rates were set by law. Savings usually accrued lower interest than the level of inflation. People were therefore discouraged to gather deposits, and bank loans were both desirable and fairly difficult to obtain since inflation decreased the value of repayment. Nepotism, even corruption, was an inevitable side effect. Labor disputes and strikes were a regular feature, and economic growth, steady in the long term, ebbed and flowed from one period to another.

The political system was fairly stable. Although the constitution of 1944 granted the head of state formal powers, including the right to refer laws from the *Althing* to a national referendum, the president of Iceland became primarily a figurehead, a dignified symbol of national unity. Sveinn Björnsson was succeeded by Ásgeir Ásgeirsson, an experienced politician. Upon his retirement, the archeologist Kristján Eldjárn became the president. In 1980, the election of his successor made headlines in the international media. Vigdís Finnbogadóttir, a former theater director and French teacher, became the first democratically elected female head of state. While this success was a notable step on the road for more gender equality in elected offices, there was still a long way to go. In the 1970s, women comprised only 5 to 6 percent of all town council persons and MPs. Still, in 1983, another step was taken: a new Women's List stood in parliamentary elections for the first time and gained 5 to 10 percent in all elections until 1995. By then, the number of female MPs had also risen to almost a quarter.

The longevity of the Women's List was an aberration. From 1944 to 1994, the four main political parties received most votes in elections, with smaller candidacies appearing at times but never lasting more than two terms in parliament. The Independence Party usually received around 35 to 40 percent of the vote on average, the Progressive Party 20 to 25 percent, and the Socialist Party (using the name the People's Alliance from 1956) got some 15 to 20 percent. Unlike the Scandinavian countries, where the social democrats were the dominant political force, the Labor Party was, with a single exception, the smallest of the four main parties in parliament, usually receiving around 10 to 20 percent. On the one hand, the party suffered from repeated splits and defections to the left. On the other, the Independents, under Ólafur Thors's successful leadership until 1963, were never a genuine conservative party and adopted in many ways the social democratic platform of state intervention, substantial taxation, and a Nordic-style welfare system.

With the exception of three short-lived minority governments, coalitions were formed. In the period 1944–1971, the Independence Party was always in power, apart from three years in the late 1950s. In the 1970s and 1980s, the Progressives were in the ascendancy, despite a constant dwindling of their traditional base in the countryside. That slide was counteracted by the political skills of their leaders, first the shrewd Ólafur Jóhannesson and then the appealing Steingrímur Hermannsson, son of the former leader and prime minister, Hermann Jónasson. With the exception of one minority government in this period, the Progressive Party was a member of a coalition with one or more political parties, holding the premiership for a total of 10 years.

In 1959, the electoral system was revamped. The country's previous 28 constituencies were reduced to 8, and the system of proportional representation was used to distribute seats between the parties in accordance with their share of the vote. Although the inbuilt imbalance in favor of the rural regions was reduced, it still existed. In the 1980s, the number of MPs was increased from 60 to 63, and the urban regions of Reykjavík and the Reykjavík peninsula were given greater weight in the electoral system. In the parliamentary elections of 1995, two-thirds of all voters resided in these two constituencies. Yet they received only 49 percent of the MPs.

The 1950s witnessed a continuous herring drought and a halt to the expansion of the fishing fleet. More freezing plants were constructed, still, and the cod fishery was fairly steady. In the early 1960s, a coalition of the Independence Party and the Labor Party relaxed the regulated economy by reducing a complex web of levies and controls. Having assumed power in 1959, the government that came to be known as the Restoration Regime lasted three four-year terms, a unique feat since Icelandic coalitions rarely lasted more than one term, if that. In 1963–1970, the coalition was led by Bjarni Benediktsson, former foreign minister and Ólafur Thors's successor as head of the Independence Party. In his tenure, the stubborn and controversial Benediktsson grew in popularity. Tragically, in 1970, he perished in a fire at the prime minister's Thingvellir residence with his wife and grandson.

One reason for the longevity of the Restoration Regime was its good fortune in fisheries, despite an ignominious decline in the trawling industry. *Ingólfur Arnarson* and the other innovation trawlers were getting old, and often their crews became a mishmash of worn-out trawlermen and drunkards because almost all the hardworking fishermen went for the herring. In the early 1960s, that source of prosperity suddenly showed up again to the north and east of Iceland. Aided by technical advances, including the use of radar to find the shoals, for half a decade, the Icelanders enjoyed a true bonanza. But then the stocks collapsed, primarily because of incessant overfishing, although complex changes in the ocean's ecosystem played a role as well.

The sudden shock led to rising unemployment, a malevolence that had been absent since the 1930s. In 1969, around 1,000 Icelanders left the country and sought work abroad. The following year, almost 1,400 followed. This was a sizable share of the population that by then had just risen to 200,000 people. A number of Icelanders settled in Australia, but most of the emigrants went to Scandinavia. Ultimately, many returned, and the temporary migration did not have a lasting effect; it was nowhere near the exodus to North America almost a century before.

Still, just like in the old days, increased diversification of the economy had become a dire necessity. Farming, the age-old basis of sustenance, had grown beyond all rational limits. Around 1960, the number of sheep in the country reached 850,000, the highest number ever. Agricultural produce more than satisfied the need in Iceland, and profitable exports were not cost-effective. Subsidized overproduction became a financial burden. Around 1980, quotas on the production of lamb, beef, and dairy products were introduced. Subsequent attempts to supplement traditional farming with aquaculture or the breeding of mink and other fur-bearing animals usually ended in costly failure.

Other revenues had to be sought. In 1965, the state and Reykjavík City Council founded the National Power Company to oversee the construction of hydropower stations that would provide energy for the public and heavy industry as well. In 1969, a power station in Thjórsá River was completed, very near the location chosen by Einar Benediktsson and his associates in the first decades of the twentieth century. In the same year, an energy-hungry aluminum smelter that was owned by a Swiss conglomerate began its operations close to Hafnarfjördur.

The power station demonstrated the victory of humankind over untamed nature. The aluminum plant provided stable employment and ample revenue, even though most of the profits went abroad. But just like the passionate

Sigríður Tómasdóttir had protested plans to harness the magnificent Gullfoss waterfall, some people called into question the heavy industrialization of Iceland. In 1956, the Icelandic Nature Association was founded, partly to prevent the destruction of wetlands near the origins of Thjórsá. They were the world's largest nesting area for the pink-footed goose. Ostensibly, however, they had to be flooded in order to make an important reservoir for the planned power station. The most ardent supporters of this new wave of industrial progress saw no need to care for geese or, for that matter, spare natural beauties like Dettifoss waterfall in the north, although by then Gullfoss would hardly have been ruined.

The peaceful campaign for the wetlands was aided by the intervention of famous scientists and the World Wildlife Fund. Halldór Laxness also protested that a type of bird that had discovered Iceland thousands of years before humans was then to be driven away because of shortsighted greed. In 1981, after years of wrangling, most of the wetlands were declared a protected area. Even so, the 1970s and 1980s witnessed the expansion of heavy industry that was furnished through new power stations. Also a rapid increase in the fishing fleet bore testimony to the incessant desire to maximize the use of Iceland's natural resources. On this, all political parties were united although they quarreled about specific details. The great majority of the population concurred as well. It was almost as if the Icelanders wanted to show the likes of Alfred Cobban and Julian Huxley that they could not only survive but also thrive on their inhospitable island.

Material prosperity increased but economic policy still left a lot to be desired. In the late 1970s, the incessant inflation in Iceland led to the introduction of indexed loans and mortgages. During the postwar years, pay negotiations between trade unions and the state or employer associations resulted in salary increases that were also linked to the rate of inflation. A vicious, or at least a semiautomatic, spiral had been created. Finally, in 1990, an agreement was reached on a novel compromise, labeled the Social Contract. The government at the time was a center-left coalition, but the initiative came from the trade unions and employer associations. While the unions agreed not to insist on inflation-indexed pay rises, their contracting parties pledged to prevent increases in the price of services and goods. At long last, the economic evil of rampant inflation had been eradicated.

In the 1970s, the use of hydroelectric power had continued with the construction of two power plants in the Thjórsá region. A new ferro-silicone factory used a fair share of the additional energy produced. Furthermore, the harnessing of geothermal power began. Since settlement times, Icelanders had enjoyed nice baths in hot springs; the chieftain-poet Snorri Sturluson even had a hot tub constructed near his farm. In the postwar years, the use of hot water to warm houses had spread around the country, and in 1969, a small geothermal power plant was constructed near Lake Mývatn in the north. A bigger station of this kind was built nearby in the mid-1970s.

That project was greatly obstructed, however, by volcanic activity nearby that began in 1975. At times, it even seemed that constant earthquakes and a series of small eruptions and lava flow would demolish this novel addition in Iceland's nature-harnessing campaign. After a decade, the unrest quieted and the power station became a profitable venture. Nonetheless, the trouble had demonstrated the volatile relationship between humans and nature. People had not become its masters.

To be sure, Icelanders certainly still realized the forceful and destructive nature of their surroundings. In 1947, 1970, 1980–1981, and again in 1990, the infamous Mount Hekla erupted, without fatalities or serious damage to land or livestock, but on the first occasion, ash reached as far as Finland. In 1961, there was a big eruption in the Askja caldera in the interior north of Vatnajökull glacier. A few years later, a team of U.S. astronauts undertook a series of exercises in that inhospitable region of lavas and mountains, in part because of the educated guess that it might in some ways resemble land-scape on the moon. In 1963, an underwater eruption created the new island of Surtsey to the south of the Westman Islands. Rather embarrassingly, a team of French journalists were first to set foot on the island. A decade later, a dormant volcano on the biggest of the Westman Islands awoke with a start. During the night of January 23, 1973, almost all of the 5,500 islanders were evacuated as the volcano spewed ash and lava. Overall, the catastrophe destroyed for good more than 500 of the town's 1,350 houses. Miraculously, only one person died. The eruption lasted half a year, and afterward, a majority of the islanders returned.

Needless to say, the unexpected eruption destroyed the winter season in the Westman Islands, one of Iceland's biggest fishing ports. At the beginning of the 1970s, yet another breakthrough had occurred in the history of the Icelandic fishing industry. During this decade, 86 stern trawlers were added to the fleet. These new vessels (which got their description from the fact that the trawl was hauled in at the stern and not by the side as before) greatly expanded the total fishing capacity. But the mass of fish in the sea was not endless. As new trawlers were purchased, fish scientists and even the fishermen themselves, who were inclined to distrust the words of overeducated landlubbers, began to warn that the stocks of cod, haddock, halibut, and other precious fish might be depleted unless the catches were controlled. In 1984, after some halfhearted attempts to limit fisheries by other means, a quota system for demersal fish was introduced. Based on fishing catches in the previous three years, vessels were allocated their share of a total allowable catch. That figure, which varied from year to year, was based on recommendations from the Marine Research Institute but decided by the minister of fisheries who was often tempted to raise the limit for political reasons. In 1990, the transfer and sale of fisheries quotas were permitted. Although the fish stocks did not grow immediately, the restrictive system seemed to have prevented their ultimate demise, as happened in the North Sea and other waters belonging to member states of the European Economic Community (EEC).

With the introduction of the quota system, Icelandic decision-makers had finally learned the lessons they should have taken in from the nonappearance of the herring in the late 1940s and its near-destruction in the late 1960s. The riches of the sea were not endless. Sustenance was based not only on exploitation but also on preservation.

Did whaling provide a similar lesson? In the 1950s, Iceland's sole whaling company ignored a proposal by the International Whaling Commission for a temporary ban on the hunt for blue whales. In 1982, after a number of failed attempts in the previous decade, the commission agreed to a moratorium on commercial whaling from 1986. Icelandic whaling continued, however, under the pretext of scientific catches. Late that year, two activists with links to the Sea Shepherd marine conservation organization vandalized the whaling station in Hvalfjördur and sank two whaling boats in Reykjavík harbor. In 1992, Iceland left the International Whaling Commission.

By that stage, scientific evidence strongly indicated that the small number of minke, fin, and sei whales caught off Iceland did not harm the stocks. Also in a general context, the economic importance of the effort was next to nil. For many Icelanders, however, whaling had become a symbol of sovereignty, the right to control their own natural resources as they saw fit. Protests abroad and boycott campaigns by environmental organizations like Greenpeace only increased their resolve and were not overly damaging in any case. Still, the Icelandic authorities had to think about the country's image for economic reasons. The fast-growing tourism sector was arguably the most sensible addition to the two sources of foreign revenue, fisheries, and heavy industry, especially because it could be a vital lifeline for the countryside.

Aviation shortened the distance between Iceland and the outside world. Soon after the end of World War II, two Icelandic airlines began scheduled flights to European destinations. In the early 1950s, one of them, Loftleidir Icelandic, launched the United States–Iceland–Luxembourg route, which soon became popular because the company was outside the international aviation authority and could therefore offer lower prices than its competitors. In the 1960s, it thus became known as the hippie airline. In 1973, rising oil prices and the economies of size in the aviation industry led to the merger of the two airlines under the name Icelandair.

During the 1950s, the number of people arriving in Iceland by sea or air rose from around 4,000 people each year to more than 12,000. In the late 1960s, the hippie airline factor multiplied that figure, and by 1994, almost 180,000 passengers came to the country. Tourist brochures emphasized the stunning nature of Iceland, the land of fire and ice. Some tourists ventured into the interior, but most of them visited a few key sites: Thingvellir, Gullfoss, the nearby Geysir hot spring, and Lake Mývatn in the north.

The tourists were welcomed. Icelanders realized that the nature could be a source of income even if it was simply left untouched. Often the visitors were asked: "How do you like Iceland?" The query demonstrated a certain sense of minority complex among the population. Despite the steady decolonization in the postwar period, Iceland was still one of the smallest nations in the UN. Then again, the question was asked in the fairly safe knowledge that it would receive a positive reply. First, the foreign guests usually expressed their admiration for the pristine nature, a few power stations and factories notwithstanding. Second, and more importantly in Icelandic minds, the apparently free and open society was often revered. Those visitors who knew the history were also apt to add that the Icelanders, apparently so poor and helpless less than a century ago, had managed to construct a modern welfare state.

This was a fact. At the end of the twentieth century, Iceland was among the world's richest countries, per capita, having been among Europe's poorest at its start. During the century, gross national income multiplied 46 times; per capita the increase was 14-fold. Even the weather kept improving. A period of relatively cold years, including winters when pack ice interrupted fisheries, started in the mid-1960s but ended 20 years later. The increase in temperature that started then could possibly be attributed to the strengthening of the Gulf Stream and a corresponding decline of the cold Labrador Current from the Arctic Ocean. Global warming may also have had its effect, but average summer temperatures in Iceland remained low in comparison with other European countries and the North American continent: 50–55°F in the more populated southern part of the country. However, the winters were relatively mild, around 32°F in the south.

Wind and rain were common features, and candid visitors might therefore have commented, when asked how they liked Iceland, that they did not enjoy the weather. But was there anything else to complain about? In 1990, the UN issued its Human Development Index for the first time, measuring life expectancy, education, standard of living, and quality of life for countries worldwide. Along with Sweden, Denmark, Norway, Switzerland, Japan, and Canada, Iceland was ranked at the very top. In short, it was safe to say that the Icelanders had never had it so good.

PERSONAL FREEDOM IN A WELFARE STATE

Despite economic, structural or personal ills like rampant inflation and nepotism, the ever-increasing prosperity of the Icelandic state laid the conditions for a Nordic-style welfare state. The main characteristics of that model included extensive state involvement, comprehensive social security, and a drive toward equality in all aspects of society.

The important law on social security from 1936, mentioned previously, had included provisions on unemployment benefits. The financial means were lacking, however, and it was only after a prolonged strike in 1955 that this part of the welfare system was achieved, much later than in Scandinavia. In the mid-1960s, again after a long strike, the state, the employer associations, and the trade unions reached agreement on the construction of inexpensive apartments in Breidholt, a new suburb of Reykjavík. In 1969, the unions and the employers also decided on the foundation of a common system of pension funds. Five years later, all wage earners were required by law to pay into a pension fund.

In 1946, a new law on education increased the period of compulsory education to the age of 15. At that stage, there were three high schools in the country, but starting in the 1960s, new institutions were established. Near the end of the century, dozens of schools could offer high school diplomas, and around 60 percent of all girls and 40 percent of boys at the age of 20 graduated. In 1994, total educational expenditures amounted to almost 6 percent of Iceland's GDP (gross domestic product), higher than in most other Western countries.

In the postwar period, the number of nursery schools multiplied as well. It was only in the early 1970s, however, that the state began to finance their running. By 1994, 80 percent of all 3- to 5-year-old children attended the publicly run preschools. It seems safe to say that around the middle of the twentieth century, few foresaw such an extensive role by the authorities in the upbringing and education of children.

In the postwar period, the health of Icelanders continued to improve. Their average life expectancy increased, from around 65 to 70 years in 1940 to 77 years for men and 81 years in the case of women. More hospitals and old age homes were built, and by the end of the century, health care amounted to more than 8 percent of Iceland's GDP. It also accounted for almost a quarter of the state's expenses. Alongside with Switzerland and Scandinavia, there were more doctors in Iceland, per capita, than in other countries. Thus, the state provided a tightly knit safety net for its subjects. Naturally, some lamented the heavy taxation it required. People of that persuasion sometimes wondered as well whether social security did not create the selfish assumption that the authorities should solve everyone's problems and act as the great leveler, restraining the individual will to succeed in the name of all-encompassing equality. Was the state becoming too involved in people's lives? With hindsight, that was perhaps the key political question of the period.

The answer can never be clear-cut. Personal freedom certainly expanded in the latter half of the twentieth century. Simultaneously, inherent inequality in society decreased. Although salaries and material wealth varied greatly, visiting tourists and foreigners who settled in Iceland often noticed the near-total absence of a class system in the country. Everyone spoke to each other on first-name terms, and there was no education- or affluence-based difference in dialect. The names of the prime minister and the bishop of Iceland appeared in the phonebook. The honorific form of address, so common in many European countries, had all but disappeared. Writing home from Reykjavík, diplomats from communist countries were especially impressed with this sense of egalitarianism.

Racial discrimination was hardly a cause for concern because Iceland was still a homogeneous society. The very few non-whites or people of non-Christian faiths who settled in the country were generally accepted. Still, most or all of them suffered isolated or repeated instances of racial abuse or religious intolerance. In 1956, more than 50 Hungarians were received in Iceland, having fled the Soviet invasion of their country. In 1979, and again in the early 1990s, around 100 Vietnamese refugees also moved to Iceland. In total, up to 1994, Iceland accepted 204 refugees. Travelers could also find seasonal work in the fishing industry, sometimes coming from as far as Australia or New Zealand and using this means to finance a trip of a lifetime. Still, only a small number of foreigners settled in Iceland, and if they took up Icelandic citizenship, they were compelled to adopt an Icelandic name in order to preserve the patronymics tradition. Only in the mid-1990s was this rule abolished.

As for gender equality, that improved in society as a whole, not only with regard to presentation in the *Althing* or town councils. The need for day cares rose because more wives and mothers took on full-time work. In 1960, a third of all married women in Reykjavík and other large towns were on the labor market. A decade later, that number had risen to 51 percent. In 1975, surveys showed, however, that women received less than half of men's salaries for similar work, and late that year, the weaker sex in Iceland caught the world's attention. On October 24, 1975, the vast majority of women in the country took the day off, whether at home or in the workplace. In that way, they demonstrated the importance of their contribution to society and the intolerant gender inequality in wages and domestic work. The following year, new equality laws banned gendered discrimination in the workplace. They did not encompass people's homes, still, and in 1980 it was estimated that working wives spent an average of 33 hours a week doing household chores or attending to children. Their husbands put in about seven hours. Also the wage differential was far from abolished despite the law, and that was still the case at the end of the century.

As before, many men resisted the drive for full equality between the sexes, and the argument was often made that children needed their mother at home. Some women agreed, including those who went to work but did so guilt-ridden. Nonetheless, this short overview of the equality struggle should be seen as a story of progress and optimism.

Similarly, even though women did most of the work at home, those duties got lighter by the year. Around 1960, a consumption revolution began in Iceland, to use a phrase by historian Eggert Bernhardsson that mirrors the notion of an industrial revolution in the country at the dawn of the century.[2] The household appliances, which began to arrive in large quantities from the United States during and immediately after World War II, spread to most homes. Besides, Icelandic firms started mass production of refrigerators, washing machines, cookers, and vacuum cleaners. There were more types of furniture to choose from. Telephones became a regular appliance and car ownership increased. In the first decades after the war, most of them were imported from the United States and Britain. German vehicles were also well-liked, especially the Volkswagen Beetle. Moreover, from the early 1950s, cars were imported from the Soviet Union and later from the German Democratic Republic, Trabant, Volga, and Lada being the best-known types. In the 1970s, Japanese cars entered the scene, and since the early 1980s, Toyota has been the most popular type in the country. In the early 1990s, Guam topped the world list of car ownership with slightly more than one vehicle per inhabitant. In the United States, the average was 1.8 people versus one vehicle and then Iceland followed, with two inhabitants for each car.

Communications became easier, although coastal shipping routes were reduced or abolished, and in 1972, the cruiser *Gullfoss* sailed for the last time from Iceland to European ports. Instead, domestic flight routes were established, and the road system was gradually improved. The ring road around the country (excluding the Westfjords) was finally completed in 1974 when the numerous glacial rivers south of Vatnajökull were bridged. And while passenger ships ceased operations, the era of holiday vacations in warmer climates had begun. In 1959, the first flight from Keflavík to Mallorca took place. From then on, other tourist spots in Spain and elsewhere around the Mediterranean were frequented each year by sun-hungry Icelanders.

In 1947, the first telephone conversation between Iceland and North America took place. In 1980, satellite telecommunications began, and a few years later, all phone numbers in the country were connected to the automatic system. The old temptation of listening into other people's conversations could no longer be satisfied. Also mobile phones were entering the scene as well as digital telephone offices and underground optical fibers, which replaced the old telegraph poles.

The ability to relax, communicate, and travel had proliferated. So had the ability or freedom to love. In the 1960s, the introduction of the contraceptive pill revolutionized sexual relations and changed the family structure. During the nineteenth century, a married woman could expect to give birth to five children, on average. By 1980, that number had dropped by half, and in 1995 it was down to two newborns. Then the set also included non-married mothers. In the postwar period, the marriage rate in Iceland, like other Nordic countries, was lower than that in other Western states, and births out of wedlock were rarely a cause for consternation. Also in the 1960s and early 1970s, the divorce rate rose considerably and then stabilized. This demonstrated the fact that both wives and husbands were to a greater degree able to take one of the most fundamental decisions of their lives, to part with their spouse if things did not work out for them.

In 1975, another action was also deemed to be a fundamental right for women: with the passage of a new law, a pregnant woman could have an abortion on either medical or social grounds. In reality, this meant that if she wanted this option, she could have it. In 1976–1980, the average number of abortions per 1,000 live births was 110, and by 1994, that figure had risen to 175. In that year, the corresponding number for the United States was 321. The issue of abortion was not a subject of primary importance in Icelandic politics or among the public. For the majority of the population, it was a sign of increased tolerance and choice. Even so, an undercurrent of prejudice and bigotry could always be detected. In 1975, the year when abortion for social reasons was legalized and women demanded equality en masse, a gay person came out of the closet in Iceland for the first time. Describing his sexual orientation in a magazine interview, well-known actor and musician Hördur Torfason was harassed and found himself forced to emigrate to Copenhagen, although he regularly visited Iceland. In 1978, a few dozen homosexuals, mostly men, established a new association of gays and lesbians. In the 1980s, the spread of AIDS reached Iceland. By 1994, 35 persons (the vast majority homosexual or bisexual males) were known to be infected and 26 had died. This modern but selective version of the epidemics from previous centuries raised more sympathy than animosity toward gay people. In 1996, homosexual couples were entitled by law to live together in civil union. Although the state Lutheran church did not yet allow gay marriages, the legal right to love another person of the same sex was almost complete.

The permissive society had arrived, to use a popular description of a social order where norms have been liberalized. Was it good, overall? Throughout the twentieth century, Iceland was known abroad as a crime-free country where people did not have to lock the doors of their homes and murders were hardly committed. While the homicide rate was indeed low, if only because gun-ownership was rare, the positive image was false or skewed. Thefts and petty crimes occurred and disruptive juveniles were regularly sent to detention centers in the countryside. One case that aroused extraordinary attention in the 1970s was the disappearance of two men whose bodies were never found. A group of young people were arrested, found guilty, and given prison sentences of up to 16 years, the longest stretch permitted in Icelandic law.

For the more conservative members of society, the convicted youngsters were dropouts, druggies, or hippies, sad specimens of a society that was sliding toward decadence, sin, selfishness, and indulgence. Older people were especially tempted to compare the Icelandic youth with a mythical image of the dawn-of-the-century generation who were to have marched together into modernity under the banner of *All for Iceland*.

Indeed, were not all the negative currents of the present coming from abroad? In the first years after World War II, national and international currents continued to clash. For a telling example, in 1951, the Icelandic Folk Dance Society was formed, and that same year, after the return of U.S. troops to the country, a radio station began to operate on the military base. Despite the good intentions of the folk dance enthusiasts, the young generation found it old-fashioned and passé. Conversely, they tuned eagerly in to the U.S. radio with its wide selection of light music and entertainment.

The outside world was more fun than Iceland's past. In 1956, rock and roll reached the country. Teenagers were enraptured by Elvis Presley and other musicians, not to mention movies like *Rock around the Clock* or *Shake, Rattle and Roll*. At the start of the 1960s, people around the Faxa Bay region could also watch the TV station on the U.S. base if they invested in sufficiently strong antennas. *Bonanza*, *I Love Lucy*, and other entertainment programs on the "Yankee station," as it was known, proved very popular. The town of Keflavík, next to the military base, also became the cradle of Icelandic rock music and home of the country's most popular band in the 1960s, *Hljómar* (The Sounds). In that decade, jeans and long hair typified the Icelandic youth, just like in most other parts of the Western world. At the start of the 1970s, the use of drugs like marijuana, hashish, and LSD had spread to Iceland although, for most people, alcohol remained the stimulant or sedative of choice.

Some of the new trends were clearly destructive and had to be resisted. The authorities tried to tackle the smuggling of drugs. Alcohol abuse, admittedly an old harm in society, also began to be seen as a disease that could be treated with correct care. In a more dubious way, the sale of alcoholic beer was prohibited until 1989. Other efforts by the state and the more purist elements of society to stem the tide were equally questionable. Initially, rock music was hardly played on the Icelandic state-run radio, and in the 1960s, the majority of the Icelandic intelligentsia demanded that the U.S. television broadcasts be confined to the base itself. That change finally occurred in the mid-1970s when cable transmission was introduced.

The 1970s witnessed the growth of two tabloids that changed media coverage in the country, with less reverence for public figures and more sensational reporting on well-known individuals, crimes, or corruption. This new emphasis contributed as well to the demise and ultimate disappearance of the outdated organs of the political parties, with the exception of *Morgunbladid*, although that morning paper distanced itself more than before from the Independence Party.

In 1966, the Icelandic state had launched its own TV station. It was only on the air a few hours a day and not on Thursdays or in July each year. Furthermore, it was deemed to have an educational and constructive role to play. Light entertainment was probably not as common as the great majority of the population would have wished. In 1986, privately run radio (radio stations) were allowed to air, offering mostly pop music. That year, a private TV channel was also launched, primarily broadcasting U.S. television programs and movies.

The public was happy with this world of increased choice that, coupled with the introduction of video tapes and rentals, transformed traditional pastime, especially in the evenings. No longer could the authorities decide that Thursday nights be television free and preserved for meetings, clubs, or other human interactions (the principle of no-Thursday transmissions came to an end in 1987). Then again, the official and intellectual struggle against the influence of English on Icelandic language and culture continued. The long resistance against *bye* and *okay*, which began in World War II, seemed to be lost as the decades passed. The same could be said about bastardized words like *sjoppa* and *jeppi* (shop and jeep), which crept into the language during the war. These negative descriptions of new words were used by venerable experts in Icelandic who also fought in vain against the popular practice of using English names for various establishments. The law forbade it, but by the 1980s, Reykjavík had fast-food places like Winny's, Chick King, and American Style, the discotheque Broadway and the nightclubs Bonny and High Voltage.

Rapid change was the only thing constant in society. Public attempts to defend stability were doomed to fail. Nowhere was this more apparent than in the incessant urbanization of Iceland. Only in the 1970s, when the Progressive Party was highly influential on the political scene, was it temporarily halted with the provision of stern trawlers that provided ample work in coastal villages and towns, while near-unlimited production in the countryside kept people busy there. It could not last, however. The quotas on fish, sheep, and cattle that were introduced also applied to humans, as it were. With restrictions on catches or production, people had little reason to stay on farms or in fishing villages—especially after the fisheries licenses could be bought and sold—with devastating consequences for some fishing ports. Admittedly, fish and fish products were still a vital export, and agricultural produce contained an important part of the daily diet. But as the twentieth century came to a close, only 4 percent of all Icelanders were employed in farming and some 8 percent in fisheries and the fishing industry.

More than two-thirds of the population lived in Reykjavík and nearby towns, including the Reykjanes peninsula. In many ways, Iceland had become a city-state. A sign of the times was the spread of local museums around the middle of the century that preserved for later generations a glimpse of a disappearing life in the countryside. Simultaneously, those who moved to Reykjavík formed regional societies to maintain their connections with the places where they grew up. Similarly, children from Reykjavík and other towns were sent to work on farms in the summertime, often in their parents' old district. The authorities aided this half-nostalgic custom by having summer vacations much longer than in other Nordic or neighboring countries.

The old suspicion against Reykjavík and the coastal towns, coupled with the feeling that Iceland's true identity lay in the countryside, did not disappear. But the capital grew by the year. In 1950, it had 56,000 inhabitants. Most of them still lived inside the Ring Road and knew their neighbors quite well. Around 4 percent of the city population lived in the soldier-barracks from the war. These dwellings were often in poor condition and were gradually eradicated. Instead, the number of apartment blocks increased, especially in new suburbs like Breidholt.

In the first decades of the postwar period, stores were small and specialized, but in 1970 the first supermarket opened in Reykjavík and in 1987 the first shopping mall. Reykjavík kept its position as the country's metropolis. It also boasted the National Symphony and the National Theater, both founded in 1950, and the University of Iceland was the only institute offering academic degrees until the University of Akureyri began its modest existence in 1987. Reykjavík was also the seat of the national sports stadium, although the vicinity to the U.S. base meant that basketball was primarily popular in Keflavík and other towns on the Reykjanes peninsula.

In the first years after World War II, Icelandic track and field athletes enjoyed a short-lived period of fame, winning a series of medals on the international scene. In 1956, the first Olympic medal was won (silver in men's triple jump) and a second one followed in 1984 (bronze in men's judo). Per capita, such achievements were quite satisfactory, and the same could be said about chess, with Iceland producing more grandmasters than other nations (again per capita, of course).

In the arts, the postwar years were first marked by the growing influence of abstract art and then, from the 1960s, the introduction of neo-surrealism, pop art, and neo-Dadaism. All were concepts, which the more conservative-minded section of society found hard to comprehend. In the world of fiction, Halldór Laxness kept his prominence, in particular after he was awarded the Nobel Prize for literature in 1955. In general, the postwar generation of writers focused on the fast changes taking place around them, the flight from the countryside and the sometimes uneasy adaptation to urban and Americanized life. While this sometimes made for onerous reading, an unpretentious novelist like Gudrún frá Lundi was popular—even if she was mocked in literary circles—for her easily read stories about rural life and romance. Likewise, translated thrillers by internationally renowned writers usually topped the sales charts, and love stories, science fiction, or Westerns were always popular.

As for the music scene, disco and punk made their double impact in the 1970s and onward. In the late 1980s, the female singer Björk achieved worldwide fame with the alternative rock band The Sugarcubes. Symbolically, this strange-looking untypical Icelander denoted the merger of Icelandic and international culture as well as the end of Iceland's isolation and remoteness.

At the same time, paradoxically, Iceland seemed to be losing its strategic importance, so evident during World War II and then throughout the Cold War. And that could be a bad loss. Although the ideological, political, and sometimes military struggle between East and West had bitterly divided the nation, the vital position of Iceland in the middle of the North Atlantic had brought various material and tactical benefits. In that sense, the Cold War had also been a good war.

THE UNSINKABLE AIRCRAFT CARRIER

Although the United States and the Soviet Union were united in the fight against the Axis powers, many policy makers in Washington worried that the end of World War II would rekindle an inevitable schism between the communist camp and the Western world. Thus, the conclusion was reached that a continued presence in Iceland would be beneficial. In other words, U.S. military thinkers shared the view of British Premier Winston Churchill, who allegedly referred to the island during the war as the unsinkable aircraft carrier.

Already before the end of hostilities, the U.S. authorities indicated that they wished to remain with their forces at Keflavík airfield and the naval base in Hvalfjördur. Also they wanted to construct military installations on the outskirts of Reykjavík. A formal but secret request for a long-term lease of land on these lines was made in October 1945. Ólafur Thors, by then premier in the Innovation Regime, turned it down and appealed to the Americans to moderate their demands. While the prime minister and his Independence Party fellows did not want to sever all security links with the United States, they realized that the Socialists would never accept the sweeping request. A watered-down compromise was found, the running of Keflavík airport by a U.S. civilian company with the tacit understanding that in times of crisis, it could swiftly be turned into a proper military base. Still, for the Socialists, this solution was a cheap façade. The Innovation Regime came to an end.

In the next five years, Iceland was placed firmly in the Western camp. Although the principle of neutrality still appealed to many Icelanders, the majority of politicians—with the obvious exception of the Socialist Party—concluded that economic and strategic considerations called for close cooperation with the United States and their allies in Western Europe. In 1948, Iceland began to benefit from the Marshall Plan, the U.S. restoration program for the war-ravaged nations of Europe. Having enjoyed enormous economic prosperity during the conflict, the Icelanders then received per capita a far greater share of the total funds than any other nation. The notion that impoverishment would benefit the Socialists was an important reason for this generosity.

In 1949, Iceland became a founding member of NATO, the North Atlantic Treaty Organization, with the provision that foreign troops would not be situated on the island in peacetime. The tension between the desire for neutrality and the grudging awareness of the need for protection in the ever-deepening Cold War determined this outcome. In 1951, however, after the outbreak of war in Korea, the majority of pro-Western politicians in Iceland agreed to the return of U.S. troops. Without defenses, they worried, the island would be an open prey for the Soviets.

At most, the foreign military forces numbered around 5,000 people. The main base was at Keflavík, where fighter planes were stationed, ready to confront sudden aggression. Naval facilities were also built at Hvalfjördur, and four radar stations around the island observed flights by Soviet bombers and fighter planes. A key link in a chain of underwater listening posts from Greenland to Britain was constructed on the shore near Keflavík base. In the 1950s, there were also plans to build a second airport and position nuclear missiles in Iceland. The Icelandic government resisted the intended airport, however, and the missiles were deemed to be more useful elsewhere.

By the 1960s, few statesmen in Reykjavík or Washington considered a Soviet invasion or a communist takeover likely, except as part of a nuclear war. The need for defensive forces diminished, but the surveillance facilities were as important as before. Throughout the Cold War, the U.S. authorities and the NATO leadership felt that Iceland could indeed be compared with an unsinkable and indispensable aircraft carrier in the North Atlantic.

It was not a happy ship in all respects. Remembering the problematic effects of foreign forces during World War II, the Icelandic authorities had severe restrictions put on soldiers' movements outside the base. Furthermore, they repeated the insistence from the war that "no negroes" be stationed in Iceland. This racist demand was made in secret but would certainly not have been opposed by the bulk of the population. By the 1970s, times had changed and the policy, which was never liked in Washington, was abolished.

Even the most ardent supporters of Western defense cooperation during the Cold War considered the U.S. troops in Iceland a necessary evil. As elsewhere, the conflict between East and West was waged on the cultural front, with the predominantly left-wing intelligentsia denigrating rightist writers and thinkers. Both superpowers tried to advance their cause. To take descriptive examples, the U.S. Information Service might screen a film about NATO, *Alliance for Peace*, while the Soviet-Icelandic Cultural Society, headed by Halldór Laxness, showed Sergei Eisenstein's *Battle for Stalingrad*. Both superpowers were involved in limited espionage, especially the Soviets who constantly—and even clumsily—tried to obtain information about the U.S. military installations on the island.

In Iceland, the Keflavík base provided an additional cause for friction in society. The debates over radio and television broadcastings offer but one proof of that. The smuggling of goods from the base was a constant problem and the entertainment facilities, nightclubs, and parties there were alluring as well. Many youths, especially in Keflavík and nearby, considered the base a welcome addition to a society that did not necessarily offer much excitement. The older generation and the authorities begged to differ.

In material terms, the Keflavík base was an important source of employment and income. In the early 1950s, up to 20 percent of Iceland's foreign currency revenues accrued from the base. By the 1960s, that share had declined to around 10 and 5 percent in the late 1980s. That was still a significant portion. Also from the 1950s to the mid-1970s, around 1,200 Icelanders worked on the base each year. The allocation of well-paid jobs and construction work for the U.S. military was a political commodity, mostly held by the two biggest parties in the postwar period, the Independence Party and the Progressives, although the smaller Labor Party was also involved. Favoritism and corruption was rife.

At the national level, Icelandic governments obtained generous loans and assistance from the United States and other Western states because of the perception that otherwise the Socialists would grow in popularity. Even a civilian airport terminal that opened in 1987 was largely financed by the United States (since it could be used for military personnel if need be). At times, Western diplomats and politicians complained that Icelandic ministers used the communist bogey to blackmail them. Although that was an exaggeration, the analogy was not totally unfounded. Icelandic statesmen knew that the importance of facilities in Iceland could be used as a trump card in negotiations about financial assistance. Thus, while left-wing coalitions twice planned to expel the U.S. forces, nothing of the kind happened. On the first occasion, in 1956, the promise of more economic assistance certainly influenced the decision to withdraw the request, although heightened tension in the world—the Soviet invasion of Hungary and the Suez crisis—was also at play. In the latter case, during 1971–1974, only the Socialists sincerely wanted the Yankees out, whereas the Progressive Party, the leading party in the coalition, had primarily agreed to that demand to get into power.

The end of the Cold War in 1991 drastically changed the Icelandic security environment. As Colin Powell, chairman of the Joint Chiefs of Staff put it, "the only Soviet bombers now approaching the United States from the direction of Iceland were those on their way to an open house at their new 'sister' unit at Barksdale Air Force Base in Louisiana."[3] While the U.S. authorities wanted to downgrade their presence, in 1994, a center-right regime in Iceland managed to secure a promise that at least four fighter jets would always be stationed in Iceland, offering some defense in times of crises or in the event of a possible terrorist attack. As before, the Icelandic authorities did not want to have U.S. facilities in Iceland for surveillance purposes only. But in reality, the stationing of four fighter jets was more symbolic than valuable, apart from the fact that they were accompanied with a helicopter squadron that was a vital backup for the small Icelandic coast guard service.

Icelandic statesmen might be excused for having lamented the passing of the good Cold War. Gone were the days when the strategic importance of Iceland could be used to gather favors. Financial loans and economic benefits have already been mentioned, but the political and diplomatic advantages were also valuable. In that context, Cold War and Cod War were closely intertwined.

At the end of World War II, the United States shaped the development of the law of the sea by proclaiming unilaterally sovereignty over its continental shelf, extending up to 200 nautical miles seaward, as well as the right to regulate fisheries in the waters above it. Other states quickly followed suit. Iceland did so in 1948, and the following year, the 1901 Anglo-Danish treaty on the three-mile territorial sea around the island was denounced, with the stipulated two-year notice. Encouraged by a ruling by the International Court of Justice, which stated that Norway could proclaim a four-mile limit, Iceland took that step in 1952. Britain, however, was not ready to accept the extension. A ban on the landings of Icelandic wet fish was imposed. Initially, it seemed bound to hurt since the British market was of high importance. But sensing a way to play on fissures within NATO and bolster its image in Iceland, the Soviet Union offered to buy Icelandic fish in return for oil and other commodities. The import ban was no longer effective and the rulers in Washington worried about increased Soviet influence in Iceland because of British intransigence. In 1956, the embargo was lifted.

By 1958, it was clear that the international community was moving toward an agreement on even wider limits. In spring, a UN conference on the law of the sea failed to reach a binding agreement, but the Icelandic authorities decided to act, nonetheless. On September 1, a 12-mile fishing limit took effect. Again, the British trawlermen were enraged, and this time the government in London decided to offer them naval protection. At significant cost, Royal Navy warships escorted the trawlers to the fishing grounds off Iceland. Meanwhile, another UN Conference narrowly failed to ratify the principle of a 12-mile limit and Icelandic statesmen and officials repeatedly warned U.S. diplomats that British imperial bullying was destroying all support for NATO and Western cooperation in the country. In 1961, Britain backed down. Iceland had won the first Cod War, a term which British journalists invented, tongue in cheek.

In return for British acquiescence, the Icelandic center-right coalition at the time had pledged to refer possible further disputes to the International Court rather than acting unilaterally. For the next decade, peace prevailed, but in 1971, a new center-left regime decided to move the fishing limit to 50 miles—and ignore the provision about the International Court. Britain and West Germany, which also had fishing interests off Iceland, protested but to no avail. The new limit was imposed on September 1, 1972. The British government was unwilling to use naval protection again, costly and politically sensitive as it had been. However, the Icelandic coast guard vessels wielded a new secret weapon—scissor-like cutters that slashed the trawl wires. Egged on by the trawling interests in British fishing ports, the Royal Navy sailed up north again.

This second Cod War came to an end with a two-year truce in 1973, but then the conflict flared up again, even though the International Court intervened and ruled in Britain and West Germany's favor. That judgment was ignored in Iceland and ran in any case counter to the prevailing current. By the mid-1970s, it seemed clear that a 200-mile Exclusive Economic Zone would ultimately be ratified internationally, offering states full sovereignty over the seabed and unilateral fishing rights. The Icelandic authorities, worried by clear signs of overfishing, decided not to wait for a final agreement on these lines. In late 1975, a 200-mile fishing limit was declared and the third Cod War broke out. This time, coast guard vessels on wire-cutting runs repeatedly collided with British warships and other protection vessels, and it was truly a miracle that no lives were lost. Tempers ran high on both sides, and in

February 1976, Iceland severed diplomatic relations with Britain, the first and only case so far of such a step being taken in a dispute between two NATO member states. That signal was heard loud and clear in London, not to mention Washington.

In the summer of 1976, Britain gave in once more. All states recognized the 200-mile limit, which, with the conclusion of the UN Convention on the Law of the Sea in 1982, became the general rule. With its progressive policy, Iceland had played a role in that outcome. It was not a key role, still, as many Icelanders like to think. Nor were the Cod Wars the only wars that Britain lost as they are fond of declaring. The fishing disputes were not wars in the proper sense of the word. Had the Royal Navy been allowed to use the weapons at its disposal, the tiny Icelandic coast guard fleet could have been immobilized in a matter of days. The strategic environment and the negative effects of using firepower against a small state without any military forces restricted Britain's options.

At the UN, other venues, and the international media, the Icelanders found it easy to portray themselves as a nation reliant on fish as its single source of income, facing the might of a (former) colonial power. Indeed, Iceland usually supported the cause of emerging nations that had achieved independence or were struggling to do so. However, when national interests were at stake, pragmatism and real interests outdid sympathy and ideology. Thus, the Icelandic authorities did not support the independence struggle in Angola or Mozambique as convincingly as might have been expected. The important fishing market in Portugal had to be considered. Furthermore, in relative terms, Iceland's contribution to development aid was always significantly lower than the amount from most other Western nations. In fact, until the 1970s, the Icelanders were rather recipients than benefactors of such assistance.

Apart from NATO and the UN, independent Iceland became a member of the pertinent international organizations. At the end of World War II, Iceland had five embassies—in Copenhagen, London, Stockholm, Washington, and Moscow. By 1994, there were 12, and the diplomatic service had grown accordingly. In 1952, Iceland was a founding member of the Nordic Council, a consultative assembly that focused primarily on cultural cooperation. In 1971, the Danish authorities began to return to Iceland the precious manuscripts that Árni Magnússon and others had collected and preserved in Copenhagen in previous centuries. Feelings of animosity toward the Danes all but vanished after this generous act. Until 1999, when English took over, Danish was the first foreign language of instruction in Icelandic schools. For many politicians and the intelligentsia, the Nordic connection had to be fostered in an era of globalization and Americanization. Agreements with the other Nordic countries also opened up work and study opportunities.

In short, Iceland was a fully functioning independent state on the international scene. During the disintegration of the Soviet Union in 1990–1991, the Icelandic government, led by Labor Party leader and foreign minister Jón Baldvin Hannibalsson, even managed to punch beyond its weight by giving vocal and active support for the Baltic struggle for independence. In August 1991, Iceland became the first country to resume diplomatic relations with the newly liberated countries of Estonia, Latvia, and Lithuania. In general, however, Iceland was of course restrained by its smallness, and some definitions of "state independence" mention national military forces as a prerequisite for that description. But lack of those hardly affected the Icelanders' upbeat image of themselves. The idea of creating an Icelandic army was never seriously discussed.

A cross-political aversion to joining the European integration process was also a testimony to the overwhelming importance of independence in Icelandic minds. The growing prosperity during the postwar years seemed to certify the traditional view of history that the people of Iceland had fared best when they ran their own affairs. Although some politicians and officials wondered in the late 1950s and early 1960s whether Iceland might benefit from joining the newly established EEC, the reliance on fisheries and uncompetitive agriculture seemed to make membership unfeasible. Instead, Iceland joined the European Free Trade Association in 1970. Neither did the country apply to enter the EEC in the 1970s, unlike Denmark (which joined) and Norway (which rejected membership), or Finland and Sweden, which both became members of the renamed and more integrated European Union in 1995.

Still, by the start of the 1990s, Iceland had embarked on its own European journey. It was to bring material benefits, increased educational, business, and work opportunities. Unfortunately, it also invited the risk of excess and arrogance. Hubris lay ahead.

NOTES

1. "Lífsskilyrðin á Íslandi eru erfið," [Living conditions in Iceland are rough], *Morgunbladid*. Sept. 17, 1949.
2. Eggert Thór Bernhardsson, *Saga Reykjavíkur. Borgin II* [The history of Reykjavík] (Reykjavík: Idunn, 1998), 39–40.
3. Colin Powell, *My American Journey* (New York: Random House, 1995), 550–551.

7

European Iceland: Integration, Excess, and Collapse (1994–2012)

GOOD-BYE AMERICA, HELLO EUROPE

At the start of 1994, the population of Iceland had reached 265,000. A short recession in the first years of the decade seemed to be over, and the coalition of the Independence Party and the Labor Party, which came to power in 1991, had successfully carried through a key part of their platform: On January 1, 1994, Iceland became a member of the European Economic Area (EEA). Best described as a halfway house between full EU membership and exclusion, the EEA offered Iceland access to the EU's common market under the principle of the four freedoms—freedom of movement of goods (excluding agriculture and fisheries), persons, services, and capital. All member states of the European Free Trade Association (EFTA), except Switzerland, joined the area. After the EU expansion of 1995, however, only Iceland, Norway, and Liechtenstein remained on the EFTA side.

Iceland's entry into the EEA was hotly debated. No issue had ever been discussed for as long in parliament, with the opponents in the Progressive Party and the leftist People's Alliance insisting that it involved an intolerable loss of sovereignty. Furthermore, the reciprocal nature of membership was said to entail the risk of foreigners flooding the sensitive job market in Iceland, purchasing property, and vast tracks of land. Thus, more than 30,000 voters petitioned President Vigdís Finnbogadóttir to put a law on accession before national referendum. Her predecessors had never used that constitutional entitlement and in the end she rejected the appeals, arguing that the president should only interrupt the law-making process in the most extreme, even war-like, circumstances.

By entering into the EEA, the Icelandic authorities pledged to incorporate all relevant EU legislation into their own national body of law. It was not surprising, therefore, that concerns about the infringement of sovereignty should arise. As one of the country's foremost law professors put it, Iceland's legal code had been transformed as swiftly and fundamentally as it did when the new laws that accompanied subjugation to the king of Norway took ef-fect in the late thirteenth century. The change involved laws on trade and commerce, competition, customer protection, employer rights, and vari-ous other fields. By the mid-2000s, Iceland had adopted up to 80 percent of the EU's directives and regulations that concerned the common market and the four freedoms. Moreover, this was an ongoing process as new missives constantly came from Brussels, the EU headquarters, to be promptly imple-mented in Iceland.

Why, then, did Iceland not go all the way and join the EU? In 1994, a ma-jority of Icelanders wanted to apply for membership, according to some opin-ion polls. But entry into the EU was not on the government's agenda, and the following year, the dominant Independence Party replaced the pro-EU Labor Party with the Progressives who were more skeptical or outright against entry. That coalition was to last until 2007, equaling the record duration of the Restoration Regime of 1959–1971. Another record was also broken. The strong-willed leader of the Independence Party, Davíd Oddsson, had become prime minister in 1991 and did not leave the post until 2004, having stayed longer in power than anyone else, including the party's old icons, Ólafur Thors and Bjarni Benediktsson. Indeed, the new kingpin seemed to have rescued the party from the difficulties it had suffered since Benediktsson's untimely death in 1970.

Although many Independents were at least willing to consider EU mem-bership, Oddsson was dead set against the idea. However, neither he nor other prominent politicians suggested that Iceland should leave the EEA. The ma-jority of statespersons, bureaucrats, and the public argued that the country was sharing the main benefits of the EU—access to the common market of member states—without the negatives of full membership where national sovereignty and Iceland's control over its fishing grounds would be lost.

The debates and opinions on the EEA demonstrated an anxiety about for-eign encroachment versus the desire for integration. The new environment certainly improved higher education options. Icelanders benefited from the EU's popular student exchange program, and the number of people enrolling in European universities increased. Business and finance opportunities also opened up. By 1998, foreign asset holdings by Icelanders equaled some 23 billion Icelandic *krónur*, about a fifth of that amount in the United States. Six years later, the figure had risen to the relatively grand sum of 250 billion *krónur*. Almost all these new foreign investments were in Europe, less than 10 percent in the United States and other parts of the world. Iceland's ties to the home continent were growing by the year.

Internationalization was the buzzword of the time. A number of Icelandic companies—in the fishing sector, retail, or even pharmaceuticals—launched or expanded their operations abroad. Icelandair modified its aircraft fleet and multiplied its destination network, with the international airport at Keflavík serving as a hub for transatlantic flights. As a result, the number of tourists traveling to Iceland proliferated, from 201,000 in 1997 to 566,000 in 2011. By then, more people (around 10,000) worked in the tourist sector than in agriculture and fisheries combined. For a while, Reykjavík became known as the capital of cool, but unspoiled and majestic nature seemed to appeal most to the visitors.

Simultaneously, the Icelanders had, like other nations on the globe, entered the era of incessant globalization with its effects on culture, language, and lifestyle. In the 1990s, an official word committee regularly discussed possible translations of the term Internet, akin to the pure Icelandic words *sími* (old word for thread) for telephone, and for computer the ingenious innovation *tölva* (a combination of the words for a number and a soothsayer). Maybe it was a sign of the times that this time no Icelandic term caught on; the Internet would simply be known as that. By 2006, 83 percent of all Icelandic homes were connected to the net while the corresponding figure in EU member states was just more than 50 percent. Stipulations about the duty to have subtitles on all foreign broadcasts in Iceland were depreciated with greater access to satellite TV stations. In the early 2000s, Icelandic programs accounted for only around one-fifth of all broadcasting time by the main privately run channel, and up to half for the state-run station. Movie attendance was higher, per capita, in Iceland than all other countries except the United States. Although the Icelandic movie industry emerged in the late 1970s, with around 80 films produced since then until the end of the century (as compared with seven between 1926 and 1977), Hollywood pictures all but monopolized the movie theaters.

It is true that many Icelanders used their free time for hikes in Iceland, reading Icelandic literature, and listening to Icelandic music. Still, the alleged uniqueness of Icelandic culture was slowly fading as entertainment flowed from abroad at an ever-increasing pace. Such were the universal pros and cons of globalization.

Similarly, Iceland's apparent innocence seemed to be a thing of the past. Yes, the country remained gun-free, apart from hunting rifles, and the Reykjavík underworld was not as rough as in many bigger cities. But drug-related crimes and violence were on the rise. Around 1995, strip clubs even sprung up and satisfied a clear demand. By then, prostitution had also become an undeniable fact. In the late 2000s, changes in the penal code made it punishable by fines or imprisonment to offer payment for sexual acts or to benefit from prostitution. Most of the striptease girls came from abroad, especially Eastern Europe, after the eastward expansion of the EU, which granted them easier access to Iceland through the EEA agreement. For these women, controversial work on a faraway island was predominantly an opportunity to escape poverty at home. With similar rationale, others sought more mainstream positions in the country. In the mid-1990s, immigrants accounted for less than 2 percent of the population in Iceland, but by 2008, that number had quadrupled to 8 percent. Most of them came from European countries, and about half of those hailed from Poland. Also in 1996–2008, Iceland received more than 300 refugees, primarily from the war-torn parts of former Yugoslavia. The minority of non-Europeans arrived primarily from the Philippines, Thailand, and Vietnam.

The bulk of the new arrivals found employment in the fishing industry, non-skilled construction work, cleaning, or other low-paid vocations that did not appeal to native-born Icelanders. Many hospitals and old age homes were primarily kept clean by Asian women, and in some of the small fishing villages of the Westfjords, first- or even second-generation Poles came to provide the mainstay of the workforce. Still, fears about foreigners flooding Iceland did not come true. Few of them mastered the Icelandic language, a prerequisite for success in the country, and neither did they necessarily intend to stay for good.

The impact of foreign-born persons in Iceland on the actual running of society was minimal. Two Icelanders with that background briefly sat in the *Althing* (permanent MPs can be substituted temporarily), one of them U.S.-born and the other a Palestinian who came to Iceland in 1995 as a stateless person. The brief presence of these two individuals in the *Althing*, the ancient and most Icelandic of institutions, carried a symbolic message of growing internationalization in society. Otherwise, it had no lasting meaning. Both represented established political parties, and foreigners or foreign-born citizens did not form political or cultural pressure groups of any kind. Neither did racist and xenophobic right-wing groups or parties gain a foothold in Iceland, as was the case in other Nordic countries. Apart from neutral nods at the workplace, a growing number of children with foreign-sounding names in preschools and schools, publicized celebrations of national holidays, and the occasional news about foreign gangs or nationality-based and alcohol-imbued nightlife fights, Icelanders and immigrants seemed mostly to live in two separate worlds on the island.

Meanwhile, the people of Iceland continued to be affected by developments abroad. The world-shattering events of September 11, 2001, with subsequent tension and wars, decreased yet further the U.S. will to maintain a military presence on the island, even if it had greatly diminished already since the Cold War era. In the spring of 2003, the Icelandic government agreed to be part of the U.S.-initiated Coalition of the Willing in the impending invasion of Iraq, partly hoping that a grateful U.S. administration would continue to station the minimum number of four fighter planes at the Keflavík base. In the ongoing U.S. War on Terror, however, military and financial resources were deemed to be more useful elsewhere. Iceland was, as one NATO official put it in the summer of 2003, "strategically on the edge of nowhere."[1] The following year, all maritime surveillance aircraft were removed from Keflavík, and in early 2006, despite continued pleadings by Icelandic diplomats and statespersons, the U.S. authorities declared their intention to close the whole base. The fighter planes flew away, and on September 30, 2006, the last military personnel left. From then, the country has been without permanent military forces, although NATO units undertake regular air patrols. Also the defense treaty from 1951 remained in force, and the United States was committed to the island's military protection, if by other means. Nonetheless, in strategic, political, and even economic terms, the American age was over in Iceland.

THE ICELANDIC ECONOMIC MIRACLE

While membership of the EEA was a key objective of the center-right regime that came to power in 1991, privatization was deemed to be of equal importance. From then until 2003, the state sold its shares in more than 20 public companies, including the State Herring Factories, a giant in its time, the Public Travel Bureau, and three state-owned banks that had dominated the banking sector. The authorities claimed that the companies would be more competitive and profitable in a free market environment. Yet suspicions about nepotism and political machinations inevitably arose. This was especially apparent with the privatization of the banks around the turn of the twenty-first century. One of them was sold to a group of businessmen with ties to the Progressive Party, another to a team led by entrepreneur Björgólfur Gudmundsson and his son, Björgólfur Thor Björgólfsson. The duo had amassed great wealth in post-Soviet Russia and appeared to benefit from strong links to the Independents, the other party in the governing coalition of the day.

Almost immediately, the privatized banks ballooned in size, launching operations and branches in various European countries. At the same time, Icelandic entrepreneurs and companies also began to look beyond Iceland's shores. In previous decades, foreign markets had primarily been the preserve of fish and wool exporters, the shipping industry, and the airlines. Indeed, some of the new successful companies had roots in the fishing industry, like Marel, which manufactured food processing machinery, initially only for fish but moving into poultry and other fields. Also there were entrepreneurs in the established fields of aviation and shipping who felt restrained and entered into the exhilarating world of acquisitions and takeovers. In early 2007, for instance, the Icelandic investment company FL Group, which originated within Icelandair, had become the largest shareholder in the mother company of American Airlines.

In Britain, another Icelandic enterprise made inroads into the retail market. During the 1990s, the young Jón Ásgeir Jóhannesson and his father, Jóhannes Jónsson, had built a supermarket empire in Iceland. In the following decade, they founded an international investment firm that was given an enigmatic Icelandic name, Baugur (an old word for ring or circle) with the popular suffix *group*. Acquiring such household names as Hamleys, known as the world's largest toy store, and Oasis, the fashion chain, Baugur Group gained international recognition.

In the Baltic and Nordic countries, especially Denmark, Baugur Group and other businesses also purchased stores, hotels, and even newspapers. Meanwhile, Björgólfur Thor Björgólfsson built a vast business empire in Eastern Europe, a familiar world thanks to his dealings in Russia in the 1990s. The moneymaking projects included takeovers of pharmaceutical and telecommunications firms. In 2005, Björgólfsson became the first Icelander to appear on *Forbes Magazine*'s list of the world's wealthiest people.

At the same time, wealth apparently accrued in Iceland. In the opening years of the new century, the worth of shares in the banks and the international companies grew steadily on the Icelandic Stock Exchange, which had come into being in the 1990s. The value of real estate increased, and mortgages for up to 100 percent of the asking price were offered. Vehicles were also purchased on credit. In both cases, loans could be taken in foreign currencies like Swiss Francs and Japanese Yen, with interest rates enticingly low. Unemployment was negligible, despite the influx of foreign workers. Purchasing power rose by the year. More students than ever were registered at the Icelandic universities, including two recently founded private institutions. Law and business were particularly popular subjects. Big-time Christmas or Easter shopping by overexcited Icelanders at Icelandic airline destinations like Dublin, London, Copenhagen, or Halifax in Canada regularly made the local news.

Jón Ásgeir Jóhannesson, Björgólfur Thor Björgólfsson, and other businessmen also acquired extensive stakes in the Icelandic media. In 2004, the center-right coalition narrowly passed a law on media ownership restrictions. However, President Ólafur Ragnar Grímsson, a former leader of the socialist People's Alliance who succeeded the retiring Vigdís Finnbogadóttir in 1996, refused to ratify the law. Although the constitution formally granted the head of state this prerogative, Grímsson's predecessors had not wielded it. The government, in particular an outraged Davíð Oddsson, insisted that it was in fact obsolete, and that the president was simply currying favor with his newfound friends. But Grímsson had his way and qualms about the corporate world's extensive media control and prosecutions about fraud and tax evasion did not upset the general picture of progress. Unsurprisingly, economists and other analysts began to talk about the Icelandic economic miracle.[2]

How was all this possible? What had changed? Where was the money coming from? Independence Party ideologues pointed to the policy of privatization, efficient fisheries through the transferable quota system, fiscal responsibility, tax and subsidy cuts, foreign ventures, and the strong financial sector. As for the evident success in the world of international business and finance, theories about inbred Icelandic superiority were proclaimed. The foremost advocate was President Grímsson. A firm believer in the abilities of small states on the international stage, he advanced in the mid-2000s a list of qualities that explained why Icelandic entrepreneurs repeatedly beat their competitors. With deep roots in the country's history, these attributes were said to include a strong work ethic, a will to take risks, admiration for adventurers like the Vikings and settlers of old, and the belief in personal trust, honor, and reputation.

Similarly, in early 2008, a state-sponsored report on the image of Iceland suggested that Icelanders envisaged themselves as proud, courageous, resilient, smart, unpredictable, undisciplined, independent, and free. Moreover, in the minds of these contemporary inhabitants, the original settlers had shared these characteristics, which had then been carried from one generation to another, in a harsh fight with nature and foreign oppressors. Academic historians protested or shook their heads over this "outdated" and nationalistic view of history, but the complacent public did not seem to care.

This use of Iceland's past, which has already been touched upon in previous chapters, was probably never as pronounced as during the economic boom in the first decade of the twenty-first century. The entrepreneurs were called Venture Vikings; they made *strandhögg*—the Viking-era word for a surprise attack from the sea—and the novel and rapid entrance into foreign markets was given the general description of *útrás*, another old term that denoted a sudden assault.

Another use of history, mentioned before, also came to full fruition. In 1996, Kári Stefánsson, previously a professor of neurology and related fields at Harvard University and other U.S. institutions, founded deCODE Genetics. Other companies were also formed, but deCODE dominated the field, if only because of Stefánsson's overpowering character and statue. The relative homogeneity of Iceland's original settlers, the smallness of the rather isolated population through the centuries, extensive genealogical facts, excellent hospital records since the early twentieth century, and DNA samples from recently deceased and living inhabitants could be used to track down faulty genes, causing hereditary or other diseases. The fact that the population in question was Caucasian appealed to the initial U.S. shareholders and pharmaceutical companies, the potential producers of drugs based on the knowledge that deCODE would extract. The company's scientists discovered key genetic risk factors for dozens of common disorders, but the big breakthrough never came, despite Kári Stefánsson's repeated promises. In 2009, after years of financial difficulties, deCODE was sold to U.S. investors. Still, its operations continued in Reykjavík, enhancing the small scientific community in Iceland. Furthermore, a popular side effect of the company's research was the new *Book on Icelanders*, a digital collection of all known family connections between about 740,000 people who have lived on the island from the settlement era to present times.

The wider database never materialized, however. In 2003, parts of a law on it were declared unconstitutional because of privacy infringements, and from the onset, the project created heated arguments about the rights and wrongs of *exploitation*, the quintessential concept with regard to Iceland's natural resources. Indeed, debates about hydropower plants and heavy industry rose again. In 2003, work began on a big power station in the interior north of Vatnajökull, including a vast dam that would turn large tracks of land into a water reservoir. The whole area was Europe's second largest unspoiled wilderness (after parts of Lapland in northern Scandinavia). Environmental organizations protested, aided by foreign activists who introduced more aggressive tactics in the struggle, with people chaining themselves to machinery on construction sites or throwing *skyr*, an Icelandic type of yogurt, at government ministers.

It was to no avail, and the average Icelander tended to label the visiting protesters as ignorant city dwellers who did not understand the realities of life on this rugged island. The Kárahnjúkar power station was finished in 2007, providing energy for a third, and by far the largest, aluminum smelter in the country. Situated in one of the eastern fjords, it augmented employment opportunities in a region that traditionally relied on fisheries.

With expansion in heavy industry, a constant rise in the number of tourists, a growing financial sector, and wide business activities abroad, the long-desired diversification of the Icelandic economy seemed all but complete. After parliamentary elections in 2007, a grand coalition of the Independence Party and the Social Democratic Alliance came to power under the premiership of Geir Haarde, Davíd Oddsson's successor as leader of the Independents. The alliance had been formed in 1999–2000, through the merger of the Labor Party and a short-lived splinter group, the Women's List, and the majority of People's Alliance members. The remainder founded the socialist, environmentalist, and euro-skeptic Left-Green Movement.

Together, the two governing parties had 43 of the 63 members of parliament and agreed to maintain in most regards a liberal outlook in economic policy. In fact, it seemed that the Independence Party's ideological admiration of Reaganomics—fewer taxes and regulations—blended well with the alliance's affection for Tony Blair's New Labor policies in Britain, which entailed a greater acceptance than before of the market economy, albeit with a strong welfare state. Also it even seemed as if nothing could go seriously wrong in the future. Perhaps the Icelanders were witnessing an end of history, to use the term that U.S. political scientist Francis Fukuyama's famously introduced after the end of the Cold War, suggesting "the universalization of Western liberal democracy as the final form of human government."[3]

To be sure, some worrying signs could be detected. By 2006, a number of foreign observers warned that the Icelandic economy was overheating and that the banking sector had grown excessively. During the two preceding years, the total assets in the three banks had grown more than threefold to 900 percent of the country's GDP, a far higher figure than in other Western countries. In 2006, Icelandic bankers found it increasingly hard to secure new credits abroad. Was retreat not necessary?

Although some Icelanders shared the overseas concerns, the authorities, the media, and the public were often tempted to disregard them as either envy or an unfamiliarity with the dynamic attributes of the Icelandic Venture Vikings. Moreover, the banks usually received good marks from rating agencies, so influential in the world of international finance. Last but not least, the banks discovered an ingenious way to finance their operations—online deposit accounts abroad with higher-than-average interest rates. Two of them became household names across Europe, Kaupthing with its Kaupthing Edge accounts in nine European countries and Landsbanki, which offered Icesave accounts in Britain from late 2006 and the Netherlands from the summer of 2008.

Thus, the general spirit of optimism survived. Incredibly enough, the authors of the 2008 report on Iceland's image, discussed before, suggested that Icelanders should demonstrate their vast capabilities to all humanity by leading a campaign of eradicating illiteracy in the world. With similar naivety, they wanted to invite children from war-ravaged countries to a week's stay on the island and then send them back as peace ambassadors from Iceland. Self-confidence was also manifested in Iceland's application for a seat on the UN Security Council, to be voted on at the General Assembly in October 2008. And when the men's team handball squad—the pride of the nation—reached the finals at the Beijing Olympics in August that year, Dorrit Moussaieff, the president's Israeli-born British wife, proudly exclaimed: "Iceland is not small, Iceland is the biggest country on earth."[4]

But then the whole thing collapsed.

COLLAPSE

In late 2007 and early 2008, the bank managers, key officials, and select cabinet ministers knew that the banks were in serious trouble. In the first half of 2008, furthermore, stock prices plummeted and the *króna* decreased sharply in value, causing immense difficulties for those who had been tempted to take out loans in foreign currencies. Then, the bankruptcy of the U.S. financial giant Lehman Brothers in mid-September turned a period of recession into the world's worst financial crisis since the Great Depression. Within a fortnight in Iceland, the state took over Glitnir, one of the three banks. By early October, it was clear that Landsbanki and Kaupthing teetered on the edge of ruin, but their huge size meant that they seemed too big to fail. Desperate measures were needed. On October 6, Prime Minister Geir Haarde addressed the nation and announced the passing of an emergency law to stave off state bankruptcy. Essentially, each of the three failed banks was divided into a bad bank and a good bank, with the former acting like an empty shell around colossal debts to foreign banks, pension funds, and other institutes that would hardly get their money back. The latter units functioned around the domestic operations of the failed bank, ensuring the running of a banking system in the country.

With the collapse of the banks, thousands of shareholders lost immense investments. People who had put their savings in money market funds were badly hit as well. Conversely, all bank deposits in Iceland were safe. However, the Icesave account holders in Britain and the Netherlands, with total assets of $5 billion, were left in the lurch. Icesave had come under Landsbanki branches in London and Amsterdam, unlike the Kaupthing Edge accounts, which had been operated in subsidiaries that were covered by national deposit protection schemes. While the Icelandic authorities simply did not have the funds to guarantee the Icesave deposits, the British side feared that Landsbanki assets in London might be channeled back to Iceland. Also EEA regulations about deposit insurances appeared to forbid discrimination between domestic and foreign accounts. Thus, the government in London took the drastic step of using legislation that had previously been applied to rogue states and terrorist organizations, to freeze all Landsbanki assets.

Before the end of the year, the British and Dutch governments had decided to cover the Icesave debts, while insisting on repayment from Iceland. Shaken by the banking collapse, the Icelandic authorities desperately needed foreign assistance. Such help, however, did not appear to be forthcoming unless the British and Dutch demands were met. With their backs up against the wall, the government in Reykjavík gave in. Loans were received and channeled through a restoration program, organized by the International Monetary Fund (IMF). That was how the mighty fell. The Icelandic economic miracle had turned into a nightmare. Iceland had been forced to accept an IMF rescue plan, like poor countries in the developing world. As a footnote to that sad tale, the bid for a seat on the Security Council failed miserably. Few wanted a near-bankrupt unarmed microstate there.

After the downfall of banks, the coalition regime tried to soldier on. It had lost all credibility and trust, however. In January, weeks of peaceful mass demonstrations were followed by more aggressive protests that at times turned violent, with people throwing rocks at the police or attempting to set fire to the *Althing*. Teargas had to be used during these unprecedented scenes. The upheaval came to be known as the pots and pans revolution since many protesters made themselves heard by banging kitchen utensils outside parliament. The government resigned, and Davíd Oddsson, cursed by many because of his previous political dominance, was ousted from his post as governor of the Central Bank. A minority coalition of the Social Democratic Alliance and the Left-Green Movement took over, led by Jóhanna Sigurdardóttir, minister of social affairs in the outgoing cabinet, and an MP since 1978. Thus, she became the first female prime minister in Iceland.

After elections in the spring of 2009, the governing parties gained a majority in parliament and continued their cooperation. Descending from the Labor Party and the People's Alliance/the Socialist Party, it could be argued that two leftist parties had for the first time achieved that feat. Also the Independence Party did not receive the largest share of the vote for the first time in its 80-year-old history. The electoral swing to the left was the voters' way of blaming the crash on the policy of privatization and liberalization, prevalent since the early 1990s.

Grudgingly, the Left-Green Movement accepted the Social Democratic Alliance's policy of applying for membership of the European Union, without actually supporting entry. The IMF program continued, with cuts in government expenditure that proved painful for a left-wing government and its different ideological agenda. Billions of *krónur* were pumped into the wrecked banking system, although the popular myth developed abroad that the Icelanders had simply let the banks fall. Also the real estate bubble burst, and house owners with hefty mortgages suffered. Currency restrictions were imposed. Purchasing power dropped. Unemployment rose sharply to around 8 percent, a high number in an Icelandic context.

Icelandic society had been shaken to its core. People mistrusted the authorities, not to mention the banks. The spirit of suspicion may have contributed to a more cynical, but honest, view of the past. Committees were formed to investigate alleged abuse in foster homes or within the church. Accusations by the victims tended to become the established truth. The infamous case in the 1970s when a group of young people were given heavy prison sentences for the murder of two men was considered a travesty of justice, although attempts to have the rulings overturned were unsuccessful.

In the summer of 2009, negotiations with the British and Dutch authorities led to an agreement on Icelandic compensation because of the Icesave accounts. In January 2010, however, President Ólafur Ragnar Grímsson, who had been harshly criticized for his undue praise of the Venture Vikings, refused to confirm a law on the agreement's ratification. In a subsequent national referendum, it was rejected by an overwhelming majority. Another more favorable solution was negotiated and passed by the Althing, but again the president intervened. Although the result was not as clear-cut, in April 2011, the voters rejected the proposed agreement. Apparently, the dispute would have to be solved in courts, either in Europe or even in Iceland. As for the president, his intervention and defense of Iceland's cause, stout but misleading at times, secured him a record fifth term in office in the summer of 2012. Grímsson's previous love affair with the now-shamed entrepreneurs was forgiven.

"We said cash, not ash," a British newspaper cartoon read in early 2010. In the midst of the Icesave dispute, a volcanic eruption underneath Eyjafjallajökull glacier spewed ash and tiny particles into the stratosphere, causing the worst disruption in aviation over Europe since World War II. The episode was a reminder of Iceland's harsh nature. Likewise, in 1995, two avalanches in the Westfjords destroyed dozens of buildings, taking the lives of 34 people. The previous year, an eruption in Vatnajökull had caused a massive gush of water and ice that destroyed major roads and bridges south of the glacier.

As devastating as natural disasters could be, they maintained or kindled an interest in exotic Iceland. Likewise, the Icesave conflict kept the country in the international spotlight, as did detailed investigations into the causes of the banking crisis. In essence, the primary reason was deemed to be the excessive growth of the banks, mostly based on borrowed money. Their managers and owners had been reckless, even greedy. Other factors included the lack of proper surveillance by the government, parliament, and state authorities, inadequate EU regulations, and various wrongdoings within the banks and the corporate world in general. The entrepreneurs who owned the banks had received loans themselves, often with insufficient collateral or none at all. Stocks prices had been maintained superficially high and cross-ownership was widespread. In short, the 'economic miracle' had been a charade.

According to the Icelandic constitution, parliament could indict ministers for misdemeanors in office. In the autumn of 2010, a narrow majority agreed to charge former Prime Minister Geir Haarde with recklessness in the buildup to the banking crisis. Since the vote on the issue was on political lines, former ministers of the Social Democratic Alliance were not charged as well. In April 2012, Geir Haarde was found guilty on one minor aspect of the case laid against him. The process had been flawed from the start and political responsibility could not be put on the shoulders of a single individual, even if that person was the prime minister.

In early 2009, the office of a special prosecutor was established in order to investigate and lay charges concerning economic violations, gainful offences, and taxation infringements. In the following years, a few prison sentences were passed, with more undoubtedly to follow. More generally, however, after the collapse as the devastating events of 2008 were often referred to, Icelanders had to face the stark reality that in the preceding years they had been guilty of collective overspending, overconfidence, and blindness akin to the crowd in H. C. Andersen's tale about the emperor's new clothes.

By mid-2012, almost four years after the collapse, there were sure signs of economic recovery. It was slow and complex issues remained to be solved, including the Icesave dispute, the lifting of currency restrictions that hampered trade and investment in the country, and possible EU membership. Negotiations were in progress. Iceland's sovereignty over its fishing grounds would have to be secured; otherwise, an agreement on entry would never be approved in the obligatory plebiscite. In any case, the constitutional and financial crisis within the EU had greatly diminished support for accession in Iceland.

But there was progress, and the U.S. economist Paul Krugman spoke of the Icelandic sort-of miracle, an expression that government officials and supporters in Iceland were quick to highlight. Even so, it did carry an uncanny resemblance to the empty adulation about the Icelandic economic miracle, only a few years before. How ironic would it be if the history of the first decades of the third millennium would in future contain the same outline of rise, fall, and rise that characterized the traditional and nationalistic history of the preceding thousand years or so?

Looking back on the fateful year of 2008, Icelanders had hopefully learned their lessons. Pride came before the fall. Still, we could also keep in mind that 2008 was the first year in recorded history, and probably since the settlement of the island, that no lives were lost at sea. Caution, knowledge of our limitations, and respect for the forces of nature: these were the true Icelandic characteristics that offset inevitable losses and kept our ancestors alive on this inhospitable but remarkable island.

NOTES

1. Gudni Thorlacius Jóhannesson, "To the Edge of Nowhere. U.S.-Icelandic Defense Relations during and after the Cold War," *Naval War College Review* 57/4 (2004), 131.

2. See, for instance, Hannes Hólmsteinn Gissurarson, "The Icelandic Economic Miracle," http://stofnanir.hi.is/ams/sites/files/ams/hhg.ppt.

3. Francis Fukuyama, "The End of History?" *The National Interest* (summer 1989), 3.

4. See Gudni Thorlacius Jóhannesson, *Hrunid. Ísland á barmi gjaldthrots og upplausnar* [The collapse. Iceland on the edge of bankruptcy and chaos] (Reykjavík: JPV, 2009), 127.

Notable People in
the History of Iceland

Audur 'the Wise' Ketilsdóttir (ca. 830–?). According to the sagas and other written sources, her father, a Norse chieftain, conquered the Hebrides Islands off Scotland. Her husband became king in Dublin but was slain. Later their son became king of the Scots, but after his death in battle, she fled to Iceland with her entourage and settled in a fertile valley off Breidafjördur. Best known as Audur 'the Wise', she is often cited as an example of the strong women portrayed in the Icelandic sagas.

Náttfari (ca. 835–?). This common man (last name unknown) may have been the first Norse settler in Iceland. When the Swede Gardar Svavarsson departed the island in 870, after a winter's stay, Náttfari was left behind with two slaves. Supposedly, Náttfari claimed a prosperous valley, but when the settlement period began, he was driven from there to a less hospitable enclave by the sea, which has since been known as Náttfaravíkur (Náttfari's Coves). The story of Náttfari is told in the *Book of Settlements*, but there is no mention of him in Ari the Learned's *Book of Icelanders*. Maybe he felt that Náttfari was not noble enough or that since he did not sail to Iceland with the clear intention of living there, he should not be deemed a true settler.

Ingólfur Arnarson (ca. 844–900). Although his father's name was probably Björnólfur, this Norse chieftain has been known in Icelandic history and collective memory as Ingólfur Arnarson (the son of Örn), the first Norse settler of Iceland, establishing his farm in Reykjavík in 874. However, he probably arrived a few years earlier, and even so, he cannot be celebrated as the first settler. Náttfari and his slaves should rather be credited with that achievement. Furthermore, the most cautious (or suspicious) historians even doubt whether this man, Ingólfur, really existed. Nonetheless, most people probably like to hail Ingólfur Arnarson, picturing him as he is portrayed in a statue in the center of Reykjavík, the proud settler and Viking, ready for battle with a spear in his hand and a helmet on his head.

Leifur Eiríksson (ca. 940–1020). Until the artist Björk achieved worldwide fame in the late 1990s, Leifur Eiríksson was probably the best-known Icelander outside the country's shores. Then again, he was born at a time when the inhabitants of Iceland had not formed a separate identity in the Norse world, and his father, Eiríkur the Red, was born in Norway. Be that as it may, Leifur Eiríksson's place in history is secured because he has been called the first European to sail to the lands that were later known as North America, around 1000. On the journey back to Greenland, Leifur Eiríksson and his team rescued 15 shipwrecked people and hence he was dubbed the Lucky. Because of these tales, he has been credited with the European discovery of North America as the Icelanders have been apt to proclaim, rejecting the contention that Columbus should hold that honor.

Gudrídur Thorbjarnardóttir (ca. 980–1050). A chieftain's daughter, she was twice widowed before she was married and sailed to the newly discovered lands west of Greenland, shortly after 1000. There she gave birth to a son, Snorri. Consequently, the Icelanders have referred to them as the first European and 'white' mother and child on the North American continent. Gudrídur Thorbjarnardóttir converted to Christianity and legend has it that she went on a pilgrimage to Rome, where she was received by the pope. While there is no reason to doubt her existence and the fact that she traveled west of Greenland, the tale of her journey to Rome is less credible.

Ari Thorgilsson (1067–1148). A gifted scholar, he wrote the *Book of Icelanders* and was probably involved in the original making of the *Book of Settlements*. He must also have composed other works although they have not been preserved. During his lifetime, Ari was called "the Learned" because of his masterful memory. He is often referred to as Iceland's first historian, and his statement in the preface to the *Book of Icelanders* is a popular maxim in works about the past: "Whatever is incorrect in these writings, it is vital to adhere to that which is more truthful."

Snorri Sturluson (1179–1241). A chieftain, priest, poet, and writer, he is among Iceland's literary giants, as well as having played a key role in the civil strife that led to the dissolution of the Icelandic Commonwealth in the middle of the thirteenth century. Once a confidant of King Hákon of Norway, the king had him executed in 1241. Snorri Sturluson wrote a textbook on poetry and pagan mythology, the history of Norwegian kings, and probably other works, although they have not survived the passage of time.

Arngrímur Jónsson (1568–1648). He was related to Bishop Gudbrandur Thorláksson at the Hólar see in northern Iceland. After studies there, he graduated from Copenhagen University and became a priest and the bishop's right hand at Hólar. In his tenure, Thorláksson was angry at what he felt were erroneous and slanderous descriptions of Iceland by scholars abroad. He therefore asked Jónsson to compose more truthful accounts of the island and its history. In 1609, Arngrímur, then known as "the Learned," published in Latin the history of Iceland. Portraying the first centuries of settlement as a glorious period when free men constructed a prosperous society, he set the tone for those who followed during the national awakening of the nineteenth century.

Árni Magnússon (1663–1730). A passionate collector of manuscripts and books, he completed a degree in theology at Copenhagen University. Instead of returning home to clerical living, he began a scholarly and archival career that centered on the collection and preservation of old Icelandic documents. In 1702–1712, Magnússon stayed in Iceland and collected information for a census and a land register. Married but with no children, manuscripts were his love and passion. In 1728, however, disaster struck. The great fire of Copenhagen destroyed thousands of items, including invaluable sources on Icelandic history and culture. Fortunately, most of the saga manuscripts were rescued, but Árni Magnússon was heartbroken and passed away two years later.

Skúli Magnússon (1711–1794). An official, entrepreneur, and visionary, Magnússon has been hailed as the founder of Reykjavík, a notable exception of drive and foresight during the miserable eighteenth century, with its epidemics, natural disasters, and economic and political mishandling. In 1749, Skúli Magnússon became the first Icelander to hold the office of treasurer in the country. He had a manor built at Videy island off Reykjavík and initiated various plans for the improvement of the Icelandic economy. Before Magnússon's death, most of these initiatives had ended in failure. Some of them were doomed to do so, while others suffered from the lack of knowledge and enthusiasm among the population or the enmity of Danish merchants who preferred the status quo.

Magnús Stephensen (1762–1833). A son of a governor and a vice governor's daughter, Stephensen (a family name, not a patronymic) was as stately born as an Icelander could be at the time. Receiving a degree in law from Copenhagen University, he was the treasurer in Iceland for a short while, and when the country's provincial court was founded in 1801 (after the abolition of the old *Althing*), he became the chief justice. A convinced follower of the Enlightenment with its emphasis on rationality, humanism, and social reform, Stephensen was considered lenient in his verdicts, unlike so many before him. Still, he chided his fellow Icelanders for idleness and apathy. Throughout the nineteenth century, the Stephensen family was powerful in governing circles in Iceland, a heavy-handed clique as the opponents branded them.

Thurídur Einarsdóttir (1777–1863). A notable exception to the gendered roles in society during her time, she was for decades the forewoman (captain) on a rowing boat, having started fishing with her father at the age of 11. Known for her combined skills of caution and daring, she was popular among fishermen. The roughness at sea required her to wear men's clothes. For this, she received a special license from the local sheriff. Thurídur Einarsdóttir was in no sense a campaigner for women's rights. Still, she demonstrated in practice that women were capable of breaking the male-made confines of her time.

Jónas Hallgrímsson (1807–1845). Arguably, Iceland's most beloved poet. After home education and studies at the school at Bessastadir, the gifted Jónas went to Copenhagen, abandoned his law studies, and switched to literature and the natural sciences, without completing a final degree. Along with other Icelanders in Copenhagen, he was influential in the national awakening, the demands for increased rights from Denmark. Primarily, however, Jónas Hallgrímsson is known for his poetry—odes to Iceland, elegies, love poems, and other popular compositions.

Jón Sigurdsson (1811–1879). Iceland's undisputed national hero, a flag bearer in the struggle for independence from Denmark, and an intelligent man of many skills. Jón Sigurdsson first reached fame in Iceland when he led protests against Danish dictates at the national assembly of 1851. Although he spent most of his adult life in Copenhagen, he was a member of the *Althing* for decades. He was almost always elected its president and thus became known as President Jón. A true nationalist, Jón still realized that the prerequisite for progress in Iceland was economic advancement, based on foreign trade and modernization. Apart from his political work, Jón Sigurdsson was a valuable historian and antiquarian. Indeed, he used his expert knowledge of Icelandic history to advance his arguments for increased sovereignty from Denmark. For decades after his death, President Jón was praised beyond sensible limits. In recent years, he is usually seen in a more balanced light.

Bríet Bjarnhédinsdóttir (1856–1940). A pioneer in the Icelandic women's movement, she studied at a women's school in 1880–1881, graduated with the highest marks but was unable to pursue further studies because of her gender. In 1887, Bjarnhédinsdóttir delivered a public lecture in Reykjavík on women's rights, the first address of that kind in the country. In 1894, she led the formation of the Icelandic Women's Association, and the following year, she launched a magazine dedicated to women's rights. In 1907, Bríet Bjarnhédinsdóttir was a prime mover in the foundation of the Icelandic Women's Rights Association, and from 1908 to 1920 (with the exception of four years), she was a member of the Reykjavík town council. Within the women's movement, she was sometimes disputed but few doubted her dedication to the cause of gender equality.

Hannes Hafstein (1861–1922). Iceland's first minister and a popular poet. Having received a law degree from Copenhagen University, he became sheriff in Iceland and elected member of the *Althing* in 1900. As a leader of the Home Rule Party, Hafstein (a family name) became Iceland's first minister in 1904, residing in Reykjavík. Reigning for five years, which were marked by economic advances, he oversaw progress in many fields, but in 1908, he and his party suffered a bad loss because of a proposed treaty on Iceland's relationship with Denmark that the electorate roundly rejected. In 1912, Hafstein became minister again, but his second period in power was marred by disappointments and the loss of a loving wife. Known for his stylishness and wit, Hafstein helped to foster a feeling of self-confidence among the Icelanders, who were unsure whether they could actually stand on their own feet in the world. Similarly, his nationalistic and romantic poems gained him widespread popularity.

Sigrídur Tómasdóttir (1871–1957). She was the daughter of simple parents on a farm near the famous waterfall Gullfoss. In the early 1900s, she protested moves to build a hydropower station, which would destroy the waterfall, often traveling by foot the 55 miles to Reykjavík to voice her opposition. Sigrídur Tómasdóttir has become a symbol of environmentalism in Iceland. While her fervent devotion to the cause should not be disparaged, the true reason why the waterfall was not harnessed—and thus destroyed—lay in the fact that a power station at Gullfoss was not economical at the time.

Björg C. Thorláksson (1874–1934). She studied at a women's school and taught there afterward. In 1897, she went to Copenhagen, where she graduated from college and began her studies in philosophy at Copenhagen University. A year later, she married scholar Sigfús Blöndal and worked with him on a massive Danish-Icelandic dictionary. In the 1920s, she resumed her studies (and divorced her husband). In 1926, she became the first Icelandic woman to complete a doctoral degree in philosophy and related fields from the University of Sorbonne in Paris. Although her research was well received in the academic world, she was unable to secure an academic position, almost certainly because of gender discrimination.

Jóhanna Egilsdóttir (1881–1982). Born to a poor housewife and a farmer in southwestern Iceland, she worked on a farm when, in 1904, she married a laborer from the neighborhood and they decided to move to Reykjavík to seek a better life. Burned by the poverty and injustices she felt in society, Egilsdóttir joined a women's trade union, became its vice chairperson in 1923 and head from 1935 to 1962. In a positive sign of how the times changed, in 1978, when Jóhanna Egilsdóttir was almost 100 years old, her granddaughter, the future prime minister Jóhanna Sigurdardóttir, was first elected to the *Althing*.

Gudrún Árnadóttir (1887–1975). She married in 1910 and lived on a farm with her husband for 30 years. In her youth, she had loved writing, a pursuit that she renewed in retirement. In 1946, at the age of 59, she published her first novel, and others followed annually until 1973 (with a single exception). Writing under the name Gudrún frá Lundi (Gudrún from Lundur, her birthplace), the works describe country life in Iceland at the start of the twentieth century, in plain and sometimes romantic terms. While literary experts were apt to denigrate her style, the general public was captivated by the stories. Year after year, Gudrún frá Lundi topped the list of most borrowed books at Icelandic libraries.

Halldór Laxness (1902–1998). The most influential writer in twentieth-century Iceland. The young Laxness loved reading and writing and wrote his first newspaper article at the age of 14, publishing his first novel three years later. At one stage, he adhered to the Catholic faith but mostly pledged allegiance to communism until disillusionment took over in the 1950s. Adopting the name of the farm where he grew up, Halldór Laxness wrote primarily about life in Iceland, both at present and in previous ages. Apart from numerous articles, plays, and poems, he wrote more than 50 books, which have been translated into more than 40 languages. In 1955, Halldór Laxness was awarded the Nobel Prize for literature.

Vigdís Finnbogadóttir (1930–). She studied at French universities, in Copenhagen, and at the University of Iceland. In 1972, she became the director of the Reykjavík Theater, a post she held until 1980. That year, after a close race against three (male) candidates, she was elected president of Iceland, thus becoming the first democratically female head of state. Admired for her elegance and linguistic skills, she took a leading role in the promotion of Icelandic products and companies abroad. She also advanced causes that were dear to her—the protection of the Icelandic language, children's education and welfare, and soil reclamation. Vigdís Finnbogadóttir was a popular president although her last term in 1992–1996 was marred by a few controversies, in particular her decision not to veto a law about Iceland's entry into the European Economic Area.

Jóhanna Sigurdardóttir (1942–). A former flight attendant, she entered parliament for the Labor Party in 1978. In January 2009, at the height of political and social turmoil, she became prime minister, a post she has held since. Always known for her tenacity, even inflexibility, admirers praise her principled stand while her detractors accuse her of diffidence and reclusiveness. A mother of two sons, Jóhanna Sigurdardóttir divorced her husband. In 2002, she entered into a civil union with her female spouse, and after legal changes in 2010, they got married.

Davíd Oddsson (1948–). Iceland's most prominent politician at the beginning of the twenty-first century and Central Bank governor during the great banking crisis of 2008. In 1982, the charismatic but controversial Oddsson became mayor of Reykjavík for the Independence Party, a post that he held until 1991. He was then elected party chairman, entered parliament, and also became prime minister. Advocating privatization and liberalization, Davíd Oddsson ruled supreme in Icelandic politics until he surrendered the premiership in 2004. Nobody has held the post longer. Oddsson was then foreign minister for a year, but in 2005, he left parliament and resigned from the party chairmanship. During these years of transition, he was diagnosed with cancer but he overcame that illness and took on the post of Central Bank governor until early 2009, when a left-wing regime forced him out of office. While his admirers claim that this insightful statesman did everything in his power to avert the banking crisis of 2008, his adversaries insist that he made matters worse by his intransigence and right-wing ideology.

Jón Páll Sigmarsson (1960–1993). Four times winner of the World's Strongest Man tournament, he was an athlete and powerlifter who gained international fame and embedded the image of Icelanders as strong and sturdy Vikings. This was not the least because of his shouting "I am a Viking" after an apparently impossible achievement in the numerous contests he took part in. A pleasant, larger-than-life character, Jón Páll Sigmarsson died of a genetic heart condition.

Björk Gudmundsdóttir (1965–). Known both abroad and in Iceland under her first name, Björk is the country's best-known artist and arguably the most famous Icelander in the nation's history. Björk's musical talents were apparent from an early age, and as a teenager, she was the lead singer in a punk rock band. At the age of 20, she formed the Sugarcubes, a group that was to thrust her to the international stage. When the band broke up six years later, Björk embarked on a solo career that has led to 10 records, material wealth, and superstardom.

Björgólfur Thor Björgólfsson (1967–). Hailed before the international financial crisis of 2008 as Iceland's first billionaire, the entrepreneur Björgólfsson at one stage reached the top 250 in *Forbes Magazine's* list of the world's richest persons. The crash greatly diminished his worth and tarnished his reputation in Iceland and abroad, although he has stoutly denied all accusations of misdemeanor or greed. Even when the going was good, however, the flamboyant Björgólfsson had not managed to shake off suspicions about murky dealings in Russia, which were said to have laid the foundations for his business and investment empire. Having been the richest of the rich, Björgólfsson is often seen as the symbol of the Icelandic businessmen who, before the crash, seemed invincible in their quest for ever more fame and fortune.

Bibliographic Essay

There are a number of general surveys on Icelandic history from the settlement to present times. Gunnar Karlsson's *Iceland's 1100 Years: History of a Marginal Society* (London: Hurst, 2000) is the most thorough and academic, if dry at times. A shorter version, which was written for the general reader, is *A Brief History of Iceland* (Reykjavík: Mál og menning, 2nd ed., 2010). For a solid, factual survey, see Gudmundur Hálfdanarson, *The A to Z of Iceland* (Lanham, MD: Scarecrow Press, 2010).

A traditional view of Icelandic history is offered in Jón R. Hjálmarsson, *History of Iceland: From the Settlement to the Present Day* (Reykjavík: Forlagid, 4th ed., 2009). A fresher and more radical perspective can be found in Sigurdur Gylfi Magnússon, *Wasteland with Words. A Social History of Iceland* (London: Reaktion Books, 2010).

Recent historical and archeological views and findings on the discovery and settlement of Iceland are summarized in a short overview, *The Settlement Exhibition* (Reykjavík: Reykjavík City Museum, 2006). In 2000, the Smithsonian Institution celebrated the Norse discovery of Greenland and North America by an exhibition and a publication, William W. Fitzhugh and Elisabeth I. Ward (eds.), *Vikings: The North Atlantic Saga* (Washington, DC: Smithsonian Institution, 2000). For a more scholarly text, see James H. Barrett (ed.), *Contact,*

Continuity, and Collapse: The Norse Colonization of the North Atlantic (Turnhout: Brepols, 2003).

The settlement period and the Icelandic sagas have long been a source of interest outside Iceland. The following works offer various insights and interpretations: Jesse Byock, *Medieval Iceland. Society, Sagas, and Power* (Berkeley: University of California Press, 1988), and *Viking Age Iceland* (London: Penguin, 2001); Gísli Sigurdsson, *Gaelic Influence in Iceland: Historical and Literary Contacts* (Reykjavík: University of Iceland Press, 2nd ed., 2000); Jenny Jochens, *Women in Old Norse Society* (Ithaca, NY: Cornell University Press, 1995); Jónas Kristjánsson (transl. by Peter Foote), *Eddas and Sagas. Iceland's Medieval Literature* (Reykjavík: Hid íslenska bókmenntafélag, 4th ed., 2007); William Ian Miller, *Bloodtaking and Peacemaking: Feud, Law, and Society in Saga Iceland* (Chicago, IL: University of Chicago Press, 1990); Orri Vésteinsson, *The Christianization of Iceland: Priests, Power, and Social Change 1000–1300* (Oxford: Oxford University Press, 2000).

It could be said that the 1300s–1800s, which have traditionally been dubbed the dark ages in Icelandic history, certainly deserve that description when it comes to works in English on the period. Compared to the wealth of literature on the first centuries of settlement in Iceland, the scarcity is blatant. Readers must primarily be referred to general surveys, but two delightful primary sources can also be suggested. The first is an adventure tale, equal in excitement to the modern movies of Indiana Jones: Jón Ólafsson (transl. by Bertha S. Phillpotts), *The Life of the Icelander Jón Ólafsson, Traveller to India, Written by Himself and Completed about 1661 A.D. With a Continuation, by Another Hand, up to his Death in 1679* (London: Hakluyt Society, new. ed., 1967). Second, the eyewitness account by Pastor Jón Steingrímsson of the tremendous volcanic eruption at Laki in 1783–1784 is equally thrilling: Jón Steingrímsson (transl. by Keneva Kunz), *Fires of the Earth: The Laki Eruption 1783–1784* (Reykjavík: University of Iceland Press, 1998).

Social changes in the nineteenth century are described in Gísli Ágúst Gunnlaugsson, *Family and Household in Iceland 1801–1930: Studies in the Relationship between Demographic and Socio-Economic Development, Social Legislation, and Family and Household Structures* (Uppsala: Uppsala University, 1988). For an uncritical survey of Jón Sigurdsson's life and the independent struggle, see Hallgrímur Sveinsson (transl. by Haukur Ingason), *We Call Him President: The National Hero of Iceland* (Brekka in Dýrafjördur: Vestfirska forlagid, 2011).

The emigration to North America in 1870–1914 has been described in detail by Jónas Thór, *Icelanders in North America: The First Settlers* (Winnipeg: University of Manitoba Press, 2002). A more personal aspect can be found in Birna Bjarnadóttir and Finnbogi Gudmundsson (eds.), *My Parents: Memoirs of New World Icelanders* (Winnipeg: University of Manitoba Press, 2007).

Biographical sketches of Icelandic nineteenth- and twentieth-century writers are offered in Patrick J. Stevens (ed.), *Icelandic Writers* (Detroit: Gale, 2004). A biography of Halldór Laxness must also be mentioned: Halldór Gudmundsson, *The Islander: A Biography of Halldór Laxness* (London: MacLehouse Press, 2008).

A brief survey of the island's importance during World War II is provided in Thór Whitehead, *Iceland and the Struggle for the Atlantic 1939–1945* (Reykjavík: Aeronautical Society of Iceland, 2007). A more detailed description is in Donald F. Bittner, *The Lion and the White Falcon: Britain and Iceland in the World War II Era* (Hamden, CT: Archon Books, 1983).

The strategic importance of Iceland during the Cold War is underlined in works by the country's foremost experts in the field. Thór Whitehead covers the first decades in *The Ally Who Came in from the Cold: A Survey of Icelandic Foreign Policy 1946–1956* (Reykjavík: University of Iceland Press, 1998). The story is told from beginning to end in Valur Ingimundarson, *The Rebellious Ally: Iceland, the United States, and the Politics of Empire 1945–2006* (Dordrecht: Republic of Letters, 2011).

A number of books have been written about the Cod Wars between Iceland and Britain. The view from the British bridge, so to speak, is offered in Andrew Welch's lively account, *The Royal Navy in the Cod Wars: Britain and Iceland in Conflict 1958–61, 1972–73, 1975–76* (Liskeard: Maritime Books, 2006). The present writer has published two books on the disputes: *Troubled Waters. Cod War, Fishing Disputes, and Britain's Fight for the Freedom of the High Seas, 1948–1964* (Reykjavík and Hull: North Atlantic Fishing History Association, 2007), and *Sympathy and Self-Interest. Norway and the Anglo-Icelandic Cod Wars* (Oslo: Norwegian Institute for Defence Studies, 2005).

Iceland's reluctant attitude toward the process of European integration is described expertly in Baldur Thórhallsson (ed.), *Iceland and European Integration: On the Edge* (New York: Routledge, 2004). Einar Benediktsson, a former diplomat, offers an interesting view in *Iceland and European Development: A Historical Review from a Personal Perspective* (Reykjavík: Almenna bókafélagid, 2003).

Increased calls for environmental protection and suspicions about the benefits of heavy industry are summarized in a polemic by writer Andri Snær Magnason, *Dreamland: A Self-Help Manual for a Frightened Nation* (London: Citizen Press, 2008). From the onset, the spectacular collapse of the Icelandic banking system in 2008 was a source of great interest abroad. A few books on the subject have already been published. Papers about impending difficulties were reprinted in Robert Z. Aliber and Gylfi Zoëga (eds.), *Preludes to the Icelandic Financial Crisis* (Basingstoke: Palgrave Macmillan, 2011). Impressions abroad are provided in Daniel Chartier, *The End of Iceland's Innocence: The Image of Iceland in the Foreign Media during the Crisis* (London: Citizen

Press, 2010). For the bankers' views, biased as they may be, see Ásgeir Jónsson, *Why Iceland? How One of the World's Smallest Countries Became the Meltdown's Biggest Casualty* (New York: McGraw-Hill, 2009), and Ármann Thorvaldsson, *Frozen Assets: How I Lived Iceland's Boom and Bust* (Chichester: John Wiley & Sons, 2009).

The internet contains a multitude of reliable and not-so-reliable information on Icelandic history. The following websites can be recommended:

http://am-dk.net/fasnl/—a research project on the heroic sagas

http://www.arnastofnun.is/page/arnastofnun_al_boekur_land_thjod—a list of books in foreign languages on Icelandic culture and history

http://baekur.is/en—a digital library of books, primarily pre-twentieth century

http://eudocs.lib.byu.edu/index.php/History_of_Iceland:_Primary_ Documents—a collection of primary sources from earliest times to the twentieth century

http://www.government.is/—the official website of the government of Iceland

http://handrit.is/en/—a digital library of manuscripts

http://www.iceland.is/—the official website for current information on Iceland

http://www.library.wisc.edu/etext/jonas/—the poetry and prose of Jónas Hallgrímsson, translated by Dick Ringler

http://www.statice.is/—Statistics Iceland

Index

About the Author

GUÐNI THORLACIUS JÓHANNESSON is a research fellow at the Reykjavík Academy, Iceland, and the president of the Historical Society of Iceland. Previously, he was a postdoctoral fellow at the University of Iceland and later assistant professor at Reykjavík University. An author of eight books and numerous articles on Icelandic contemporary history, he specializes in Iceland's foreign relations, especially fishing disputes with other nations, the development of the presidency, and Iceland's spectacular economic collapse of 2008. Jóhannesson holds a Ph.D. from Queen Mary, University of London; an M.St. from St. Antony's College, University of Oxford; an M.A. from the University of Iceland; and a B.A. from the University of Warwick, England. He lives in Reykjavík with his wife and four children.

Other Titles in the Greenwood Histories of the Modern Nations
Frank W. Thackeray and John E. Findling, Series Editors

The History of Afghanistan
Meredith L. Runion

The History of Argentina
Daniel K. Lewis

The History of Australia
Frank G. Clarke

The History of the Baltic States
Kevin O'Connor

The History of Brazil
Robert M. Levine

The History of Bulgaria
Frederick B. Chary

The History of Cambodia
Justin Corfield

The History of Canada
Scott W. See

The History of Central America
Thomas Pearcy

The History of the Central Asian
Republics
Peter L. Roudik

The History of Chile
John L. Rector

The History of China, Second Edition
David C. Wright

The History of Congo
Didier Gondola

The History of Costa Rica
Monica A. Rankin

The History of Cuba
Clifford L. Staten

The History of the Czech Republic
and Slovakia
William M. Mahoney

The History of Ecuador
George Lauderbaugh

The History of Egypt
Glenn E. Perry

The History of El Salvador
Christopher M. White

The History of Ethiopia
Saheed Adejumobi

The History of Finland
Jason Lavery

The History of France
W. Scott Haine

The History of Germany
Eleanor L. Turk

The History of Ghana
Roger S. Gocking

The History of Great Britain
Anne Baltz Rodrick

The History of Greece
Elaine Thomopoulos

The History of Haiti
Steeve Coupeau

The History of Holland
Mark T. Hooker